The Tyndale Old Testament Commentaries

General Editor:
PROFESSOR D. J. WISEMAN, O.B.E., M.A., D. Lit., F.B.A., F.S.A.

1 and 2 SAMUEL

1 and 2 SAMUEL

AN INTRODUCTION AND COMMENTARY

by

JOYCE G. BALDWIN, B.A., B.D.
formerly Principal, Trinity College, Bristol

INTER-VARSITY PRESS

Inter-Varsity Press
38 De Montfort Street, Leicester LE1 7GP, England
Email: ivp@uccf.org.uk
Website: www.ivpbooks.com

First published 1988
Reprinted 1991, 1992, 1995, 1997, 1999, 2001

Text set in Baskerville 10/10 pt
Phototypeset by Input Typesetting Ltd, London SW19
Printed and bound in Great Britain by
Creative Print and Design Wales, Ebbw Vale

British Library Cataloguing in Publication Data
Baldwin, Joyce, *1921–*
   1 and 2 Samuel
   1. Bible. O.T. Samuel – Commentaries
   I. Title.   II. Series
   222′.407

   ISBN 0–85111–842–9

Inter-Varsity Press is the publishing division of the Universities and Colleges Christian Fellowship (formerly the Inter-Varsity Fellowship), a student movement linking Christian Unions in universities and colleges throughout Great Britain, and a member movement of the International Fellowship of Evangelical Students. For more information about local and national activities write to UCCF, 38 De Montfort Street, Leicester LE1 7GP, email@uccf.org.uk, or visit the UCCF website at www.uccf.org.uk.

GENERAL PREFACE

THE aim of this series of *Tyndale Old Testament Comment-aries*, as it was in the companion volumes on the New Testament, is to provide the student of the Bible with a handy, up-to-date commentary on each book, with the primary emphasis on exegesis. Major critical questions are discussed in the introductions and additional notes, while undue technicalities have been avoided.

In this series individual authors are, of course, free to make their own distinct contributions and express their own point of view on all debated issues. Within the necessary limits of space they frequently draw attention to interpretations which they themselves do not hold but which represent the stated conclusions of sincere fellow Christians.

The books of Samuel carry the history of God's people Israel through from the period of the judges to their first experiments in monarchy. The tragedy of Saul (the first in the line of kings) and the triumphs of his successor David (in spite of his long struggle with Saul and later within his own family) hold many lessons for the modern reader. The other main character in the book, Samuel, was also an influential leader of the nation, as prophet, priest and judge. These books are rich in the frank stories of individuals – good and bad – and set the scene for the subsequent history of the divided kingdom. All of this Joyce Baldwin handles with keen appreci-ation both of their literary and spiritual value, showing that the books of Samuel still have power to speak to us in the late twentieth century.

In the Old Testament in particular no single English trans-lation is adequate to reflect the original text. Though this commentary is based on the Revised Standard Version, other translations are frequently referred to, and on occasion the author supplies her own. Where necessary, Hebrew words are transliterated in order to help the reader who is unfamiliar

5

with the language to identify the precise word under discussion. It is assumed throughout that the reader will have ready access to one, or more, reliable rendering of the Bible in English.

Interest in the meaning and message of the Old Testament continues undiminished and it is hoped that this series will thus further the systematic study of the revelation of God and his will and ways as seen in these records. It is the prayer of the editor and publisher, as of the authors, that these books will help many to understand, and to respond to, the Word of God today.

D. J. WISEMAN

CONTENTS

AUTHOR'S PREFACE

THERE is a sense in which everyone who writes a commentary on any book of the Bible climbs on the shoulders of previous commentators. The books of Samuel have been particularly well served in the last two or three decades, not only by commentaries but also by scholarly research on technical and detailed matters (some of which have been raised by manuscript finds), as well as on literary techniques and on theological interpretation. The resulting literature, in several languages, amounts to a mini-library. One recent bibliography consists of 259 entries, but that would certainly be incomplete now because contributions are being published all the time. Why then another commentary on 1 and 2 Samuel?

For many years I was engaged in teaching the Old Testament to men and women in training for the Christian ministry world-wide. Such students, as well as lay people in the churches, rarely have the time or opportunity to pursue the scholarly literature, and can be trenchant in their questioning of its relevance! My aim has been to 'set the scene' in the Introduction by indicating the present state of Samuel studies, and in the Commentary to include what seems to me most important for an understanding of the text. A high degree of selection was imposed by the length of book envisaged for the series, and those who need a more detailed and technical commentary will find great help, as I myself have done, in the outstanding books by Dr R. P. Gordon. I regret that his commentary was still unpublished when I needed to consult it in the writing of 1 Samuel. Many others to whom I am indebted will be obvious from the footnotes, but even so the list would not be complete, if only because over the years the writings of others have become part and parcel of my own thinking.

There are several people to whom I wish to express my

thanks. Dr Gordon McConville of Trinity College, Bristol, has been generously helpful with his comments and suggestions, and Trinity's librarian, Su Brown, has cheerfully taken trouble to obtain just what I needed for reference. Professor D. J. Wiseman and other readers of the manuscript have also provided stimulus and helpful ideas, for which I want to express my gratitude. Above all, thanks are due to God for the books of Samuel, which, though written at least two and a half millennia ago, continue to speak and to generate faith in Israel's Rock, who in Christ established David's kingdom for ever.

JOYCE BALDWIN

CHIEF ABBREVIATIONS

Alter	R. Alter, *The Art of Biblical Narrative* (London: George Allen & Unwin, 1981).
ANEP	J. B. Pritchard, *The Ancient Near East in Pictures Relating to the Old Testament* (New Jersey: Princeton University Press, 1954; ²1969).
ANET	J. B. Pritchard (ed.), *Ancient Near Eastern Texts Relating to the Old Testament* (New Jersey: Princeton University Press, ²1955; ³1969).
AOTS	D. Winton Thomas (ed.), *Archaeology and Old Testament Study* (Oxford: Oxford University Press, 1967).
AV	English Authorized (King James) Version, 1611.
BA	*Biblical Archaeologist.*
BAR	*Biblical Archaeology Review.*
BASOR	*Bulletin of the American Schools of Oriental Research.*
BDB	F. Brown, S. R. Driver and C. A. Briggs, *A Hebrew and English Lexicon of the Old Testament* (Oxford: Oxford University Press, 1906).
BeO	*Bibbia e Oriente.*
BJRL	*Bulletin of the John Rylands Library.*
Bright	J. Bright, *A History of Israel*, The Old Testament Library (London: SCM Press, ²1972).
BT	*The Bible Translator.*
CBQ	*Catholic Biblical Quarterly.*
DOTT	D. W. Thomas (ed.), *Documents of Old Testament Times* (London: T. Nelson & Sons, 1958).
Driver 1909	S. R. Driver, *Introduction to the Literature of the Old Testament* (Edinburgh: T. & T. Clark, ⁸1909).
Driver 1913	S. R. Driver, *Notes on the Hebrew Text of the Books of Samuel* (Oxford: Oxford University Press, ²1913).
EOPN	A. R. Millard and D. J. Wiseman (eds.), *Essays on the Patriarchal Narratives* (Leicester: Inter-Varsity Press, 1980).

11

Eslinger	L. M. Eslinger, *Kingship of God in Crisis, A Close Reading of 1 Samuel 1–12* (Sheffield: Almond/JSOT Press, 1985).
ET	English Translation.
ExpT	*The Expository Times.*
Fokkelman 1981	J. P. Fokkelman, *Narrative Art and Poetry in the Books of Samuel, A full interpretation based on stylistic and structural analyses*, vol. 1 *King David (II Sam. 9–20 & I Kings 1–2)* (Assen: Van Gorcum & Co., 1981).
Fokkelman 1986	J. P. Fokkelman, *Narrative Art and Poetry in the Books of Samuel, A full interpretation based on stylistic and structural analyses*, vol. 2 *The Crossing Fates (I Sam. 13–31 & II Sam. 1)* (Assen: Van Gorcum & Co., 1986).
GNB	Good News Bible: Today's English Version, 1976.
Gordon 1984	R. P. Gordon, *1 & 2 Samuel*, Old Testament Guides (Sheffield: JSOT Press, 1984).
Gordon 1986	R. P. Gordon, *1 & 2 Samuel, A Commentary* (Exeter: Paternoster Press, 1986).
Gottwald	N. K. Gottwald, *The Tribes of Yahweh, A Sociology of the Religion of Liberated Israel, 1250–1050 B.C.E.* (London: SCM Press, 1980).
Gunn 1980	D. M. Gunn, *The Fate of King Saul, An Interpretation of a Biblical Story* (Sheffield: JSOT Press, 1980).
Gunn 1982	D. M. Gunn, *The Story of King David, Genre and Interpretation* (Sheffield: JSOT Press, 1982).
Heb.	Hebrew.
Hertzberg	H. W. Hertzberg, *1 & 2 Samuel, A Commentary*, The Old Testament Library (London: SCM Press, 1964).
HUCA	*Hebrew Union College Annual.*
IBD	J. D. Douglas *et al.* (eds.), *The Illustrated Bible Dictionary*, 3 vols. (Leicester: Inter-Varsity Press, 1980).
IDB	G. A. Buttrick *et al.* (eds.), *The Interpreter's Dictionary of the Bible*, 4 vols. (Nashville: Abingdon Press, 1962).
IDBS	K. Crim *et al.* (eds.), *The Interpreter's Dictionary of*

	the Bible Supplementary Volume (Nashville: Abingdon Press, 1976).
JB	The Jerusalem Bible, Standard Edition, 1966.
JBL	*Journal of Biblical Literature.*
JCS	*Journal of Cuneiform Studies.*
Jobling	D. Jobling, *The Sense of Biblical Narrative: Three Structural Analyses in the Old Testament (1 Samuel 13–31, Numbers 11–12, 1 Kings 17–18)* (Sheffield: JSOT Press, 1978).
JSOT	*Journal for the Study of the Old Testament.*
JSS	*Journal of Semitic Studies.*
JTS	*Journal of Theological Studies.*
JTVI	*Journal of Transactions of the Victoria Institute.*
Keil and Delitzsch	C. F. Keil and F. Delitzsch, *Biblical Commentary on the Books of Samuel* (Edinburgh: T. & T. Clark, 1866).
Kirkpatrick 1880	A. F. Kirkpatrick, *The First Book of Samuel, with Map, Notes and Introduction,* The Cambridge Bible for Schools and Colleges (Cambridge: Cambridge University Press, 1880).
Kirkpatrick 1881	A. F. Kirkpatrick, *The Second Book of Samuel, with Maps, Notes and Introduction,* The Cambridge Bible for Schools and Colleges (Cambridge: Cambridge University Press, 1881).
LXX	The Septuagint (pre-Christian Greek version of the Old Testament).
Mauchline	J. Mauchline (ed.), *1 and 2 Samuel,* New Century Bible (London: Marshall, Morgan & Scott, 1971).
McCarter 1980	P. Kyle McCarter, Jr., *I Samuel, A New Translation with Introduction, Notes and Commentary,* The Anchor Bible 8 (New York: Doubleday & Co., 1980).
McCarter 1984	P. Kyle McCarter, Jr., *II Samuel, A New Translation with Introduction, Notes and Commentary,* The Anchor Bible 9 (New York: Doubleday & Co., 1984).
McKane	W. McKane, *I & II Samuel, Introduction and Commentary,* Torch Bible Commentaries (London: SCM Press, 1963).
mg.	margin.

CHIEF ABBREVIATIONS

MS(s)	manuscript(s).
MT	Massoretic Text.
NAB	New American Bible, 1970.
NBA	J. J. Bimson, J. P. Kane, J. H. Paterson and D. J. Wiseman (eds.), *New Bible Atlas* (Leicester: Inter-Varsity Press, 1985).
NBC	D. Guthrie, J. A. Motyer *et al.* (eds.), *New Bible Commentary* (Leicester: Inter-Varsity Press, ³1970).
NEB	The New English Bible: Old Testament, 1970.
NICOT	The New International Commentary on the Old Testament.
NIDNTT	C. Brown (ed.), *The New International Dictionary of New Testament Theology*, 3 vols. (Exeter: Paternoster Press, 1975, 1976, 1978).
NIV	New International Version, 1978.
Noth	M. Noth, *The Deuteronomistic History* (1957; Sheffield: JSOT Press, 1981).
OTA	*Old Testament Abstracts.*
PEQ	*Palestine Exploration Quarterly.*
POTT	D. J. Wiseman (ed.), *Peoples of Old Testament Times* (Oxford: Oxford University Press, 1973).
RSV	American Revised Standard Version: Old Testament, 1952; New Testament, ²1971.
RV	English Revised Version, 1881.
TOTC	Tyndale Old Testament Commentary.
TynB	*Tyndale Bulletin.*
Watson	W. G. E. Watson, *Classical Hebrew Poetry, A Guide to its Techniques* (Sheffield: JSOT Press, 1984).
VT	*Vetus Testamentum.*
ZAW	*Zeitschrift für die Alttestamentliche Wissenschaft.*

INTRODUCTION

THREE characters dominate the books of Samuel: the prophet Samuel; Saul, who became Israel's first king; and above all David, the greatest and best loved of all who reigned in Jerusalem. The very sequence points to one of the main themes of the book, which is the transition from theocracy to monarchy. Under the theocracy, God by his Spirit designated human leaders as and when they were needed, whereas after the establishment of a dynastic monarchy a successor to the throne was already designated from among the king's sons. To Israel, this development seemed altogether desirable: a king would regulate Israel's life according to some agreed policy in place of the piecemeal action of individual tribes, and having organized the machinery of state and trained a standing army he would enable Israel to defeat the aggressive neighbours who plundered their crops and threatened to occupy Israel's land. In the face of strong popular demand for a king opposition finally gave way, and the account of Israel's circumstances at the time, together with the interaction of conflicting opinions and the successes and failures of the three leaders, make up the subject-matter of the books of Samuel.

Such a prosaic summary, however, fails to do justice to the ongoing fascination of these books. Simply as a source of stories to hold children spellbound they are incomparable, and moreover they provide an abundance of raw material from which to study the human condition, for they present real life with all its ambiguities but without the kind of analysis of character or motivation such as we have come to expect in modern writing. Instead, they invite the reader to reflect on the narrative in order to tease out the enigmas posed by the text, which often appears studiously to avoid reconciling apparently contradictory statements. Of course, it may be that what appear to the modern reader to be contradictions were part of an attempt to convey a two-dimensional presentation of a character or situation in as concise and straightforward a way as possible. In the absence of other literary works of a similar age with which to compare the biblical narrative, however, it is wise to be reticent in pronouncing upon its debt to its literary predecessors.

What can with confidence be said is that the books of Samuel are the product of highly developed literary art, purposively selective, often restrained, sometimes repetitive, sometimes silent, but by whatever means intending to engage the reader in an active relationship with the text.

> What we need to understand better is that the religious vision of the Bible is given depth and subtlety precisely by being conveyed through the most sophisticated resources of prose fiction . . . The biblical tale, through the most rigorous economy of means, leads us again and again to ponder complexities of motive and ambiguities of character because these are essential aspects of its vision of man, created by God, enjoying or suffering all the consequences of human freedom.[1]

The psychological complexities of Saul or David present enough food for thought to last a lifetime, as each interacts with the other and responds to circumstances. In the course of the Commentary it is intended that references should be made to some at least of the examples of outstanding artistry in these books.

An appreciation of literary qualities in the Bible in no way conflicts with a theological understanding of its message; indeed the two are inseparably linked. The very fact that the Bible has a message to proclaim which matters supremely because it relates to eternal issues means that only the best in literary art is good enough. When God has a revelation to make to the human race he will surely see to it that it is expressed in many different ways, using every literary device to ensure that what he is saying is both arresting and unambiguous, both earthed in human experience and therefore

[1] Alter, p. 22. Alter brings to his study of the Bible wide experience of literary appreciation, and to my mind succeeds in his aim 'to illuminate the distinctive principles of the Bible's narrative art' (p. ix). He concentrates on the Pentateuch and the Former Prophets, and so draws examples from the books of Samuel, among others.

always relevant to every generation, but introducing all the same the external dimension as the only appropriate context because that is the true context of all human history. The books of Samuel form a significant part of Old Testament narrative. The unusual amount of detail related about the chief characters invites the reader to get to know them as individuals and to appreciate God's dealings with each one, both of which we shall be most likely to do if we enjoy reading about them.

'Enjoy' is not too strong a word for the deep delight to be had through a sustained effort to enter into the human situations depicted here: the hurts, ambitions, spiritual aspirations and above all the failures. To some extent both Samuel and David failed, and Saul obstinately pursued his own interpretation of his kingly office in such a way as to forfeit the divine favour. Here in these people is real life as we experience it. 'The biblical writers fashion their personages with a complicated, sometimes alluring, often fiercely insistent individuality because it is in the stubbornness of human individuality that each man and woman encounters God or ignores Him, responds to or resists Him.'[1] What grips the reader of these realistic life histories is God's verdict on each life, and the reason for David's acceptance over against Saul's rejection. Truth about God's dealings with men and women is to be discovered, vividly illustrated, in the pages of the books of Samuel. In other words, the theology in these books is, in its dynamic form, revealed in human lives rather than in textbook definitions; momentous discoveries about both man and God are on offer to those who will respond to the invitation to read and ponder the lives of those depicted here.

THE BOOKS OF SAMUEL AND THEIR PLACE IN THE LONGER HISTORY

Originally one book in the Hebrew Bible, the text was first divided by the translators who framed the Greek version, where Samuel/Kings was known as 'Basileiōn A, B, C, D' (the four books of the kingdoms). This designation was modified by Jerome, when he translated the Vulgate, to 'The Four Books of Kings', and the AV retains as a secondary title to

[1] Alter, p. 189.

17

1 AND 2 SAMUEL

1 and 2 Samuel, 'The First (Second) Book of the Kings'; 1 and 2 Kings then become the third and fourth 'Book of the Kings'. This way of referring to the books we know as 1 and 2 Samuel and 1 and 2 Kings has the merit of drawing attention to the continuity between them, for the last days of David and his death are recorded not in 2 Samuel but in 1 Kings 1 – 2. The history goes on to cover the four centuries to the collapse of Judah and the destruction of Jerusalem in 587 BC. Since after the death of Solomon the kingdom divided into the two kingdoms of Israel and Judah, a parallel account of each kingdom necessitated a much abbreviated record, a remarkable exercise in selectivity. The small amount of space devoted to Saul and the forty chapters given to David by comparison is indicative of the different assessments with which these two kings were regarded.

The books of Joshua and Judges relate how the Israelite tribes entered Canaan, occupied it and settled in the land, but these books in turn look back to the dominant figure of Moses, whose life and work are recounted in Exodus, Leviticus, Numbers and Deuteronomy. The book of Genesis not only tells the family history of Abraham, Isaac and Jacob, and how it came about that Jacob and his sons settled in Egypt, but also in its opening chapters traces the human race back to its very beginnings. Similarly, when the writer of the books of Chronicles presented his interpretation of the history, he began with genealogies which span the time from Adam to King Saul.

The resulting account sets all subsequent history from whatever part of the globe in perspective, broadening our otherwise restricted horizons, and putting us in touch with people who were very much like ourselves, and yet who had discovered some of life's secrets and so had become what C. H. Dodd called 'experts in life'. 'Here [in the Bible] also we trace the long history of a community which through good fortune and ill tested their belief in God.'[1] The distinctive characteristic of the people of this community was their firm conviction that they knew God. It is this reference to God which makes history in the Bible, and therefore in the books of Samuel, distinctive. These books are not meant merely as a source of information for people who have antiquarian interests, but rather as a

[1] C. H. Dodd, *The Authority of the Bible* (London: Nisbet, 1928), p. 298.

divinely revealed commentary on human life, in which all who will may find wise guidance in the conduct of their own lives.

It is not easy to give dates to the events recorded in 1 and 2 Samuel, but Assyrian eponym lists (lists of those who gave their names to their year of office), king lists and historical texts have enabled historians to arrive at a fixed date for the battle of Qarqar, 853 BC, in which Israel's King Ahab took part. Dates for the united monarchy are arrived at by working back (or forward) from this fixed point, using the biblical data, and in this way the period *c.* 1050–970 BC is reckoned for the events of the books of Samuel. The accession of David may tentatively be dated between 1010 and 1000 BC.

At this period no great world power was seeking to dominate the Near East. Israel's battles were waged against near neighbours, whose territory bordered the land occupied by the twelve tribes, and in particular against the Philistines, a military aristocracy from Crete, small numbers of whom had settled in Canaan in patriarchal times. Soon after Israel's arrival in Canaan, however, they had arrived in force and had occupied the coastal plain of the south-west. There they set up five city-states, organized under *s^erānîm*, 'lords', and demonstrated their mastery of iron technology and their military professionalism in their attacks against Israel. Inadvertently they played an important part in shaping developments within Israel, because it was almost certainly the persistent aggression of the Philistines that led to the repeated request for a king.[1] Throughout the reign of Saul, and initially during the reign of David also, they continued to be a thorn in Israel's side; both Saul and Jonathan died at their hands, and the Philistines penetrated eastwards to Bethshan, so dominating the Jordan valley. Yet the Philistines 'assist the narrative's movement towards David's takeover . . . David's successes against the Philistines advance him at Saul's expense. Saul's attempt to use the Philistines to destroy David misfires (18:29–29). The Philistines recognize David's kingship early in the story (21:11). And they prevent his participation in the disastrous final battle (ch. 29)'.[2] Looked at in relation to the aim of the narrative, the Philistines can be shown to play a

[1] For more detail on the Philistines, see *AOTS*, pp. 404–427; *POTT*, pp. 53–78; T. Dothan, *The Philistines and their Material Culture* (Newhaven and London: Yale University Press, 1982).

[2] Jobling, p. 15.

consistent role, and to be an indispensable part of the plot. Looked at theologically, these incidents illustrate God's control of history, though the Philistines were unaware that they were serving any other cause than their own.

By the end of David's reign the political scene had been transformed. Law and order were imposed on raiding neighbours; cordial relations were established with Phoenicia, and kingdoms to the east and north became part of David's empire, of which Jerusalem was the capital. The 'land' promised to Abraham now extended from the border of Egypt to the Euphrates (Gn. 15:18–21).

COMPOSITION AND AUTHORSHIP

Ancient libraries, made up of collections of scrolls, identified them and maybe classified them by reference to their opening words or to the person of note with whom the early columns were concerned. For that reason Samuel's name was used to identify the books that bear his name. The fact that he died before David became king is sufficient evidence to forbid our attributing authorship to him. The same argument applies to 'the Chronicles of Samuel the seer', referred to in 1 Chronicles 29:29 as one of the sources for 'the acts of King David, from first to last'. Clearly the name was not intended to imply authorship.

How then did these remarkable books come into being? This is the basic question which motivated Old Testament scholars, largely in Germany, during the eighteenth and nineteenth centuries, though they did not address themselves particularly to the books of Samuel but rather to the Pentateuch. Their method was to submit the biblical text to analysis in accordance with the norms of scientific practice, and the movement became associated with the name of Julius Wellhausen (1844–1918), who gave classic expression to the theory of proposed documentary sources behind the Pentateuch.[1] His analysis of the Pentateuch was, however, closely bound up with an understanding of Samuel and of Israel's history on its broadest plan.

---

[1] J. Wellhausen, *Die Komposition des Hexateuchs* (1877), the Hexateuch being the Pentateuch together with the book of Joshua.

The Documentary Hypothesis

According to this hypothesis, four strata (J, E, D and P), each representing a different source, could be discerned in the early books of the Bible: J, the earliest, preferred the name Jahweh (or Yahweh) for God; E, a century or so later, preferred the name Elohim; D, the Deuteronomic document, was identified with the scroll found in the Temple during the reign of Josiah in 621 BC; P consisted of cultic details, lists and genealogies attributed to priestly writers, and was dated in the sixth or fifth century. According to Wellhausen's theory, the books of the Pentateuch were therefore composite documents, made up of extracts from these sources which were to be distinguished by differences of vocabulary, viewpoint and theological emphasis. Apparent discrepancies, duplications and repetitions in the biblical books were accounted for by attributing them to different sources which reflected the particular outlook of the period in which they were written.

Wellhausen too had his special interest. He was a historian in search of reliable documents from which to construct a history of Israel, and for this purpose he published in 1883 his *Prolegomena zur Geschichte Israels*,[1] a work in which he summarized his assessment of the documentary sources of the biblical books from Genesis to Chronicles, especially from the point of view of their historical reliability. In 1 Samuel 7 – 12, for example, he distinguished a later source in which Samuel is 'a saint of the first degree', acting as a theocratic leader should, urging repentance and experiencing God's vindication (1 Sa. 7:2–17; 8; 10:17 – 12:25). But this he sees as contradicting the whole of the rest of the tradition, found in 1 Samuel 9:1 – 10:16.[2] When he compared the picture of David in Chronicles with that of the books of Samuel he found in Chronicles 'a feeble holy picture, seen through a cloud of incense', and remarked, 'it is only the tradition of the older source that possesses historical value'.[3] Wellhausen's analytical method of discerning the sources behind the historical books set a pattern which has dominated critical studies ever since, despite the influence of form criticism and, more recently, appreciation of the text as the testimony of a worshipping community, with a message that is important in

[1] ET, *Prolegomena to the History of Israel* (New York: Meridian Books, 1957).
[2] *Ibid.*, pp. 248–249.   [3] *Ibid.*, p. 182.

its own right. Nevertheless, there have been many variations on the documentary theme over the years, so creating a complicated web of possibilities.

One early theory was that two sources lay behind the books of Samuel, and that the earlier was the continuation of the J document of the Pentateuch, while the later could be identified as E.[1] Although this theory was at first influential, it has not in the long term won wide support. A three-source theory, put forward by Eissfeldt, who added a conjectured source L to J and E, did not find many followers.[2] Nevertheless, whether two or three strands of tradition are postulated, most scholars have concluded that diverse origin accounts for the apparent duplications and differences of viewpoint alleged to be found in 1 Samuel. In 2 Samuel the narrative has been judged to be more a continuous whole, especially chapters 9 – 20 (together with 1 Ki. 1 – 2), which have become known as 'the Court History of David', and have been described as 'the supreme historical treasure of Samuel'.[3] These chapters win this accolade because they are judged to have been written by someone who was not only a contemporary of David, but who also knew at first hand life at David's court.

A compilation of earlier accounts, which may have included a life of Samuel, a history of the ark, and accounts of the inauguration of the monarchy, as well as annals of David's reign, would have been put together by an editor, probably during the exile. Both Joshua and Judges were thought to show signs of Deuteronomic editing, and, though in 1 and 2 Samuel Deuteronomic influence was less marked, a Deuteronomic redactor was credited with compiling these books also. Poetic passages such as Hannah's song (1 Sa. 2:1–10) and David's poems (2 Sa. 22:2 – 23:7), together with the extra information in the Appendix (2 Sa. 21 – 24), were thought to be late additions, added after the remainder of the book had taken shape.

[1] K. Budde, writing in 1890, thought he identified the J document; C. H. Cornill argued in favour of an E source in the books of Samuel (1885, 1887, 1890); T. Klähn in 1914 claimed to have proved on linguistic grounds that the J source continued into the books of Samuel, a view taken up by O. Eissfeldt (1925, 1931).

[2] O. Eissfeldt, *The Old Testament, An Introduction* (ET, Oxford; Basil Blackwell, 1965), p. 275.

[3] G. W. Anderson, *A Critical Introduction to the Old Testament* (London: Duckworth, 1959), p. 80.

Before moving on to consider more recent developments of critical scholarship, we pause at this point in order to assess the method behind the Documentary Hypothesis, which has dominated the field for well over a century. This consensus is in itself indicative of the degree to which the method suited the intellectual mood of the nineteenth century, and the continuing rationalism of the twentieth.

1. It was inevitable that questions concerning the composition of the books of the Bible should have been raised; the major problem was lack of hard evidence on which to base an answer. True, reference is made in the biblical books to documents which could be consulted at the time of writing (*e.g.* Jos. 10:13; 2 Sa. 1:18; 1 Ki. 11:41), which proves that there were 'books behind the Bible', but these are no longer extant. In the absence of factual checks, the weaknesses in the documentary theories were slow to emerge; eventually the proliferation of possibilities demonstrated how damaging to any theory was the total lack of proof.

2. Wellhausen and the others who shaped the documentary theories were thoroughly equipped scholars who brought to their task linguistic, literary and historical knowledge. They studied the text of the Bible in detail and encouraged rigorous scholarship. On the debit side, 'the text became controlled by scholars, whereas previously scholars had subjected themselves to the text. The text now was subject to their tools, methods, conclusions. The controlling factor was no longer any claim of Biblical authority but now was scientific method, which enjoyed enormous popularity and respect in this period.'[1] The ruling criterion was 'reasonableness'.

3. The outcome of the search for documents was a fragmented biblical text. The dissection process 'killed' the life-giving message inherent in the books of the Bible, yet they have never ceased to speak authoritatively, and their literary creativity, quite apart from their spiritual power, has often been noted; not least, in the books of Samuel the 'Court History of David' has been recognized as a literary gem. Thus the vitality of these books continues to reassert itself. Meanwhile modern studies of the Pentateuch are highly

---

[1] W. Brueggemann, 'Questions addressed in study of the Pentateuch', in W. Brueggemann and H. W. Wolff, *The Vitality of Old Testament Traditions* (Atlanta: John Knox Press, 1975), pp. 13–14.

critical of the classical Documentary Hypothesis.[1]

The Deuteronomistic History

The claim that a Deuteronomic editor left his mark, however lightly, on the books of Samuel has continued to find favour, especially under the influence of Martin Noth, whose significant work on the subject has been translated into English some forty years after its first publication in Germany in 1943.[2] This has proved to be one of the most enduring theories to be published during the first half of the twentieth century.

Whereas it had been usual to attribute to a Deuteronomic hand the editing of the individual books from Joshua to 2 Kings, Noth went a stage further by postulating that Deuteronomy to 2 Kings was a continuous narrative, compiled by one writer. Though this Deuteronomistic writer had made use of existing documents, he freely added his own comments and thus, from diverse material, succeeded in compiling a history which reflected certain theological viewpoints and interests, and which was, to that extent, a unified whole. Noth denied that J, E and P extended beyond Numbers, and regarded the literary sources used by the editor/author of 1 and 2 Samuel as independent units or collections. The Deuteronomistic writer was looking for a meaning in the history of Israel. 'The meaning which he discovered was that God was recognisably at work in this history, continuously meeting the accelerating moral decline with warnings and punishments . . .'[3] Thus there was a divine retribution at work in the history of the people of God, and the Deuteronomist made this the great unifying factor of his work as he commented on the course of events.

Noth's concept of a Deuteronomistic History continues to have an influential part to play in any research on the com-

---

[1] *E.g.* R. N. Whybray, *The Making of the Pentateuch* (Sheffield: JSOT Press, 1987), esp. pp. 43–131. Whybray assesses philosophical, linguistic, literary and cultural aspects of the Documentary Hypothesis, and shows how the breaking of texts into separate documents 'often destroys literary and aesthetic qualities which are themselves important data which ought not to be ignored' (p. 130).

[2] M. Noth, *The Deuteronomistic History* (Sheffield: JSOT Press, 1981), which consists of pp. 1–110 of *Überlieferungsgeschichtliche Studien* (Tübingen: Max Niemeyer Verlag, ²1957). The adjective 'Deuteronomistic' as opposed to 'Deuteronomic' is used to distinguish the hypothesis put forward by Noth.

[3] *Ibid.*, p. 89.

position of the books from Deuteronomy to 2 Kings. Indeed, as E. W. Nicholson comments in his foreword to the English edition,

> This is a 'classic' work in the sense that it still remains the fundamental study of the corpus of literature with which it is concerned, and still provides, as far as the majority of scholars are concerned, the basis and framework for further investigation of the composition and nature of this corpus.[1]

Though this assertion may need some qualification in the light of the most recent trends, its estimate of the importance of Noth's book is not exaggerated.

Yet when the Deuteronomistic historian came to narrate the events of the reigns of Saul, David and Solomon, Noth believes that he found he was dealing with traditional accounts which 'absolved [him] from the need to organise and construct the narrative himself'.[2] Here the narratives themselves agreed with the emphases which he himself wished to make, and there was therefore little that he needed to add, whereas in 1 Kings 12 – 2 Kings 25, by contrast, he both supplied the chronology and related the reigns of the monarchs of the two kingdoms to each other, in addition to passing judgment on the individual kings and on the monarchy as an institution. According to Noth, the contribution of the Deuteronomistic historian is limited in the books of Samuel to the following passages:

    i. 1 Samuel 7:2b, the chronological note: 'a long time passed, some twenty years'.

    ii. 7:7–14, which Noth connects with Judges 13:1, where the Philistines are said to have dominated Israel for forty years.

    iii. 13:1, the chronological note concerning Saul's reign.

    iv. 2 Samuel 2:10–11, the chronology of the reign of Ishbosheth, and of David's reign in Hebron.

    v. 1 Samuel 8 – 12, where the Deuteronomistic historian reveals his disapproval of the establishment of the monarchy.

    vi. 2 Samuel 5:4–5, the chronology of David's whole reign, and 5:6–12, David's conquest of Jerusalem, which enabled him to house the ark in his own city.

[1] *Ibid.*, p. ix.   [2] *Ibid.*, p. 54.

Apart from these relatively few passages, Noth attributed to the Deuteronomistic historian only occasional rearrangement of the material he found in his sources to suit his purpose (e.g. 2 Sa. 8, which chronologically belongs earlier), and he emphatically denies that 2 Samuel 7, in which Nathan pronounces concerning the future of David's house, could belong to this historian, though he may have made some insertions, notably verse 13a and verses 22–24.[1]

Noth viewed the purpose of the Deuteronomistic historian as particularly pessimistic, seeing him as speaking of Israel's 'final rejection and therefore its downfall because of its repeated apostasy'.[2] Many scholars, on the other hand, have interpreted the fact that 2 Kings ends with the release of Jehoiachin from prison as an indication of qualified optimism. Similarly, the sin – repentance – renewal theme, characteristic of Deuteronomy and well illustrated in 1 Samuel 7:3–14 and in 2 Samuel 7, is thought by several scholars to point in the same direction.[3]

In the course of developing his thesis that Deuteronomy to Kings was originally one narrative, Noth drew attention to the overlap between books, which he thought went back to the time when the whole was divided.[4] The divisions accounted for the failure of earlier scholars to identify the extent of the original work, especially as many had become absorbed in studies of the Pentateuch (or Hexateuch), and had become accustomed to think of Deuteronomy as part of that collection of books. Moreover, Noth thought that after the time of the Deuteronomistic writer, additions to Joshua/Judges (between Jos. 23 and Jdg. 2:6), and at the end of Judges and 2 Samuel, obscured the issue. Noth conjectured that in the original work speeches of anticipation and retrospection summed up the judgments of the Deuteronomistic writer. Thus 1 Samuel 12 would have brought to an end the period of the judges, while 1 Kings 8:14–53, Solomon's prayer of dedication of the Temple, would have concluded the section on the period of the early

---

[1] *Ibid.*, pp. 54–55.   [2] *Ibid.*, p. 79.

[3] *E.g.* G. von Rad, *Studies in Deuteronomy* (London: SCM Press, 1953), pp. 90–91; D. J. McCarthy, 'II Samuel 7 and the Structure of the Deuteronomic History', *JBL* 84 (1965), pp. 131–138; Gordon 1984, who comments, 'Noth's omission probably has more than a little to do with the incompatibility of the dynastic oracle with his own conception of the purpose of the History!' (p. 20).

[4] *Cf.* Dt. 34/Jos. 1; Jos. 24:29–31/Jdg. 2:7–10; Jdg. 13:1/1 Sa. 7:1–14.

kings of Israel.

Noth's contention is that the skill of this Deuteronomistic writer is demonstrated in the unity he imposes on disparate sources, for he is wholly responsible for 'the coherence of this complex of material and hence the unity of the whole history in Joshua-Kings which is clearly *intentional*, as is shown by the form of these books as we have it'.[1] Since there is no trace of Deuteronomistic editing in Genesis to Numbers, Deuteronomy must belong with the books that follow it, and on this argument Noth based his rejection of the theory that Genesis to Joshua should be seen as an entity, a 'Hexateuch'.[2] The central importance of Deuteronomy was inescapable either way; it dominated the judgment of the writers responsible for Joshua to Kings.

Sources in the books of Samuel
Already it has become apparent that, according to Noth, Deuteronomistic editing in the books of Samuel is somewhat limited. Here the Deuteronomistic writer was able to take over extensive collections of traditions, compiled long before his time. These are thought to have comprised the following sources:

  i. The Ark Narrative (1 Sa. 4:1b – 7:1), with the possible addition of 2 Samuel 6.
 ii. The Shiloh traditions (Sa. 1:1 – 4:1a), sometimes considered to be part of the Ark Narrative.
iii. Traditions concerning Saul (1 Sa. 7 – 15), collected long before the time of the Deuteronomistic editor, who would have added passages recording his disapproval of the monarchy. The reign of Saul (1 Sa. 13 – 15) is sometimes considered a separate source, hence the division sometimes made at 1 Samuel 12.
 iv. The 'History of David's Rise' (1 Sa. 16 – 2 Sa. 5:10 or 7:29).
  v. The 'Succession Narrative' (2 Sa. 9 – 20 and 1 Ki. 1 – 2).

[1] Noth, p. 10.
[2] Wellhausen, *Prolegomena*: 'From a literary point of view . . . it is more accurate to speak of the Hexateuch than of the Pentateuch' (p. 6). The suggestion was widely accepted, and continued to be employed by many scholars, including G. von Rad, into the 1950s.

1 AND 2 SAMUEL

(The delineation of sources iv. and v. owes much to L. Rost.[1])

It would be misleading to give the impression that this list of sources is universally accepted, for there are many variations in detail on the sources recognized by different scholars, even though i., iv. and v. are widely accepted. Similarly, a variety of theories characterizes the subject of the Deuteronomistic editing of the books of Samuel.[2] The absence of any means of verification tends to encourage the proliferation of theories, and inevitably leads to a certain scepticism regarding any possibility of 'assured results' in this field.

Prophetic history

Meanwhile preoccupation with Deuteronomistic theories had diverted scholarly attention from the part which the prophets may well have played in compiling collections of written documents that related to their times. At the end of the last century A. F. Kirkpatrick considered that 'contemporary prophetical histories' were probably the chief sources of the books of Samuel.[3] Moreover, he could support the supposition with evidence from 1 Chronicles 29:29, where the Chronicles of Samuel, Nathan and Gad are referred to as sources of information on the reign of David. The statement was meant to assure the reader that the resulting account rested on the most reliable authority. The idea of a prophetic history has been taken up recently by P. K. McCarter, who regards it as a middle stage in the growth of canonical books: 'Once the limited scope of the latter [the Deuteronomistic overlay] is recognized . . . it becomes apparent that it was at some pre-Deuteronomistic stage that the stories were set in their basic order, and the middle stage takes on considerable importance.'[4] At this pre-Deuteronomistic stage, therefore, there was already a continuous prophetic history. McCarter envisages this as consisting of three sections in 1 Samuel – the story of Samuel (1 Sa. 1 – 7); the story of Saul (1 Sa. 8 – 15); the story

---

[1] L. Rost, *The Succession to the Throne of David* (Sheffield: JSOT Press, 1982); originally published in German in 1926.
[2] Gordon 1984, pp. 14–22, provides a succinct account of recent trends, together with a bibliography. He notes 'the imperialist tendencies of the phenomenon of Deuteronomism in current Old Testament study', and points out that, apart from phraseological criteria, little that is regarded as characteristic of D 'is peculiar to the Deuteronomistic History' (p. 18).
[3] Kirkpatrick 1880, p. 10.   [4] McCarter 1980, p. 18.

of David's rise (1 Sa. 16 – 31) – and all three he regards as dominated by the figure of Samuel the prophet.

The prophetic viewpoint was negative with regard to the monarchy: it was a concession to a wanton demand of the people; but though the king would be head of the government, he would be subject to the word of the prophet as the spokesman of Yahweh. McCarter admits that there are affinities between this prophetic outlook and the Deuteronomic tradition, and describes it as 'proto-Deuteronomic'. He sees this as the reason why the Deuteronomistic writer needed to make only slight revision of the text before him, and then add to the continued history of David's rise in 2 Samuel 1 – 5 the 'Deuteronomistic capstone', as McCarter describes 2 Samuel 7, the theological centre of the books of Samuel.

We have taken the briefest look at the approach of a few selected scholars to the question of the sources underlying the books of Samuel. In reality, the picture is far more complicated. Nevertheless, an attempt to follow the arguments of even a few contributors is important, if only to indicate how impossible is the task of arriving at any definitive answer to the questions, 'How did these books of Samuel come to be written?' and 'What sources did their authors use?' After two hundred years of biblical criticism in the West, the fact has to be faced that even such established concepts as the Pentateuch have been shaken by conflicting theories of composition. In the absence of objective criteria there is no way, apart from scholarly consensus which endures for a while but is open to new directives, of evaluating all the hard work that has gone into the search for sources, but which has come up with so many varying possibilities. According to one recent writer, 'It is no exaggeration to say that the truly assured results of historical critical scholarship concerning authorship, date and provenance would fill but a pamphlet.'[1] The fact is that scholarly interest has been moving away from historical-critical study, partly under the influence of the methods applied in the study of secular literature, and partly, one suspects, because of the felt need to find a more fruitful approach to the study of the biblical books.

[1] D. M. Gunn, 'New Directions in the Study of Hebrew Narrative', *JSOT* 39 (1987), p. 66.

Diagrammatic summary of the main developments

	Canonical Tradition	Wellhausen	Martin Noth	Modern Literary Analysis
Genesis	Pentateuch (one book)	Hexateuch	Tetrateuch	Tends to adopt Genesis to Kings as standard unit
Exodus				
Leviticus				
Numbers				
Deuteronomy			Deuteronomistic History	
Joshua	Former Prophets	Israel's traditions assigned to 'collections'		
Judges				
[Ruth]				
1 and 2 Samuel				
1 and 2 Kings				

Recent trends

Generations brought up to look for sources do not easily abandon the method which has dominated their research and shaped their whole approach to the text. Yet a shift away from historical criticism has been taking place.

The work of Brevard Childs,[1] for example, has marked a significant change of perspective. Whereas for two hundred years theology has largely been subordinated to history – 'The cake has been history, the icing theology'[2] – the aim of Childs

[1] *E.g.* B. Childs, *Biblical Theology in Crisis* (Philadelphia: Westminster Press, 1970); *Introduction to the Old Testament as Scripture* (Philadelphia: Fortress Press, and London: SCM Press, 1979).

[2] R. W. L. Moberly, 'The Church's Use of the Bible: the Work of Brevard Childs', *ExpT* 99/4 (1988), p. 106.

rebuked the naked and unbridled use of royal authority'.[1] To be king in Israel was therefore quite a different matter from being king in the countries round about. Saul did not understand this distinction, and resented Samuel's 'interference', whereas David appreciated the point that the Lord his God was the focus of authority, and therefore he was willing to submit to the word of his prophet even though, in the eyes of the watching world, it must have seemed that David's own authority would thereby be weakened. Here lay the crucial distinction between Saul and David. The man after God's own heart submitted to God's word, obeyed his prophets, and found acceptance and forgiveness, despite his many glaring faults and failures. Saul obstinately clung to his rights as king, but lost the throne.

2 Samuel 7

This important chapter lays the foundation for the Davidic dynasty. By divine decree it is declared to be 'for ever', and yet in 597 BC Jehoachin, David's descendant, was deported, soon to be followed by his only successor on the throne, Zedekiah. Jerusalem was left in ruins, the Temple of the Lord was plundered, and there was neither relief from suffering nor ground for hope. If, as many people think, Israel's historical books were compiled at that time, the contrast between God's promises to David and the stark reality of a whole generation languishing in a foreign land put a desperate strain on Israel's faith. This climactic chapter in the books of Samuel was one to dwell upon and use to help formulate an understanding of God's purpose.

The Lord's sovereignty is established by his word to both prophet and king. What counts is not David's aspiration to build a house for the Lord, but what the Lord commands. The Lord's authority and initiative is insisted upon throughout Nathan's address to David: 'I commanded [the judges] to shepherd my people Israel' (v. 7); 'I took you from the pasture . . . I have been with you wherever you went, and have cut off all your enemies before you' (v. 8–9). In his sovereignty the Lord also declares what he will do in the future: he is Israel's Lord God, while the human king is

[1] W. J. Dumbrell, *Covenant and Creation* (Exeter: Paternoster Press, 1984), p. 138.

dependent on the supreme King whom he serves.

For his part, the Lord undertakes to exalt his servant (2 Sa. 7:9). The promise of 'a great name' is reminiscent of God's covenant with Abraham (Gn. 12:2), and suggests (though the word 'covenant' nowhere appears in these verses) that the Davidic kingship is being incorporated into the Abrahamic covenant. This is reinforced by the reference to God's people Israel dwelling in their own place, undisturbed by enemies (v. 10), a reference to Genesis 15:18–21 and Deuteronomy 11:24. Moreover, the covenant word *ḥesed*, God's 'steadfast love' (v. 15), ensures the fulfilment of the promises, which are here unconditional, though the need for chastisement is foreseen. The question is whether David's descendants will 'keep covenant', and if they do not fulfil their obligations how God can achieve his purpose of blessing.

When the books of Samuel are seen in the wider context of the history from Joshua to the end of Kings, the contrast between promise and fulfilment is sharp. The cycle of apostasy – repentance – restoration, typical of the period of the judges, was repeated in the period of the kings. It was the theme of Deuteronomy (*e.g.* Dt. 30:1–3), where the possibility of being uprooted from the land and cast into another land was faced (Dt. 29:25–28). Disintegration followed Solomon's reign, constant apostasy marked the northern kingdom of Israel, and the end came when Assyria carried away captive most of the population. Judah and Jerusalem suffered a similar fate at the hand of the Babylonians not much more than a century later. Had God forgotten to be gracious? Had his covenant promises gone for good?

The question whether the Lord would restore the kingdom to Israel was, of course, still a live issue during the ministry of Jesus, hence the popularity of the 'kingdom' theme in the teaching of Jesus, and hence also the disciples' question about the kingdom after the resurrection (Acts 1:6). By the time the Gospels came to be written, the truth had dawned that the promises to both Abraham and David had been more than fulfilled in the person and work of Jesus. The point is taken up in the very first verse of the New Testament, 'Jesus Christ, the son of David, the son of Abraham' (Mt. 1:1), and is referred to in its last chapter, 'I am the root and the offspring of David' (Rev. 22:16), as well as many times in between (*e.g.* Lk. 1:32; Rom. 1:3; 2 Tim. 2:8).

The historical David, for all his faults, came to stand for the idealized king, and the refrain 'for the sake of David my servant' (1 Ki. 11:13) spoke of mercy to Solomon and his successors, with all their shortcomings. The prophetic word in the promise of Nathan to David had given rise to 'a completely independent cycle of conceptions . . . Of the ideal, theocratic David, exemplary in obedience.'[1] Through the years, prophets and psalmists took up the hope and developed the messianic concepts even further. This hope was to endure, despite the shock of exile and the ambiguity of events in the centuries that followed it, till the dawn of the gospel era (Lk. 2:25, 38).

The creative power of the word of God was demonstrated clearly in the way the prophecy of Nathan developed over the centuries. As von Rad so helpfully expresses his understanding of Israel's history as presented by the books of Kings, 'The decisive factor for Israel does not lie in the things which ordinarily cause a stir in history, nor in the vast problems inherent in history, but it lies in applying a few simple theological and prophetic fundamental axioms about the nature of the divine word.'[2] Definite and comprehensible as these axioms were, there were nevertheless tensions between divine judgment and promised salvation. What the biblical history provides is an overview of God's judgment on individuals and nations, but particularly on Israel; yet this was the nation that had received the promises. How could the covenant between God and man stand if on the human side it was broken time and time again? Even within the books of Samuel that tension is already apparent in the human failures of Israel's successive leaders. Nor was that tension resolved during the Old Testament period; rather it provided 'the grit that caused the pearl within the oyster', provoking constructive longing for better integration of actual living with the covenant ideal, and above all longing for a king on the throne of David who would govern 'with justice and with righteousness . . . for evermore' (Is. 9:7).

TEXT

Before the middle of the twentieth century, the earliest known Hebrew manuscripts of Old Testament texts dated from about

---

[1] Von Rad, *Studies in Deuteronomy*, p. 88.   [2] *Ibid.*, p. 91.

the ninth century AD, whereas part of the Gospel of John, known as p[52], goes back as far as the first half of the second century AD. At first sight it seems strange that older copies of Old Testament books in Hebrew should not have survived, but there is an explanation. In part this was because, after the standardization of the text early in the Christian era, non-standard texts were eliminated. Then again, such was the veneration with which Jewish scholars regarded their copies of the Hebrew scriptures that, when the scrolls were worn and needed to be replaced, they carefully relegated them to a special room in the synagogue, known as a *genizah*, prior to giving them an honourable burial. In this way the scriptures were protected against improper use, but they were also unlikely to survive for the later use of interested scholars.[1]

All the more extraordinary, therefore, was the discovery of Hebrew manuscript fragments of all the books of the Old Testament (except Esther) – many of which were written before the Christian era – among the Dead Sea Scrolls, which were brought to light at the end of the 1940s. These manuscripts, including a complete scroll of Isaiah in Hebrew, renewed research and debate on the transmission of the text of the Old Testament.

So far as the books of Samuel are concerned, the Hebrew text had long been recognized as presenting problems. Already in 1871 Wellhausen had used the Greek of the LXX to reconstruct what he judged to be a more adequate Hebrew text; while Driver could write: 'The Books of Samuel . . . though they contain classical examples of a chaste and beautiful Hebrew prose style . . . have suffered unusually from transcriptional corruption, and hence raise frequently questions of text'.[2]

Attention is drawn in the Commentary to a number of places where scholars have argued in favour of preferring the LXX reading to the MT. In view of the fact that the LXX potentially represents a Hebrew text older by a thousand years than the traditional Hebrew MT, its evidence is important, though it must be noted that there is as yet no critical edition of the LXX of Samuel. The initial translation of the Pentateuch into

[1] One exception is the contents of a *genizah* in a Cairo synagogue, which included many ancient portions of the Hebrew scriptures. *Cf.* P. Kahle, *The Cairo Geniza* (Oxford: Basil Blackwell, ²1959).

[2] Driver 1913, p. i.

Greek (the only part to which the legend of the 'seventy' translators applies) was made in Alexandria during the third century BC, to meet the liturgical needs of Jews for whom Greek had become the mother tongue. Subsequently the other books were translated, though when and where is uncertain.

The books of Samuel have been well served by finds in cave 4 at Qumran. There are three fragmentary texts of these books, all of which are important for textual study: 1. a well-preserved roll containing both books, which is known as 4QSamᵃ; 2. a handful of very old fragments, which one can date 'scarcely later than 200 BC', are designated 4QSamᵇ; 3. a fragmentary manuscript of 2 Samuel 14 – 15, which is known as 4QSamᶜ.[1]

1. At the time of writing, 4QSamᵃ is still not officially published, although it has been the subject of major study, especially by E. C. Ulrich. In the past scholars had to rely partly on insight and intuition in using the LXX text critically; 4QSamᵃ, by giving access to a pre-Christian Hebrew text of the Old Testament, provides a 'control' for the text-critical use of the LXX.

Studies so far have established that there is frequent agreement between 4QSamᵃ and the LXX. Nevertheless, there are also disagreements, which need to be accounted for, and the suggestion has been made that each should be regarded as an independent source. Interestingly, where Samuel and Chronicles overlap, the text from Qumran often preserves a text much closer to the text of Samuel used by the author of Chronicles than to the traditional text of Samuel surviving from the Middle Ages (the MT).

2. 4QSamᵇ, together with a worn portion of Jeremiah and a fragment of Exodus, is thought to be a master scroll, the property of the Qumran community from its inception in the third century BC. This archaic manuscript 'obviously reflects

[1] F. M. Cross, Jr., *The Ancient Library of Qumran and Modern Biblical Studies*, revised edition (Grand Rapids: Baker Book House, 1980), pp. 40–42. Recent work on the Qumran texts of Samuel may also be found in E. C. Ulrich, Jr., *The Qumran Text of Samuel and Josephus* (Missoula: Scholars Press, 1978); and *idem*, '4QSamᶜ; A Fragmentary Manuscript of 2 Samuel 14 – 15', *BASOR* 235 (1979), pp. 1–25. For an assessment of Ulrich's work, see E. Tov, 'The Textual Affiliations of 4QSamᵃ', *JSOT* 14 (1979), pp. 37–53; E. Tov (ed.), *The Hebrew and Greek Texts of Samuel* (Jerusalem: Academon, 1980); G. Vermes, 'Biblical Studies and the Dead Sea Scrolls 1947–1987: Retrospects and Prospects', *JSOT* 39 (1987), pp. 113–128.

at many points a text which antedates both the proto-Masoretic recension and that underlying the Septuagint, though its affinities are clearly with the latter'.[1]

On the assumption that the LXX Samuel was translated in Egypt, the question arises whether texts were imported from Egypt to Qumran. Cross finds no good reason to suppose that this would be the case, and concludes that this manuscript 'is a witness to a collateral line of tradition that persists in Palestine from a time antedating the divergence of the Chronicler's Palestinian text of Samuel and the Hebrew textual tradition surviving in Egypt'. This divergence would have taken place no earlier than the fourth century BC and no later than the early third century BC.

The question remains where the Massoretic text underlying the standard English translations of the books of Samuel originated. Since Cross believes that this was neither in Palestine nor in Egypt, he conjectures that the proto-Massoretic text developed independently in Babylon, and was reintroduced into Palestine in the Hellenistic period or later. At present, however, evidence for the place of origin of the various 'families' of texts is not available. The analogy of a book like Isaiah (for the great Isaiah scroll from Qumran was in this 'standard' or proto-Massoretic text) argues that it is old.

3. The third manuscript contains parts of 2 Samuel 14 and 15, together with four fragments, and has been described in detail by E. C. Ulrich. He dates it in the first quarter of the first century BC, identifies other work by the same scribe, and exposes his idiosyncrasies as a copyist. Ulrich concludes his study, 'Despite his many lapses, he [the scribe of 4QSam^c] produced a text noticeably superior to our Massoretic *textus receptus* . . . for, having considerably enriched our knowledge of the text and text history of Samuel, [he] merits our gratitude.'[2] Though the text it provides is limited to two chapters, this manuscript adds its evidence to the early forms of the text of 1 and 2 Samuel.

The task which faces translators of the Old Testament in deciding upon a 'source text' (the version of the Hebrew from which all participating scholars will work) requires very specialized knowledge and sound judgment if all the relevant

---

[1] Cross, *Library of Qumran & Modern Biblical Studies*, p. 190.
[2] Ulrich, '4QSam^c', p. 25.

evidence is to be taken into account. The standard Hebrew text (the MT) is basic because it was itself the product of scholarly efforts to ensure that only the authoritative traditions were handed on, and every effort was made to preserve intact the text established in the early second century AD. Nevertheless, there are many places where the MT Samuel as it stands is unintelligible, partly because the language of the Old Testament is no longer perfectly known, but also because of mistakes made during copying.

A member of the Finnish Committee for Bible translation, Raija Sollamo, has published his committee's principles for establishing their text.[1] Sollamo points out that in theory it is appropriate to divide the textual history of the Hebrew into four stages: i. the oldest written texts, no longer available; ii. finally compiled and edited texts (*e.g.* the books of Samuel/Kings); iii. the consonantal text approved by Jewish scholars after AD 70; iv. the MT with vowels and punctuation inserted. The aim is to use the second stage as the source text for translation:

> There is no reason to aim for the first stage, because then literary criticism would be needed, the Bible would have to be broken up into pieces, and even so we should reach only a hypothetical source text. Even the reconstruction of the second stage is full of difficulties, and it will never succeed perfectly.[2]

The reference to 'literary criticism', or source criticism, ties up with what we have already written in connection with methods of approach. The specialist in textual studies is obliged to work with the books as they have been handed down to us, using the MT whenever it is satisfactory and the consonantal text when the vocalization appears to be mistaken and the consonants permit a meaningful translation. When neither of these is intelligible the ancient translations may be consulted; but this particular committee has great respect for the MT, and where no reliable conclusion can be reached,

---

[1] R. Sollamo, 'The Source Text for the Translation of the Old Testament', *BT* 37/3 (1986), pp. 319–322. No mention is made here of the Qumran evidence.

[2] *Ibid.*, p. 320.

tends to translate in accordance with the earlier translation tradition.

Not every translation committee is so careful to conserve tradition, however, and the translators of the NAB, for instance, have been so impressed with readings of Qumran texts published by F. M. Cross that they have incorporated them into their translation. In the books of Samuel the published *Textual Notes* record over four hundred emendations, the vast majority of them from the LXX; of these some seventy-three are supported from a Qumran text, and twenty-two follow a Qumran text without further support.[1] Thus the question is raised whether the resulting translation is to be regarded as superior to the standard versions of 1 and 2 Samuel – a matter which concerns every reader, not only those trained in textual study.

A most significant challenge to the thesis that 4QSam[a] and the LXX are generally superior to the MT of Samuel has come from Stephen Pisano.[2] His conclusion, after analysing some seventy passages where 4QSam[a] or the LXX differ from the MT by way of a major plus or minus (*i.e.* words added or missing from the text), is 'that in the vast majority of cases a large plus or minus occurring in the LXX or 4QSam[a] vis-à-vis MT indicates a further literary activity by LXX or 4QSam[a]'.[3] He therefore urges caution in emending the MT too quickly on the basis of another text, especially where large insertions or omissions are concerned, though he acknowledges that the texts of the LXX and 4QSam[a] are helpful for the restoration of the Hebrew texts where corruptions have occurred through faulty transmission.

In a review of Pisano's book H. G. M. Williamson finds his arguments convincing on some passages, but in general considers him to be rather too reluctant to depart from the MT. Williamson urges that 'Neither the Masoretic Text nor (as has become fashionable) the LXX should be given the prior benefit of the doubt, but each instance should be judged on

---

[1] *Textual Notes on the New American Bible* (Paterson, N.I.: St Anthony's Guild, no date or editor given), pp. 342–351.

[2] S. Pisano, *Additions or Omissions in the Books of Samuel: The Significant Pluses and Minuses in the Massoretic, LXX and Qumran Texts* (Freiburg: Universitatsverlag, and Gottingen: Vandenheock & Ruprecht, 1984).

[3] *Ibid.*, p. 283.

its own merits.'[1] This involves a great deal of extra work, but to weigh all the arguments in each case will eventually lead to more reliable judgments.

Two considerations may be of help to the non-specialist reader. 1. The standard Hebrew consonantal text made about AD 100 was felt to be necessary because manuscripts were in circulation which showed variants that the traditional teachers judged to be less close to the original than the best they had available. 2. Even where the Qumran texts seem to make better sense, caution is necessary because some of the early scribes (*i.e.* those at work before AD 100) were not averse to harmonizing or innovating, hence the need for an authoritative text. Once the Qumran texts have been published, so that work on them is open to public scrutiny and scholarly judgment, assessment of their part in establishing the Hebrew text should become easier. In this present Commentary some alternative readings are noted, but it is not always possible to adjudicate between them.

Even academics who have made specialist studies of the Dead Sea Scrolls (such as Geza Vermes, who has been associated with Qumran studies from the start) admit to their inability to pronounce judgment on the claims and suggestions of other scholars. Vermes finds particularly problematic the existence of so great a variety of texts prior to the second century BC, and wonders whether the lack of need for textual unity prior to this period should not be attributed 'to the unchallenged doctrinal and legal authority of the priesthood which considered itself to have been divinely appointed for this supreme doctrinal and judicial role'.[2] Socio-historical circumstances are certainly important, and, although the case is not quite parallel, one wonders how many recensions of the Scriptures there must be in China, where Christians make their own copies of books of the Bible. What should impress us more than the variety of small differences in the text is the astonishing similarity between all the books and the MSS that have to date been discovered. When the Qumran scrolls were first discovered they were expected to be strikingly different, 'being about a thousand years older than the earliest Massoretic codices', but 'the expectation did not materialize'.[3]

[1] H. G. M. Williamson in *JTS* 37 (1986), pp. 458–461.
[2] Vermes, 'Biblical Studies and the Dead Sea Scrolls 1947–1987', p. 125.
[3] *Ibid.*, p. 120.

Though there are certainly many questions that remain to be answered, considerations such as this help to keep the problems in perspective.

ANALYSIS

I. THE END OF AN ERA: SAMUEL, THE LAST JUDGE OF ISRAEL
(1 Samuel 1:1 – 12:25)
   a. The birth and boyhood of Samuel (1:1 – 4:1a)
      i. A woman's prayer is answered (1:1–28)
      ii. Hannah exults in the Lord (2:1–10)
      iii. Samuel encounters corruption at Shiloh (2:11–36)
      iv. The Lord calls Samuel (3:1 – 4:1a)
   b. Disaster, repentance and deliverance (4:1b – 7:17)
      i. Defeat and loss of the ark of the covenant
(4:1b–22)
      ii. The Philistines fall foul of the ark (5:1–12)
      iii. The return of the ark (6:1 – 7:2)
      iv. Repentance and recommitment at Mizpah
(7:3–17)
   c. The question of the kingship (8:1 – 12:25)
      i. The request for a king (8:1–22)
      ii. Saul's secret anointing (9:1 – 10:16)
      iii. Saul elected and proclaimed king (10:17–27)
      iv. Saul confirmed as king (11:1–15)
      v. Samuel hands over to Saul (12:1–25)

II. SAUL: THE FIRST KING (1 Samuel 13:1 – 31:13)
   a. Key incidents in the reign of Saul (13:1 – 15:35)
      i. Jonathan attacks the Philistine garrison (13:1–23)
      ii. Jonathan's second initiative (14:1–23)
      iii. Saul's rash oath (14:24–46)
      iv. A survey of Saul's reign (14:47–52)
      v. Samuel's final confrontation with Saul (15:1–35)
   b. David comes into prominence (16:1 – 19:17)
      i. David's secret anointing (16:1–13)
      ii. Saul needs a musician (16:14–23)
      iii. Saul needs a warrior to fight Goliath (17:1 – 18:5)
      iv. Saul's jealousy and fear of David (18:6–30)

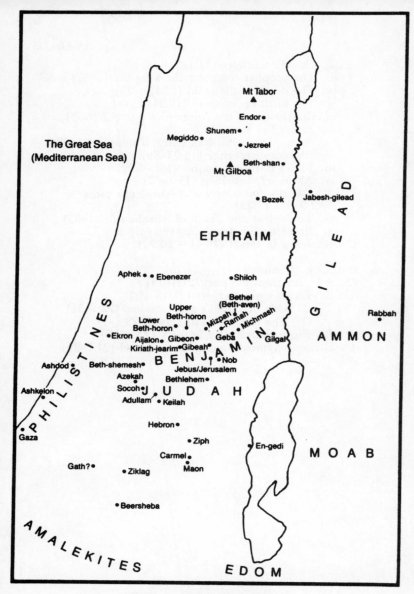

ISRAEL IN THE TIME OF DAVID

48

COMMENTARY

I. THE END OF AN ERA: SAMUEL, THE LAST JUDGE OF ISRAEL
(1 Samuel 1:1 – 12:25)

a. The birth and boyhood of Samuel (1:1 – 4:1a)

In the Hebrew text 1 Samuel 1 immediately follows Judges 21, the book of Ruth being among the 'Writings', the third division of the Hebrew scriptures. The Christian canon, by inserting the book of Ruth into the place where it belongs in the history, 'when the judges ruled' (Ru. 1:1), drew attention to the long-term theological importance of David as the forerunner of one born 'King of the Jews' in Bethlehem. Moreover, Ruth the Moabitess was among David's ancestry through Boaz, the kinsman-redeemer (Heb. *gōʾēl*), and the genealogy (Ru. 4:18–22) is another link with the Gospels (Mt. 1:5; Lk. 3:31–32).

The last chapters of the book of Judges, with their refrain, 'there was no king in Israel' (Jdg. 18:1; 19:1; 21:25), prepare the way for new developments in Israel's leadership. The 'judges' had been military as well as judicial leaders, effective in an emergency (though Samson did not fulfil his early promise), but limited by their geographical boundaries and by the nature of their office, for they did not appoint their successor.[1] At times of uncertainty due to external pressure from aggressors, Israel felt the need of a leader who would unite the tribes, have an effective standing army, and be a match for those who led their enemies to victory. It is hardly

[1] D. J. Wiseman, *EOPN*, pp. 147–149, likens the office of the so-called 'judge' (Heb. *šōpēṭ*) to that of the 'governor' (*Šāpiṭum*) at Mari. These regional governors acted on behalf of the supreme governors who had appointed them, but were responsible for law and order, diplomacy, taxation, and commercial transactions.

surprising that there were differences of opinion in Israel as to the propriety of asking for a king when the Lord was their King, and Samuel bore the brunt of the conflict in his capacity as judge, priest and prophet, after the style of Moses.

i. A woman's prayer is answered (1:1–28). Without any sense of incongruity, the book opens with an introduction to one particular family. First the husband is mentioned, but the main character in the chapter is to be the first-named wife, who was bold enough to believe that God would hear and answer her prayer for a son. The chapter records the answer to her prayer and ends with the fulfilment of her vow. Her motives may have been mixed, but her request was in line with the overarching will of God, who was preparing to bring into the world a man who would be his faithful representative and mouthpiece.

1. The opening phrase, *There was a certain man*, is identical with Judges 13:2 (*cf.* Jdg. 17:1; 19:1), so keeping continuity with the era of the judges, but introducing a new starting-point in the series of people and events selected for special mention. The site of *Ramathaim-zophim* is uncertain; in 1 Samuel 2:11 it is called simply 'Ramah', from the Hebrew verb *rûm*, meaning 'to be high': ancient towns in the vicinity were usually on hilltops. The form of the word *Ramathaim* suggests two adjacent summits on which the town was built. The longer name may distinguish this town in Ephraim from the frequently mentioned Ramah in Benjamin (*cf.*, *e.g.* Jdg. 19:13). The prominence of Ramah in 1 Samuel 1 – 7 has led to the suggestion that Ramah became the flourishing religious centre after the fall of Shiloh, and that these chapters may have been compiled and preserved there.[1] Unfortunately, in the absence of evidence, this must remain a conjecture.

Elkanah's genealogy to four generations may be an indication of his standing in society, though nothing more is known about those named here. In Chronicles, on the other hand, Elkanah is a recurring name in the descendants of Kohath (1 Ch. 6:22–30), and Samuel is shown to be a Levite in 1 Chronicles 6:33–34. But how can an Ephraimite also be a Levite? It is worth noting i. that Bethlehem is also called Ephrath in

---

[1] J. T. Willis, 'An Anti-Elide Narrative Tradition from a Prophetic Circle at the Ramah Sanctuary', *JBL* 90 (1971), p. 307.

the Old Testament (Gn. 35:16, 19; Ru. 4:11; Mi. 5:2), and that 'Ephraimite' (Heb. *'Ep̄rātî*) can denote a member of the tribe of Ephraim or a Bethlehemite; ii. that there were connections between Levites of Bethlehem and of the hill country of Ephraim (Jdg. 17:7–12; 19:1–21). If Elkanah traced some family connections to Bethlehem, it would be natural that his son Samuel should return there to offer his sacrifice (1 Sa. 16:2, 5),[1] even though the family had more frequently gathered at Shiloh, the sanctuary in Ephraim (v. 3).

2. The skilful way in which the two wives are introduced (Hannah, Peninnah, Peninnah, Hannah) prepares the reader to expect that the barren wife will become the mother of a son. *Hannah*, whose name meant 'grace', was being tested, like famous women before her (Gn. 11:30; 25:21; 29:31; Jdg. 13:2).

3–8. The high point in the family's year was the annual excursion to Shiloh for communal worship and sacrifice. Whether this was to be identified with the feast of the Lord mentioned in Judges 21:19, or whether it was simply a family festival, is not important for an understanding of the story, though it would be instructive to know whether it was one of the feasts outlined in Exodus 23:14–17.

Lord of hosts (Heb. *Yahweh ṣ̌b̄ā'ôṯ*) is first used here in the Old Testament in connection with the Shiloh sanctuary, and then occurs frequently in the books of Samuel (*cf.* 1 Sa. 1:11; 4:4; 15:2; 17:45; 2 Sa. 5:10; 6:2, 18; 7:8, 26, 27), Kings, Chronicles and the prophets. The 'hosts' were armies which, belonging as they did to the great Creator God, were composed of angels (Jos. 5:14), stars (Is. 40:26) and men (1 Sa. 17:45). The name expresses the infinite resources and power which are at the disposal of God as he works on behalf of his people.

The consistent worship offered by Elkanah and his family year by year set a positive example of faithful and godly living; the priestly leaders, by contrast, were known to be leading scandalous lives (1 Sa. 2:12–17). For the moment, however, they are simply mentioned by name, and interest is directed to the unhappy relationship between Hannah and Peninnah, both of whom attended the festival with Elkanah their husband. Although monogamy was not yet standard practice,

[1] M. Haran, *Temples and Temple Service in Ancient Israel* (Oxford: Clarendon Press, 1978), pp. 307–309, a section headed 'The Yearly Family Sacrifice'.

its advantages must have been obvious from situations such as this.

The family feast which followed the sacrifice was the culmination of the pilgrimage. Whereas no offerer ate the meat of his own sin or guilt offering, he was given back a substantial part of his own thanksgiving or 'peace' offering (Lv. 7:11–18), and this meat was enjoyed at the meal in celebration of restored fellowship with God. Peninnah regularly chose this moment to score points over Hannah. The merry chatter of Peninnah's children enjoying their *portions* would be reminder enough of Hannah's isolation, without additional taunts and innuendos. Invariably Hannah was reduced to tears and left her meal uneaten. In vain Elkanah tried to comfort her; *Am I not more to you than ten sons?* (*cf.* Ru. 4:15) was evidently a current idiom.

9–11. While everyone else enjoyed the good cheer, Hannah took the opportunity to pray at *the temple of the Lord* (v. 9). There is no record in Scripture of the building of this 'temple', and despite excavations at the site of Shiloh, modern Seilūn, about nine miles (14 km.) north of Bethel, little is known about it; no trace of it was found.[1] Whether Hannah entered the shrine or not is uncertain. She was so distraught that she seems not to have noticed the presence of Eli, and had no hesitation in presenting her desperate situation in prayer to the Lord. For her, the power of the Lord of hosts was not confined to military exploits; she believed he knew all about her and could give her a son. For her part, she would acknowledge that any son born to her was in answer to prayer, and therefore she vowed to give him back to God, who gave him. The outworking of the vow shows that she intended this quite literally (v. 24).

And no razor shall touch his head implies a Nazirite vow, like that prescribed by the angel of the Lord for Samson (Jdg. 13:5; *cf.* Nu. 6). The verb *nāzar* means 'to separate', 'to consecrate'. Hannah voluntarily undertook the vow on behalf of her son, who would be known by his uncut hair to be consecrated to the Lord. The origins of this practice appear to go back into Semitic culture. To this simple country woman, desperate

[1] What can be said is that occupation of the site was established with the Israelite conquest, and there is a gap of hundreds of years between it and earlier occupation. See the Additional Note, 'The temple of the Lord at Shiloh', pp. 65–68.

for a son, it was the appropriate way of demonstrating her gratitude.

12–18. Eli was quick to rebuke what he took to be drunken behaviour. It was a terrible mistake, but no doubt it tells us something about the problems he frequently had to contend with. Once he saw the genuineness of her need and the sincerity of her faith he did his best to reassure her. *Go in peace* affirmed his acceptance of her explanation and, though the recorded conversation does not refer to the content of her prayer, Eli added his priestly prayer for its fulfilment. *Your petition which you have made* is literally 'the asking that you asked'. The Hebrew *šā'al*, 'ask', is to be taken up in verses 27–28.

There is an instructive contrast between the Hannah who, distraught and averse to food, went to pray, and the Hannah who returned to join the family. Though outwardly her circumstances had not changed, she was now joyous and resolute, full of assurance that her prayer would be answered.

19–20. Though the family made an early start, they worshipped before setting off for home. *The Lord remembered* Hannah, as he had remembered Noah (Gn. 8:1), and his covenant with Abraham, Isaac and Jacob (Ex. 2:24), not to suggest that his memory was faulty but to indicate that he was about to work out his unfolding purpose. Accordingly Hannah gave birth to *Samuel*, meaning 'the name [of God] is El', a reference to the power of the God to whom she had prayed. Commentators have pointed out that her explanation, *I have asked him of the Lord*, suggests that the name 'Saul', from the Hebrew *šā'al*, would have been more appropriate, while some have conjectured that the incident occurred originally in connection with the birth of Saul, and has been transferred to that of Samuel. Hannah was testifying to her prayer-answering God rather than giving the strict etymology of the name.

21–23. Elkanah is careful to let nothing hinder the fulfilment of his commitments at Shiloh. Hannah shares his earnestness. Though she stayed at home until Samuel was weaned, at the age of two or three years (*cf.* 2 Macc. 7:27; weaning takes place late where there are no specially prepared foods for a baby's digestion), she had every intention of fulfilling her vow. Once she took the child to *the presence of the Lord* it

53

would be *for ever*. 4QSam^a adds at this point, 'and I will dedicate him as a Nazirite for ever, all the days of [his life]'; this expansion occurs in no other text or version.

Elkanah has no hesitation in supporting his wife's decision – *only, may the Lord establish his word*. So reads the MT, whereas 4QSam^a, the LXX and the Syriac version have 'your word', a reading that is preferable (*cf.* Nu. 30:2): *i.e.* 'may the Lord enable you to fulfil your vow'.

24. This Hannah did. She brought him to the house of the Lord at Shiloh, *along with a three-year-old bull* (Heb. 'three bulls'). Though the RSV reading, which is supported by 4QSam^a, as well as by the LXX and Peshitta, is widely accepted, there were three sacrificial offerings to be made.[1] The choice of bulls when smaller animals would have been acceptable (Lv. 12:6) is indicative of the gratitude of both Hannah and Elkanah.

And the child was young (lit. 'the child was a child'): the LXX and 4QSam^a have a longer reading here, 'and the boy was with them. And they came before the Lord, and his father killed the sacrifice as he did year by year before the Lord, and she brought the boy . . .' The inference is that between the two occurrences of the word 'child' some words were lost from the early Hebrew exemplar.

25–28. Hannah's singleminded testimony cannot have failed to impress Eli as he recalled the occasion when she had stood near him, lost in prayer. Her point is emphasized by a word play on the root *šāʾal* (*cf.* the commentary on vv. 12–18); four times it occurs, 'the Lord has granted me my *petition* which I *petitioned* him. Therefore I have *petitioned* [the verb also means 'lent'] him to the Lord . . . he is *petitioned* to the Lord'. The contrast between Hannah's selfless devotion and the self-indulgence of the priests at Shiloh (1 Sa. 2:12) highlights the cost to her of leaving Samuel there, though this is not mentioned directly. People like her were salt and light in the community. Ironically, there is here a subtle undermining

---

[1] *Cf.* G. J. Wenham, *The Book of Leviticus*, NICOT (London: Hodder & Stoughton, 1979), p. 79 n. 12. The three were 'the burnt offering . . . the purification offering that was expected after childbirth (Lv. 12) . . . and the peace offering' in fulfilment of a vow. Wenham also points out that 'An ephah of flour . . . is approximately three times the normal quantity of flour to be offered with a bull (Num. 15:9)', which would be in keeping with three bulls.

of Eli's authority: 'it will be Samuel, not his master Eli, who will hear the voice of God distinctly addressing him in the sanctuary'.[1]

ii. Hannah exults in the Lord (2:1–10). This poem expressing confident trust in the God who controls and judges the whole world is usually reckoned to be either an already existing hymn which Hannah made her own, or a later composition put into her mouth by a compiler long after her time. On the one hand, W. F. Albright says, 'Some very archaic verse has been preserved as the Song of Hannah ... It is highly probable that it does go back to the time of Samuel ...',[2] while Raymond Tournay, on the other hand, comments on the remarkable structure of the poem, and says he thinks it probably dates from the period of the second Temple.[3] Such widely divergent datings, separated by about five hundred years, indicate that the criteria of judgment are inadequate, and that at present it is impossible to date the poem with any degree of certainty. That being so, why could Hannah not have expressed her joy in this way, adapting for her purposes the poetic phraseology of early Israel? Examples in the Bible of early poetry are the Song of Moses (Ex. 15), which Albright suggests may have been 'a kind of Israelite national anthem',[4] the Song of Deborah (Jdg. 5) and the Oracles of Balaam (Nu. 23:7–10, 18–24; 24:3–9, 15–24). She may, of course, have chosen an appropriate hymn from the Shiloh collection.

The words that precede the hymn vary in the ancient versions, the MT reading 'And he worshipped the Lord there' (1 Sa. 1:28c; *cf.* AV, RV). Whether Eli or Samuel is the intended subject it is impossible to say; the RV mg. draws attention to several ancient authorities with the reading 'they' (hence RSV). One LXX manuscript omits this statement in 1 Samuel 1:28 but includes an equivalent in 1 Samuel 2:11. 4QSam[a] has 'and she left him there and worshipped the Lord', which satisfies the expectation that Hannah would be mentioned either in 1

---

[1] Alter, p. 86.
[2] W. F. Albright, *Yahweh and the Gods of Canaan* (London: Athlone Press, 1968), p. 18.
[3] R. Tournay in *Orbis Biblicus et Orientalis* 38 (1981), pp. 553–573.
[4] Albright, *Yahweh and the Gods of Canaan*, p. 11.

Samuel 1:28 or in 1 Samuel 2:11.[1]

Among the archaic features in Hannah's song, Albright includes the reference to God as a *rock* or 'mountain' (Heb. *ṣûr*), as in the Song of Moses (Dt. 32:31, 37), and the repetition of the same word rather than the use of a synonym in parallel lines of verse (*e.g. the Lord* in vv. 1, 6 instead of varying the name). He also sees parallels in verse 10 with Ugaritic texts; but whereas there kingship belongs to Baal, here kingship belongs to Yahweh (reading 'giving power to his reign' [Heb. *molkô*] where the text has *he will give strength to his king* [Heb. *malkô*]).[2] In the last line, however, *his anointed* continues to point to a king, implying that Israel had a human ruler, unless Hannah, the mother of the king-maker, had a divinely given premonition of Samuel's role (*cf.* 1 Sa. 10:1; 16:6 'the Lord's anointed'). It is more usual to suggest that, if the song was for the most part early, the reference to the king was a later addition.

Hannah certainly had something to sing about: i. she had had fulfilled her desire for a son; ii. she had proved in her own experience that the Lord, far from despising her, had known all about her and had answered her prayer (even hers!); iii. now that she had given her son back to the Lord she could sing from the fullness of joy that wells up from costly giving; iv. perhaps most telling of all, she had an unshakable assurance that her God controlled the providential ordering of the world, and therefore she need have no anxiety. Everything was in his good and capable hands. It would hardly be surprising if she adapted poetic phrases and liturgical forms current in her day. Mary was to adapt Hannah's song a thousand years later (Lk. 1:46–55), and home-made prayers still echo phraseology familiar from worship.

1. The emphasis in these opening lines is on Yahweh, the *Lord*. First there is personal testimony to personal experience of *thy salvation*, but then the psalm widens out to include in that salvation a just solution to problems throughout the world.

My heart . . . my strength (lit. 'horn') *. . . my mouth*: the whole

---

[1] Fuller detail can be found in McCarter 1980, pp. 57–58. He comments, 'The witnesses are at odds here because of the confusion caused by the insertion of the Song of Hannah'. This may be so, but there could be other explanations. The LXX has 'she went to Ramah' in 1 Sa. 2:11.

[2] Albright, *Yahweh and the Gods of Canaan*, pp. 18–19.

personality unites in exultation because of what God has done, and because of his holiness and dependability. *My mouth derides* . . . (Heb. *rāḥab* 'is enlarged over') is figurative for defeat of one's enemy by swallowing him (Ps. 35:21, 25).

2. The three lines of this verse, each beginning with *there is none* (Heb. *'ên*), provides a clear example of a tricolon, with its emphatic, short, three-stress lines. Israel's God is beyond compare. This message is conveyed by the poetic form as well as by the words.

3. *Talk no more so very proudly*: in the presence of this God, human arrogance is totally misplaced and even dangerous, in view of the Lord's way of 'balancing out' human experience. That is the meaning of *weighed* in the last line. The following verses illustrate the idea with examples of providential reversals that God has brought about.

4–5. The all-knowing Lord God sees the powerless and disadvantaged and acts on their behalf (*cf.* 'Blessed are the meek', Mt. 5:5); it is a theme that will recur in these books, notably in David's victory over Goliath (1 Sa. 17).

Those who were hungry have ceased [*to hunger*]: the RSV has added the last two words, which have no counterpart in the Hebrew (*cf.* AV, RV). A secondary meaning of the verb *ḥādal*, 'cease', has been shown to be 'become fat',[1] hence 'the hungry grow strong again' (NEB). *The barren*, like Hannah herself, are not to despair, for other childless women have *borne seven* (the ideal number; Hannah herself bore five other children, v. 21), while the one with children 'pines away' (NIV).

6. This, the most surprising couplet of all, envisages the Lord bringing people back to life from the realm of the dead. *Sheol*, the abode of the dead, is depicted as a huge underground cave, where judgment takes place (Dt. 32:22; Ps. 88:3–6), but the Lord can deliver even from Sheol (*cf.* v. 9).

7–8. A person's status in life is not to be regarded as fixed and unchangeable, for the Lord is well able to reverse it. This was good news for those of lowly birth, accustomed to poverty, because, if they looked to the Lord, they would no longer be the victims of their depressing circumstances.

He lifts the needy from the ash heap: the rubbish tip outside the city was the resort of those in deep trouble (*cf.* Jb. 2:8, 12). If

[1] Summary in Gottwald, p. 505. M. Dahood, 'Are the Ebla Tablets Relevant to Biblical Research?', *BAR* 6/5 (1980), p. 58, shows that the verbal root had this meaning in the Ebla texts.

the Lord lifts such needy people to a place of honour, it must be important that his servants co-operate with his purpose, and do not merely accept the status quo.

For the pillars of the earth are the Lord's, and on them he has set the world: the general sense of these lines is clear – the Lord has established the 'pillars' of the social and moral ordering of society. The exact meaning of 'pillars' (Heb. *mᵉṣuqê*) is not so clear, because the noun occurs only here and in 1 Samuel 14:5, where it is translated 'crag' in the RSV. The verbal root has two meanings, i. 'to constrain', 'bring someone into straits'; ii. 'to pour out', 'melt', hence 'molten pillar', a rather tenuous translation. 'Foundations' (NEB, NIV) is probably the nearest English word.

9–10. Thought of the moral order leads on to judgment after death, to which *the ends of the earth* will be subjected. This is the counterpart of verse 2: the incomparable God is the only judge. *The wicked* (v. 9b), *the adversaries of the Lord* (v. 10a), are those who pit their strength against him (v. 9c); *his faithful ones* (v. 9a) and *his anointed* (v. 10c) are by contrast those who keep covenant, who rely not on their own strength but on that of their God.

Mention of *his king* before there was a king in Israel has been the chief reason for denying the composition of this song to Hannah. Though Israel did not have a king until some years after this, the felt need for a king had been expressed in the time of the judges (Jdg. 8:22; 9). Yet the hope of a king was as old as the Abrahamic covenant (Gn. 17:6), and the process of anointing, appropriate for the setting apart of kings (Jdg. 9:15), was part of Israel's ritual. There is nothing anachronistic, therefore, in Hannah's discernment that an era of kingship was about to dawn through the ministry of her son, for she plays a prophetic role here.[1]

Interestingly, especially from the point of view of the structure of the book, the Song of David at the end of 2 Samuel picks up several of the themes of Hannah's song, including the victories granted by the Lord to 'his king . . . his anointed' (2 Sa. 22:51). It is in Hannah's song that the word 'anointed' (Heb. *māšîah*, 'messiah') is first used in con-

---

[1] Kirkpatrick 1880, p. 51: 'Hannah's song is a true prophecy . . . The failure to recognize this has led critics to deny the authenticity of the song, and to conjecture that some ancient triumphal war-paean has been erroneously placed in Hannah's mouth by the compiler of the book'.

nection with the king.

This song, appropriate on the lips of Hannah, but full of telling observations on God's overruling of human life, which give it wide application, became the model for Mary's song of thanksgiving (Lk. 1:46–55). A careful comparison of the two poems shows the same wonder at God's mercy to a humble woman in Israel, in keeping with his character through the ages as the just God who accomplishes his good purposes. There is similarity between the two songs yet they are quite distinct.

Hannah's song in its context encourages an individualistic interpretation: people from humble backgrounds do, in the Lord's providence, become important leaders. The question arises whether the song had any political overtones for the people of God. They had come into the land of Canaan, with few possessions, to find relatively wealthy cities which, under the good hand of their God, they had overthrown. 'Those formerly ruled and deprived in all the basic areas of their existence are now self-ruled, abundantly provisioned, prolifically reproduced, and socially fulfilled.'[1] Thus God's word had credibility for Israel because they could see that it worked out in tangible ways, for individuals and for the whole community. The outworking of God's judgment was as impartial as the bestowal of his blessing, and judgment was soon to fall on those who despised God's law at the very shrine to which Hannah had brought her son.

iii. Samuel encounters corruption at Shiloh (2:11–36).

11. *And the boy ministered to the Lord:* the verb 'minister' (Heb. *šāraṯ*) occurs in domestic and political contexts, but its most frequent use is for service at the sanctuary; Samuel ministered as a priest, in so far as his age permitted, under the direction of Eli.

12. *The sons of Eli,* who up to this point had simply been named (1 Sa. 1:3), now become the focus of attention. In short, they were a bad lot, *worthless men,* who *had no regard for* (lit. 'did not know') *the Lord.*

13–17. This rare description of worship in Canaan before the monarchy reveals some acquaintance with Levitical rules. Worshippers knew that the fat of the sacrifice was to be burnt

---

[1] Gottwald, p. 540.

as an offering to the Lord (v. 16; *cf.* Lv. 17:6; Nu. 18:17). Presumably they also knew that certain parts of the animal were allocated to the priests to provide them with food (Lv. 7:28–36; Dt. 18:3). Dissatisfied with what should have been adequate provisions, these men intimidated worshippers into allowing them to take a random selection of joints of meat, whether they were entitled to them or not. Protest was useless, and non-compliance was met by force (*cf.* v. 9c). In ethnic religions, ritual has to be performed exactly according to the custom in order to be efficacious; in worship of the living God, who forgives sin and is merciful, people took liberties and *treated the offering of the Lord with contempt*. This was inexcusable.

18–21. By contrast, Samuel grew up into a thoroughly wholesome lad, unsullied by their influence. The references to him, sandwiched between descriptions of the scandalous behaviour of Eli's sons, witness to the keeping power of the Lord, to whose service Samuel had been dedicated (*cf.* vv. 21, 26). Scripture takes seriously the commitment of children to his service, and Jesus was to warn against corrupting children by ungodly behaviour (Mt. 18:2–5, 10; 19:14). The example of Samuel showed up the perversity of his seniors simply by contrast.

A linen ephod was a distinctly priestly garment (1 Sa. 22:18), but what it looked like is not known. An elaborate form of ephod was reserved for the high priest (Ex. 28:6–14; 39:2–7). The *robe* which Hannah supplied for Samuel was the *mᵉ῾îl*, a cloak worn by the high priest over his ephod (Ex. 28:31), but also by others of importance (1 Sa. 15:27; 18:4; 24:4). The ordinary outer garment, called a *śimlâ*, was square and of blanket-like material, and was used as a covering at night (Ex. 22:25–27). Hannah's loving concern made sure she provided a garment large enough to allow for a year's growth in her son. Eli's prayer of blessing on the couple was abundantly answered, so that, for the one child they gave to the Lord at the sanctuary, they received five others. As the old saying puts it, 'The Lord is no man's debtor' (cf. Mt. 5:3–12).

22–25. *Women who served at the entrance to the tent of meeting*, mentioned also in Exodus 38:8, presumably served in the same ·ways as the Levites, of whom the same verb *ṣābā'* is used (*e.g.* Nu. 4:23; 8:24). It is the word also for army service, suggesting conscription, and provides the name 'Lord of hosts' (Heb.

ṣᵉbā'ôt; *cf.* the commentary on 1 Sa. 1:3–8). Immorality was an integral part of Canaanite worship, but was totally out of keeping with Israel's service to the Lord; indeed it was a sin *against the Lord.*

If a man sins against a man, God will mediate for him: the last clause could be translated 'the judges will mediate . . .' (*cf.* NIV mg.), the word *'ᵉlohîm* having this meaning in certain contexts (*e.g.* Ex. 21:6; 22:8–9), the judges acting as God's representatives in dispensing justice (Ex. 18:19–22). Deliberate sin against the Lord, by contrast, was in a totally different category. Eli's sons could not plead ignorance, and their high-handed arrogance cried out for a fall (*cf.* vv. 2, 9, 10a).

It was the will of the Lord to slay them: in the light of the events of 1 Samuel 4:11, this statement was no mere conjecture. Like the Pharaoh of Exodus 5:2, who said he had no intention of heeding the voice of the Lord, and thereafter became increasingly obstinate, until 'the Lord hardened his heart', so Hophni and Phineas sealed their own fate by their refusal to take warning (*cf.* Rom. 1:18).

26. This commentary on the growth of Samuel *in favour with the Lord and with men* provided a description of the development of the boy Jesus (Lk. 2:52), who like Samuel had to recognize God's way in an evil world, and resist temptation.

27–29. The unnamed *man of God* was the first to pronounce to Eli the destiny of his whole family in the light of the depravity of his sons. The prophetic oracle begins with a reference to the Lord's original calling of Eli's ancestor in Egypt. Though Eli was called an Ephraimite in 1 Samuel 1:1, because he lived in Ephraimite territory (*cf.* 1 Ch. 6:66), his Levitical descent is now implied in that his 'father' was chosen to serve as priest. 1 Kings 2:27 implies that Abiathar, who was a priest in David's time, was related to Eli (*cf.* 1 Sa. 22:20 and 1 Sa. 14:3), and 2 Samuel 8:17 shows the connection with Zadok, who descended from Aaron (1 Ch. 24:1–4). In the light of the provision made for the remuneration of the priests, there was no excuse for the greed which led to extortion of *the choicest parts of every offering.* Eli is involved in the sin: *Why then* [do you (plural)] *look with greedy eye?* The RSV has followed the LXX (which is now supported by 4QSamᵃ), whereas the AV and RV, following the MT, have 'kick at' (*cf.* 'Jeshurun waxed fat, and kicked', Dt. 32:15), a telling metaphor, but both translations run into difficulty at the end of the clause.[1] Eli is accused of honouring his sons before God, because he permitted the abuses to continue.

30–34. The punishment is now spelt out in a solemn pronouncement of the (repeated) divine word, or 'oracle of the Lord' (Heb. *nᵉ'um Yahweh*). The promise of priestly service *for ever* was conditional upon faithfulness on the part of the family, a condition which applies to God's promises even when it is not explicitly stated. The principle is summed up in a memorable proverb (just four words in the original Hebrew), *those who honour me I will honour, and those who despise me shall be lightly esteemed.* Its truth can be tested from the events of the book. Its outworking in the family of Eli will unfold in 1 Samuel 4 (but see also 1 Sa. 22:11–23; 1 Ki. 2:27), and Eli will see the given sign (v. 34) fulfilled before his own death.

35. The Lord will supply himself with *a faithful priest . . .* and *will build him a sure house.* The words 'faithful' and 'sure' represent the same Hebrew adjective, *ne'ᵉmān* and create a balance which matches the principle which has just been established. The double meaning of this word, the root of which gives us the familiar 'Amen', underlines the connection between faithfulness (to the covenant, understood) and security (*cf.* Is. 7:9b for the negative expression of the same point). This faithful priest will not merely keep the law, but will discern the mind of the Lord and do it; so Christians are to be 'sons of your Father who is in heaven' (Matt. 5:45) and those who have 'the mind of Christ' (1 Cor. 2:16). There is a second reference to the anointed one, 'my messiah' (*cf.* v. 10), the king whom the priest will serve. A contemporary is indicated; the word 'messiah' has been coined, but it does not yet have the status of a title. If David was in mind, the priest was likely to be Zadok (1 Ki. 2:35).

36. Poverty will be the lot of survivors of Eli's family because they have been demoted from office; hunger will drive them to beg for even menial jobs at the sanctuary. Thus the reversal of which Hannah sang came about before her eyes.

iv. The Lord calls Samuel (3:1 – 4:1a). However many books are written on the subject of God's calling, for each individual who receives that call a mystery remains: Is this

---

[1] For more detail, see Gordon 1986, p. 86.

an authentic message from God, and if so how am I to know that? Samuel received that calling through an audible voice, but he did not at first correctly identify its source. The message he received had all the direct force of truth, but final verification that he had heard the voice of God came only later, when events vindicated God's word. It was a word he might well have wished he had not heard, and it tested his strength of character and resolve.

1. Samuel was still the young apprentice, learning from Eli and subject to him. Nothing indicated that the Lord was about to inaugurate a new era; indeed *the word of the Lord was rare* (Heb. *yāqār*, 'highly valued'); times of greater blessing had evidently been known, when people had more readily received guidance from the Lord. As it was, Samuel had not had opportunity to experience the receiving either of an oracle or of a vision.

2–4. *At that time . . . the Lord called* is the sense; the description in between sets the scene more fully. Eli's failing eyesight meant that Samuel did his duty by sleeping in *the temple*; *the lamp* which was kept burning from evening to morning (Ex. 27:21) *had not yet gone out*, so the time was most likely early morning.

5–9. It says much for Samuel's self-discipline that he got up three times in the early hours in response to what he thought was Eli's call. His willing obedience was a qualification for receiving God's word.

Now Samuel did not yet know the Lord: he had not had personal experience by which to recognize the Lord's call (*cf.* v.1).

10. *The Lord came and stood forth*, so becoming visible as well as speaking. Samuel now received both word and vision.

11. *Ears . . . will tingle*, an expression which is used when a specially severe judgment is pronounced (2 Ki. 21:12; Je. 19:3).

12–14. Once again Eli bears the brunt of the punishment, because, as head of the house, responsibility was his for seeing to it that blasphemy did not go unchecked. The history of his sons' insubordination no doubt went back to their youth, when it should have been possible to discipline them. As it is, the whole family will be condemned and *the iniquity of Eli's house shall not be expiated by sacrifice or offering for ever*. Provision was made in the ritual for sacrifice on behalf of the sin of the priests, but such sacrifice covered only unwitting sin (Lv. 4:2;

cf. Lv. 4:13, 22, 27). Sin committed 'with a high hand', in deliberate disregard for God's law, such as Eli's sons had committed, could not be dealt with by any sacrifice. Eli himself had foreseen a disastrous judgment (1 Sa. 2:25), a prophet had already pronounced the decline of his family (1 Sa. 2:31); now the Lord himself pronounces the inescapable doom of Eli's house.

15–18. Under the weight of so severe a message, Samuel *lay until morning*. How could he broach such a subject with the venerable old man to whom he was responsible? He need not have feared, for Eli took the initiative and solemnly charged Samuel to tell him the whole message. Moreover, he accepted graciously all that he heard, though the further pronouncement of God's judgment can only have added, in his old age, great sadness and apprehension of the future. Nevertheless, what the Lord does is *good*; Eli acquiesces in his will.

Such was Samuel's introduction to the prophetic calling. Though he had been committed to priestly service from his earliest days, there is now a new dimension to his ministry, for he has received the word of the Lord, and he unites with his priestly office a prophetic task. This will bring him to prominence in the land at a time when people need to know the word of the Lord to them, for they are facing powerful enemies. Already Samuel is learning that his words will not always be easy either for him to speak or for his hearers to receive, but he will continue to deliver God's message without fear of the consequences, and so establish God's rule in the land.

19–4:1a. Samuel's growth to manhood was marked by continuing public recognition: *the Lord was with him*, authenticating his ministry by the fact that what Samuel said proved to be right. Thus *all Israel from Dan to Beersheba*, that is, from the northern to the southern borders, was at one in acknowledging Samuel's God-given authority. Indeed he was *a prophet of the Lord*, who continued to receive the revelation of his word, a *nābî'*, one called to special duty by God to declare his word. The derivation and meaning of the Hebrew term have been much debated, but the most likely origin of *nābî'* is an Akkadian verb *nabû*, 'to call to duty', especially the call of a man by the gods.[1] The experience of Samuel in this chapter and

---

[1] So W. F. Albright, *From Stone Age to Christianity* (New York: Doubleday Anchor, ²1957), p. 303, 'The king is repeatedly termed "the one whom the great gods . . . have called". '

throughout his life certainly bears out such a derivation, for the whole emphasis is upon the Lord's initiative. The Lord speaks, his servant hears and obeys. Samuel has no choice; his own will is submitted to the command of God. The Lord for his part honours his word and his servant, who finds his security in his God, and so can stand fearless before the great one of the earth. Samuel's role is altogether different from that of a religious practitioner, seeking to cajole the deity into conformity with his desires. Quite the reverse is true: Samuel stands unequivocally for the demands of the Lord upon his people. The outcome must be either repentance and reform, or certain punishment.

Samuel, like Moses, is to be the leader *par excellence* in Israel, fulfilling in himself the roles of judge, priest and prophet, yet his greatness is most clearly seen in appointing others, Saul and David, as kings in the land. Thus he pointed, not to himself, but to the Lord's anointed, by whom 'the Lord will judge the ends of the earth' (1 Sa. 2:10).

Additional Note: The temple of the Lord at Shiloh

The Temple of the Lord was built by Solomon in Jerusalem, as is well known, but the Old Testament provides no explanation of this temple at Shiloh, where the tent of meeting was set up after the conquest of Canaan (Jos. 18:1). Shiloh was the main sanctuary of the Israelites throughout the period of the judges (Jdg. 21:19), but when the wood-frame tent was replaced by a more permanent structure is not known. The word *hêkāl*, 'temple', 'palace', presupposes a building. It is used of the holy place of Solomon's Temple, but not of the corresponding area of the tabernacle. Similarly, the words for 'door' and 'doorpost' (1 Sa. 1:9; 3:15) require a solid structure, and not merely a tent with movable curtain.

Shiloh was the central shrine, because it housed the ark of the covenant, but it may not have been the only temple of the Lord in Israel during the judges period. The tribe of Dan is recorded as installing a centre for worship (Jdg. 18:30–31) at the city they renamed Dan; it was to be revived as a cultic centre by Jeroboam I, who also refurbished Bethel for worship (1 Ki. 12:28–29). Built at about the same time as Solomon's was the temple at Arad, the only excavated Israelite temple. Yohanan Aharoni is adamant:

There is no doubt that this is an Israelite temple in the full meaning of that word, a house of Yahweh in biblical terms, not just a shrine built in the Israelite period . . . In the various stages of excavation, there was not found even one object relating to idol worship . . . Furthermore, there were found in it some inscriptions with the names of known priestly families, such as Pashhur, Meremoth, and the sons of Korah. There is no doubt, therefore, that this is an Israelite temple.[1]

Its plan was different from that of the Jerusalem Temple in some important respects: it had only one room instead of two, and it was a broad room in contrast to the elongated structure of the Jerusalem Temple. A niche was formed in the long western wall by a recess, a sort of 'holy of holies', while a courtyard outside the long eastern wall contained the altar of sacrifice, constructed of earth and unhewn stone (Ex. 20:24–25). Small rooms round the courtyard would provide accommodation for the duty priests. Similar temples of the Canaanite period, with one broad room and a central niche, have been found also at Hazor, Lachish and Megiddo; it could well be, therefore, that the Shiloh shrine was of the same style, in keeping with the practice of the country.

A building of this sort makes good sense of the references in 1 Samuel 1 – 3. Samuel slept within the temple, 'where the ark of God was', in its niche along the west wall, while Eli had his quarters somewhere in the rooms around the outer court. Plans of the Arad temple even show a bench seat each side of the door, such as Eli may have regularly used (1 Sa. 1:9).[2] All the sacrificial ritual and the preparation of the meat for the worshippers took place, of course, in the open courtyard.

Danish excavators in the 1920s and 1930s failed to find evidence of the Shiloh temple. Excavation of Shiloh was resumed in 1981 as part of a regional study of the territory of Ephraim by Israeli scholars. They opened nine areas of excavation, some of them close to those of the earlier Danish expeditions. Since then, some important conclusions have been reached about the history of Shiloh, though it remains

[1] Y. Aharoni, *The Archaeology of the Land of Israel* (London: SCM Press, 1982), p. 229.
[2] *Ibid.*, photograph 31, model of the reconstructed temple at Arad.

true that no trace of the temple there has come to light, probably because the highest point of the tell, where it was most likely to have been built, has been weathered to bedrock. Nevertheless, from the earliest levels of building onwards, objects used in worship have been found:

> There are accumulating indications of cultic continuity at the site – from the Middle Bronze II period onward; that is, the sacral tradition at Shiloh long antedates the Israelites. A sanctuary probably stood here as early as the Middle Bronze Age [1650–1550 BC], and this may have been of central importance to the development of the site. Even after the destruction of the fortified Middle Bronze site . . . cultic activity continued in the late Bronze Age, despite the absence, as far as can be determined, of any real settlement . . . The history of Shiloh in the Middle and Late Bronze Ages helps us to understand why Shiloh was chosen as the first Israelite cultic centre.[1]

Surveys have shown that the territory of Ephraim was inhabited by only a small sedentary population just before the arrival of Israel; and in view of the fact that Shiloh was an old traditional site for worship, it was an obvious choice for the site of the tabernacle.

Indications of the date when organization round the sanctuary at Shiloh began are gained from excavated buildings on the western side of the tell, which Israel Finkelstein takes to have been annexes to the cultic complex that stood farther up-hill. Storage vessels abound, indeed 'the Iron Age pottery of Shiloh is one of the richest accumulations of pottery finds at any early Israelite site'.[2] These vessels may have been used to store offerings brought by worshippers to the sanctuary (1 Sa. 1:24). The building is dated *c.* 1200–1000 BC.

Within a radius of three to four miles of Shiloh, twenty-two settlements have been found belonging to this period, a higher density of population than anywhere else in Ephraim so far discovered.

Evidence of a dramatic destruction of the buildings at Shiloh abounds. The storage vessels mentioned above all bear marks of burning which are visible in Finkelstein's photograph.

[1] I. Finkelstein, 'Shiloh Yields Some, But Not All, of Its Secrets', *BAR* 12/1 (1986), p. 39.
[2] *Ibid.*, p. 38, where a photograph shows eight different shapes of jar.

Charred raisins remained in one of the jars. The building which housed the pottery had collapsed in a fierce fire, dated about the middle of the eleventh century BC, which would tie up with an attack by the Philistines, after their victory at Ebenezer. Though this event is not recorded in 1 Samuel, it was long remembered, and well served Jeremiah's purpose in warning about the imminent destruction of Jerusalem (Je. 7:12; 26:6; *cf.* Ps. 78:60–64).

b. Disaster, repentance and deliverance (4:1b – 7:17)

i. Defeat and loss of the ark of the covenant (4:1b–22).
The Lord's reiterated warning to Israel went unheeded, and relationships with the Philistine neighbours to the west became strained. Already in the time of the judges the Philistines had made incursions into Israel's territory, and had occupied some of it so successfully that the tribe of Dan had migrated to the north (Jdg. 18). Their aggression dominates the background and the military events during the time of Samuel and Saul.

1b. The Hebrew (and therefore most of our versions of the text) implies that Israel was the aggressor in the battle, but the LXX preserves a longer text, seemingly omitted accidentally from the Hebrew MT, but printed in the JB. Part of this includes the text: 'It happened at that time that the Philistines mustered to fight Israel and Israel went out . . .'[1] According to this extra information, Israel was forced into battle by the Philistine attack.

Aphek was over twenty miles north of Ekron, the northern-most of the five cities of the Philistines (the others being Ashdod, Ashkelon, Gaza and Gath), and in the foothills to the west of Shiloh. The threat was obviously against the central sanctuary there. *Ebenezer* was to be named in a victory a little later (1 Sa. 7:12); if the two battles happened in the same spot, it was situated between two towns, and was probably not inhabited at the time Israel encamped there.

2. *About four thousand men*: the Hebrew *'elep*, 'thousand', may have designated at this time a unit of soldiers of a particular size, unknown now, but numbering considerably less than a

---

[1] This verse provides a good example of haplography, an omission caused because the eye of the scribe slipped from the first occurrence of the verb for 'went out' (in v. 1a) to the second (in v. 1b).

thousand.[1] It is generally agreed that the 'thirty thousand' of verse 10 is an impossibly large number, given the military strategy of the period, with a mere handful of men achieving victory on occasions (*e.g.* Jonathan's exploits in 1 Sa. 14:6–15). Whatever the number of casualties, it is evident that the defeat at Aphek was decisive.

3. Defeat had evidently been unthinkable and immediately questions as to the reason were asked by *the elders* who had accompanied the troops. If they had heeded the words of Samuel, they would not have been surprised. They were right in assuming that the Lord was responsible for their defeat, but wrong in thinking that a parade of the *ark of the covenant* would compensate for their neglect of the Lord's ethical demands. The 'ark' or 'chest' contained the very law of God to which Israel was committed under the covenant initiated by the Lord himself. To think that the presence of the ark with them would reverse their fortunes without any change of heart in Israel's leaders was a measure of their insensitivity to spiritual things.

4. *The Lord of hosts . . . enthroned on the cherubim*: as well as containing the Lord's teaching, the ark was 'the footstool of his throne' (*cf.* 1 Ch. 28:2). The cherubim of beaten gold at either end of the gold-covered box flanked his footstool (Ex. 25:10–22). But most important of all, this was the 'mercy seat' where the Lord would meet with his people and give them his word (Ex. 25:22), and it was the Lord's presence which made it a powerful symbol, to be held in awe. By this point in the narrative the names *Hophni* and *Phinehas* strike an ominous note after the twofold pronouncement of doom upon them by prophetic utterance.

5–9. The *mighty shout* that resounded through the hills was a bid for victory in the coming battle, but the Philistines were curious to know what had provoked such confidence. Direct speech keeps the reader in touch with the very thoughts of the contestants

A god has come into the camp . . . These are the gods who smote the Egyptians: the Philistines assumed that Israel's religion was like their own – polytheistic. Nevertheless they had heard

---

[1] *Cf.* R. E. D. Clark, 'The Large Numbers of the Old Testament', *JTVI* 87 (1955), pp. 82–92; G. E. Mendenhall, 'The Census Lists of Numbers 1 and 26', *JBL* 77 (1958), pp. 52–66; J. W. Wenham, 'Large Numbers in the Old Testament', *TynB* 18 (1967), pp. 19–53.

something of the events of the exodus, though the account is garbled, and they were duly respectful with good reason (1 Sa. 6:4). Having had the upper hand, and having enslaved Israel, as the Egyptians had done, they were not prepared to become *slaves to the Hebrews*. Other people referred to the Israelites as Hebrews (*cf.* v. 6), but the Israelites preferred their distinctive name with its reference to Jacob/Israel, and the calling of God. 'Hebrew' (Heb. *'ibrîm*) evidently had a wider connotation, maybe racial, the stock from which the people of God were taken, or maybe social, groups that lived by invading the territory of others, or by serving as slaves or mercenaries.[1]

10–11. Though the reader has been prepared for the outcome, this decisive victory for the enemies of the Lord is still a shock to Israel's army, because it turns their expectations upside down. *They fled, every man to his home* means that the army melted away. It disappeared, not by command, but of its own accord. *And the ark of God was captured*, words which become a solemn refrain in the next few verses, and underline the enormity of the disaster. In the Old Testament it is equalled only by the fall of Jerusalem in 587 BC. The very foundations of the world were shaken. By comparison, the deaths of Hophni and Phinehas were both just and expected, but they did not prevent the tragedy that their faithlessness brought to the whole country.

12. It was a good twenty miles (34 km.) from Aphek to Shiloh; considering that the route was predominantly up-hill into mountainous country, the runner needed to be in good shape to cover the ground *the same day*. His dishevelled appearance indicated that he was mourning; he would be seen to bring bad news.

13–15. *Eli was sitting upon his seat by the road watching:* the LXX (and v. 18) reads 'beside the gate', where he would be

---

[1] Gn. 10:21 traces the genealogy of Eber, the ancestor of the *'ibrîm*, so indicating a racial grouping, from which eventually a particular man, Abram, was chosen to head up the people we know as Israel. In texts of the second millennium BC people called *ḥa-BI-ru* feature widely, and they have been popularly identified with the *'ibrîm*; this would make them a social or occupational group, but the identification is disputed on linguistic grounds. Even so, the term does sometimes have a certain derogatory sense, and in this context the Philistines are claiming political superiority. A meaning such as 'serfs' would fit well here.

70

certain not to miss the arrival of any messenger.[1] Despite his blindness, Eli is described as *watching*, straining every nerve.

For his heart trembled for the ark of God: though his father's heart must have been anxious about his sons, Eli had his priorities right. Despite his effort not to miss the messenger, the first Eli knew of his arrival was the alarming roar of voices from the city (v. 14).

16. Recognizing that Eli is blind, the messenger identifies himself as having come from the battlefield.

17–18. Though Eli was prepared for the disastrous news, at his age it was enough to cause his death, maybe from a heart attack which made him fall backwards from his seat in the gate. The fourfold announcement grew increasingly alarming, until it reached its climax in the capture of the ark of God. It was this last calamity that ended Eli's long life.

He had judged Israel forty years: the LXX, maybe under the influence of 1 Samuel 7:2, has 'twenty years'. Like the judges before him, Eli had been the sole leader, God's appointed ruler in Israel. At his age of ninety-eight, he could well have been in control for forty years.[2] As a priest, Eli would be succeeded by his sons, but the possibility that they might take over his wider leadership seems to have been in mind. Eli's failure to discipline them is therefore a national disappointment, even before it becomes a national disaster. It raises the whole question of hereditary leadership. How can a succession of godly men be assured if a leader such as Eli is unable to provide sons who can be trusted?

19–22. The chain of events is not yet completed. One further death takes place in Eli's family. The wife of Phinehas, her labour pains induced by the shocks she had received, died after giving birth to a son. Though this birth was good news,

---

[1] McCarter reconstructs the Hebrew on the basis of the LXX, and reads 'Now Eli was in a chair atop the gate watching the road', and in v. 18, '[Eli] fell backward from his chair over the gate-tower' (McCarter 1980, p. 111; a whole page is devoted to the textual variants). Merely on the grounds of common sense, this reading seems unlikely to be right. The fact that he could not see (v. 15) would deprive him of any advantage in climbing the tower, while his age and obesity (v. 18) would make him unlikely to attempt the exercise!

[2] A. E. Cundall, in A. E. Cundall and L. Morris, *Judges and Ruth*, TOTC (Leicester: Inter-Varsity Press, 1971), p. 32, suggests that forty may be a round figure representing a generation.

she did not answer or give heed. She was preoccupied with the divine judgment that had befallen Israel, summed up in the name *Ichabod* (Heb. *'i kābôd*, 'alas for the Glory [of Israel]'). The glory of Israel was the Lord, the footstool of whose throne had been captured by people who gave him no honour, for whom he was not resplendent with glory. *The glory has departed* indicates that, though the Philistines possess God's 'footstool', they have not captured Israel's God. The Lord is in control of the situation. He has withdrawn from the ark. But what then can become of Israel?

The fact that the child lived is a reminder that Eli's family was not entirely wiped out at this time (*cf.* 1 Sa. 2:31–33, 36). There are further references to Eli's family in 1 Samuel 14:3 (*cf.* 1 Sa. 22:9; 2 Sa. 19:11; 1 Ki. 2:27). As these references show, the family failed to prosper.

As for Shiloh, it ceased from this time to have any importance as a centre of worship, though it is mentioned occasionally, as for example in 1 Kings 11:29 and 15:29 in connection with Ahijah the Shilonite. It was still inhabited in the time of Jeremiah (Je. 41:5), but for Jeremiah the destruction of the 'place' was an object-lesson for his contemporaries, who regarded the Jerusalem Temple as indestructible. They should go and see what the Lord had done to the 'place that was in Shiloh' (Je. 7:12, 14; 26:6, 9). The implied destruction of the temple at Shiloh is nowhere recorded, but it is usually assumed that the Philistines razed it after the capture of the ark. For those who wrote these chapters the ark of God was far more important than the shell of a building that remained once the ark had been removed. When the ark was finally returned to Israel, it was set up at Nob, among the hills to the north-east of Jerusalem and within sight of that city (Is. 10:32).

ii. The Philistines fall foul of the ark (5:1–12).

In order to appreciate the events that follow, it is necessary to know a little more about the Philistines, who feature prominently at this period in Israel's warfare, and who were eventually to give their name to the country – Palestine.

Their name, *p^elištîm* in Hebrew, *prst* in Egyptian texts, first appears in Egyptian royal inscriptions of 1185 BC, though the 'Sea Peoples' of which they were part were named two centuries earlier, in the Amarna Letters, and small numbers of Philistines had settled in the Gaza area in patriarchal times.[1] They belonged originally in the region of Asia Minor, but migrated via Caphtor (Am. 9:7), that is Crete, first to Egypt, and later, between 1200 and 1050 BC, they settled on the coastal plain of south-west Canaan. No mention is made of Philistines in Joshua, so they must have been later arrivals than Israel in Canaan. There is some evidence that they may have come in the first instance as mercenaries of the Egyptians, who had nominal control of Canaan at that time.

The Philistines adapted easily to their new environment, taking over the city-state organization they found, and apparently absorbing the Canaanite language, for there appears to have been no language barrier between them and the inhabitants, particularly Israel. In this chapter they prove equally ready to adopt another deity in addition to their own, and such syncretism was totally alien to the whole revelation given to Israel of Yahweh, the Lord of hosts, visible and invisible. Militarily, the Philistines were highly organized and well disciplined, added to which they possessed advanced weapons made of iron, as opposed to bronze (1 Sa. 13:19–23). To be overcome by enemies such as these was alarming, and reminiscent of bondage in Egypt, but without the advantage of the Lord God 'on their side'. There was, moreover, determination on the part of the Philistines to dominate the population and make them slaves (1 Sa. 4:9).

1–3. The ark of God was taken as a trophy of war to the city of *Ashdod*, some nineteen miles (30 km.) to the south, and set up there in the temple dedicated to the god *Dagon*, whose image dominated the shrine (*cf.* the temple of Dagon at Gaza, where Samson lost his life, Jdg. 16:23–30). The name *Dagon* (or Dagan) is Canaanite in origin;[2] perhaps this god was the head of the Philistine pantheon, which included Ba'al-zebub, the god of Ekron (2 Ki. 1:2–3), and Ashtaroth (1 Sa. 31:10), together with other idols (1 Sa. 31:9). Now, in the temple of Dagon,

the contest is not between Israel and Philistia, but between Israel's God and the gods of the Philistines. In this regard, as also in the shared plague motif, these chapters recall the

[1] *EOPN*, p. 147.
[2] 'Dagon was known, under the form Dagan, with weather and fertility aspects, from the third millennium in the Near East', T. C. Mitchell, *AOTS*, p. 414.

Exodus story . . . The motivation is the same: 'on all the gods of Egypt (or "Philistia") I will execute judgments' (Exod. 12:12), and so, in the cities of Philistia, Israel's God shows himself again as 'a man of war' (cf. Exod. 15:3), wreaking havoc wherever the 'captured' ark is taken, in a veritable parody of a victory tour.[1]

And parody it certainly is, when Dagon is found prostrated before the ark of the Lord.

4–5. The following morning the parody is intensified when Dagon is found dismembered as well as flat on his face before the ark, while his head and hands lay on *the threshold*. The account is quite specific about the special custom at Ashdod, but avoiding treading on the threshold is a widespread taboo in ethnic religions.

6. As if the downfall and fragility of Dagon had not yet been enough to demonstrate his impotence, and the superiority of Yahweh, a third event proclaims the point. The population of Ashdod and its environs recognized the terrifying plague that struck their city as *the hand of the Lord* at work. The LXX adds 'And rats appeared in their land, and death and destruction were throughout the city' (*cf.* NIV mg.). It is well known that rats carry bubonic plague, which causes painful swellings of the lymph nodes, or buboes, in the armpits and groin. Untreated, the disease is fatal in well over half of those who contract it.[2] Little wonder there was panic, if this was the illness they suffered, but D. J. Wiseman points out that bubonic plague is attested only many centuries later in Syria and Libya.[3] The interpretation given by Josephus that the disease was dysentery seems less likely, though a recent writer proposes a tropical form of bacillary dysentery.[4]

7–8. There was a consensus that the cause of the outbreak of disease was the presence among them of the ark of the God of Israel, and subsequent events proved the Philistines were not mistaken. There are, according to the Bible, spiritual dimensions of cause and effect in addition to the clinical diag-

[1] Gordon 1984, p. 35.

[2] P. Wingate (ed.), *The Penguin Medical Encyclopaedia* (Harmondsworth: Penguin Books, 1972), p. 333, art. 'Plague'.

[3] D. J. Wiseman, 'Medicine in the Old Testament World', in B. Palmer (ed.), *Medicine and the Bible* (Exeter: Paternoster Press, 1986), p. 25.

[4] J. F. D. Shrewsbury, *The Plague of the Philistines* (London, 1964), pp. 33–39, and referred to in Wiseman, 'Medicine in the OT World', p. 25 n. 64.

noses of illness and its causes (see, *e.g.*, Num. 11:33; 1 Cor. 11:29–30). By removing the ark elsewhere, the Philistines believed that Ashdod would find healing. *All the lords (s‘rānîm) of the Philistines* conferred and agreed to send the ark to *Gath*. *Seren* is probably a Philistine term for the ruler of a city-state, one of their words which has survived. Though each city had its *seren* (1 Sa. 6:4), these leaders co-operated in time of crisis. Gath (Tell es-Safi) is twelve miles (19 km.) east of Ashdod, in the Elah valley which opened a route into the Judean hills.

9–12. When the disease struck Gath, the ark was sent north to *Ekron*, to the dismay of the inhabitants. The decimated population wanted no more to do with the ark.

The cry of the city went up to heaven: in desperate straits the Philistines prayed to a God greater than their local deities.

iii. The return of the ark (6:1 – 7:2). Everyone acknowledged that the God of Israel had not been conquered, though the ark was captured. Indeed the ark had become a liability, too dangerous to keep, and yet problematic to return without incurring further loss.

1–4. Their *priests* and *diviners* used their specialist powers to indicate the 'correct' method to adopt in order to placate the God of Israel. The writer shows no interest in the method used in deciding what to do; clearly a costly gift was required as a *guilt offering* (Heb. *’āšām*), to make compensation for the wrong committed, and to ward off further suffering. Healing could be expected to follow. The idea of compensation is present in Israel's guilt offering also (*cf.* Lv. 5, esp. v. 14–16).

And it will be known to you why his hand does not turn away from you: there is a difficulty in the MT here, which does not make easy sense. The Qumran text 4QSam^a is in line with the LXX in reading, 'When you have been ransomed, why should his hand not turn away . . . ?', and this could well have been the original sense.[1] The ransom, *five golden tumours and five golden mice*, represent the five Philistine cities, and their rulers, all of which suffered.

5–6. Here for the first time in the MT mention is made of *mice that ravage the land*. Whether or not a connection was suspected between the mice and the disease, it is clear that

[1] For further detail, see McCarter 1980, pp. 129, 133.

loss of crops was a further anxiety. The Philistines were threatened with ruin. By presenting gold mice and tumours (*'opelîm*, a word which also means 'fortified cities' and so has a double meaning), the costly offering will depict their plagues and at the same time request the removal of both, as they *give glory* (Heb. *kābôd*) *to the God of Israel*. This the Philistines do by paying tribute to him, and so acknowledge his lordship over them.

Why should you harden your hearts?: evidently there was some support for opposing the proposal. The opposition of the Pharaoh to the release of the Israelite slaves was evidently well known beyond the bounds of Israel, as was the fact that he gained nothing by it but extra plagues on his people (*cf.* Ex. 9:35 – 10:2). In the end the Pharaoh had to give in, so the Philistines would be wise to delay no longer.

7–9. An experiment is set up to test out whether or not the Lord had been responsible for the plagues, for they might have happened quite by chance. Every effort was to be made to do the reverent thing: the cart was to be new and the cows unyoked. Since the cows were unused to pulling a cart, and had calves dependent on them, all their instincts would be to turn back. If, contrary to expectations, they pressed ahead with the precious load, that would be proof that the Lord had been responsible. It was understood that the cows would be sacrificed to the Lord. *Bethshemesh*, in the valley of Sorek, was south-east of Ekron, within the border of Judah. It is listed as a Levitical city in Joshua 21:16.

10–12. Contrary to nature, the cows made no attempt to return to their calves, though they lowed after them, so fulfilling the sign that the Lord had been afflicting the Philistines.

13–16. The circumstantial evidence makes the narrative vivid, as if written by someone present. The mound which covers the ancient site stands on a ridge between two valleys which meet on the west. Since wheat would be grown in the valleys, it is understandable that the Philistines would come upon the harvesters at work before reaching Bethshemesh itself. *Wheat harvest* time was May/June. Nothing is known of this *Joshua* in whose field the cows halted. Work ceased in order that everyone could join in joyous worship, the large stone presumably providing a natural altar for the sacrifice of both cart and cows, though it also served as a table on which to place the ark and the Philistines' offerings. A wide outcrop of rock could have served both purposes. Satisfied that their sacred objects had been safely received, the Philistine lords could return home.

17–18. The five city-states belonging to the Philistines are now named; each served as the administrative centre of the villages around, so that the whole country was represented.

19. Trouble instead of blessing came even to Bethshemesh, which belonged to Israel, because the ark of God was not accorded due reverence. *He slew seventy men of them* is a correction made also by the NEB and NIV (*cf.* the AV, which translates the Hebrew, 'he smote of the people fifty thousand and three-score and ten men'). The much smaller number seems more likely to be right because Bethshemesh was only a small town. It is still not clear why the population as a whole should have been afflicted; a clue is provided, however, by Josephus, who says that those who had touched it, 'not being priests', were not worthy to touch the ark.[1]

20–21. Since Bethshemesh was a Levitical city (Jos. 21:16), it is strange that no priests were available to see that the ark was not profaned. *Who is able to stand before the Lord, this holy God?*: death may have been caused by disease which spread from Philistine contacts, but it served to strike due awe in the minds of those who had dared to look into the ark.

To whom shall he go up away from us?: The presence of the holy God with the ark was fraught with danger; it was perilous to keep him in the vicinity, hence the approach to *Kiriath-jearim*. Why this place rather than one of the ancient sanctuary sites should have been chosen is obscure. It was some fifteen miles (24 km.) east-north-east of Bethshemesh, near the borders of Judah, Dan and Benjamin (Jos. 15:9, 10, 60; 18:14, 15); its alternative name, Baalah (Jos. 15:9), may indicate that it had been a Canaanite high place, like Shiloh, and therefore associated with worship, albeit of another god.

7:1–2. The transfer of the ark was safely completed; we are not told whether *Abinadab* and his son *Eleazar* were priests, though the name Eleazar was associated with priestly genealogies (Ex. 6:23), and the family continued to serve the ark until David took the ark to Jerusalem (2 Sa. 6:3). *Twenty years* probably belongs to the Mizpah incident, as NIV indicates. The period between the death of Eli and David's accession was almost certainly more than twenty years.

[1] Josephus, *Antiquities of the Jews*, 6.1.4.

And all the house of Israel lamented after the Lord: the Hebrew construction is unusual, hence the tentative translations (*e.g.* RV mg. 'was drawn together after'; NIV 'mourned and sought after'). There was a feeling that all was not well, and Samuel recognized this as the moment when he could call for repentance and recommitment. The absence of Samuel from the scene in 1 Samuel 4 – 6, which is often accounted for in terms of literary sources (the Ark Narrative having been attributed to a different source from that of Samuel's career), has a bearing on God's dealings with Israel. Samuel would no doubt continue his regular work, but he waited for the right moment before calling a national convention.

iv. Repentance and recommitment at Mizpah (7:3–17).

3–4. This was an outstanding event in the lifetime of Samuel's contemporaries. It would be interesting to know how he communicated with *all the house of Israel*; messengers must have summoned the tribes to Mizpah, and they would have conveyed at least to distant places his call to repentance also. *Foreign gods and the Ashtaroth*, were adopted by Israel from the population around. Ashtoreth (pl. 'Ashtaroth') was worshipped over a wide area as the goddess of fertility, love and war (Gk. 'Astarte'), and plaques of naked female figures from the Bronze and Iron Ages in Palestine are numerous. The *Baals* were the corresponding male deities. This depraved cult had become widespread at this period, involving Israel in breaking the first and second commandments, and resulting in loathsome sexual indulgence. The Canaanite way of life was totally opposed to everything Israel should have stood for as the people of God, and therefore repentance, if it was to be credible, had to entail renunciation of this foreign worship. Samuel now resumed his prophetic ministry to Israel as the Lord's spokesman, and as intercessor on behalf of Israel. Both tasks he was able to fulfil only because the Lord had called, appointed and equipped him, and because the people recognized and accepted his authority. They did as he said, and *served the Lord only*.

5–6. The day of confession and fasting at *Mizpah* was the culmination of Samuel's programme of reform. Mizpah (modern Tell en-Nasbeh) was in Benjamite territory, on the main north-south road across the hills, and only five miles (8 km.) north of Jerusalem. The first walled city on the site was founded *c.* 1100 BC, during the Israelite period, and it was one of the places on Samuel's regular circuit (v. 15). It commanded views through the valleys to the west, had already been a rallying point (Jdg. 20:1), and after the fall of Jerusalem even became the capital (2 Ki. 25:23).

They *drew water and poured it out before the Lord*, evidently as a symbol of the washing away of communal guilt, for which Samuel prayed (*cf.* La. 2:19; Mk. 1:4) – the visible sign reinforcing the divine response to the confession of sin.

Samuel judged the people . . . at Mizpah (*cf.* v. 15): In this instance his role as judge involved a pastoral concern, with particular reference to the covenant relationship between an apostate people and their holy God. So far as we know, only Gideon among the 'major' judges came near to playing such a role (Jdg. 6:25–27), though Deborah was both prophetess and judge (Jdg. 4:4). In the person of Samuel the role of judge took on prophetic and priestly significance.

7. The name *Mizpah* meant 'watchtower' – it was a vantage-point for military purposes and was itself visible from a distance. The Philistines, hearing of the great gathering of Israelites, supposed an attack to be imminent and moved up to take the initiative in the battle (*cf.* Jdg. 20:3a, 14). It was a testing moment for the Israelites, who had been defeated so decisively in the previous encounter (1 Sa. 4:10–11).

8. The circumstances, however, could not have been more different. Instead of the brash, misplaced confidence in outward symbols (1 Sa. 4:3), there was genuine if timid faith in the power of their God to save them from their enemies, expressed in the request to Samuel, *Do not cease to cry to the Lord our God for us.* Two thoughts are combined: 'do not cease from us' or 'keep silent from us', expressing dependence on Samuel's support; and 'do not fail to pray', indicating ultimate dependence on the Lord.

9–11. The *whole burnt offering* in this instance was offered in penitence and as a gift to secure the Lord's favour, 'a pleasing odour to the Lord' (Lv. 1:13). Though the approaching Philistines threatened to interrupt the worship, and action seemed imperative, faith held out, and *the Lord thundered with a mighty voice.* The weather frequently played a part in the outcome of a battle (Jos. 10:11; Jdg. 5:4, 20, 21; *cf.* 1 Sa. 2:10; Ps. 18:13). It is surprising that, in a land subject to earthquakes, more frequent reference is not made to this alarming phenomenon as an instrument of the Lord's intervention (though Amos, *cf.* Am. 1:1; 8:8, *etc.*, and other prophets do so use it). Intimidated by the thunder-storm that broke up their battle lines, the Philistines fled downhill towards their own territory, while the Israelites had the double advantage of height from which to hurl their missiles on the enemy below, and growing confidence in their likely victory. *Beth-car*, mentioned only here, has not been identified. The enemy was decisively defeated.

12. So remarkable a deliverance could not be allowed to sink into oblivion, hence Samuel's memorial-stone, set up like our war memorials in a prominent place. But Samuel's stone recalled not the names of the dead but the living Lord God, the Helper of his people. *Ebenezer* means 'stone of help' or 'stone of the Helper', a name frequently applied to the Lord (*e.g.* the refrain 'He is their help and their shield' in Ps. 115:9–11). The explanation of the name, *Hitherto the Lord has helped us*, can mean either 'as far as this geographical spot', which fits the context well, or 'until now'; the Hebrews loved to use words and expressions with double meanings, and most likely kept both senses here. The reminder of prayer answered in the past would encourage faith in God for further blessing:

> We'll praise Him for all that is past,
> And trust Him for all that's to come.[1]

Jeshanah is a correction of the Hebrew, which read *hᵃšēn*, 'the tooth', probably with reference to a tooth-like crag. 'Jeshanah' is supported by the LXX and Syriac readings, and could be identified with the Jeshanah mentioned in 2 Chronicles 13:19.

There is a problem over the naming of Ebenezer in this chapter, raised by the occurrence of the name in 1 Samuel 4:1b. Two different places may have been called by the same name. This simple explanation is adopted in the marginal note of the JB, for example; in which case the name would have served to recall the original battles against the Philistines, which ended in defeat, alongside this later incident, which reversed past failure. The two encounters with the Philistines were intended to be seen in relation to one another, and the totally different outcome vividly illustrated the importance of Israel's relationship to the Lord. Even an apostate people

---

[1] The last two lines of the hymn 'How good is the God we adore' by Joseph Hart (1712–1768).

could find the Lord again if they truly came in penitence and faith.

13–14. As the result of the Lord's help, and under the leadership of Samuel, Israel enjoyed a threefold benefit: i. the Philistines *were subdued* (after their forty-year period of supremacy, Jdg. 13:1) for a time, but not indefinitely (they were to make even greater inroads into Israel's territory in the days of Saul); ii. border cities from Ekron to Gath came under Israel's control, and land which the Philistines had captured was restored; iii. there was peace, not only between Israel and the Philistines, because *the hand of the Lord was against the Philistines all the days of Samuel* (*cf.* 1 Sa. 5:6, 7, 9), but also *between Israel and the Amorites*. The name 'Amorites' is used loosely to cover the Canaanite population, who regarded the Israelites as less of a threat to them than the Philistines, and so ceased to harry Israel. 'Canaanite city-states would have been indirect beneficiaries of Israelite successes in resisting or driving back the Philistines, and vice-versa.'[1] It was a natural sequel.

15–17. The whole section ends with a summary of the ministry of Samuel, which is to be followed by one aspect of his work looked at in detail (1 Sa. 8 – 16).

All his life he *judged Israel* – three times the fact is stated (the RSV's *he administered justice* is simply a variant to improve the English style); but, as has already become plain, the settlement of legal matters was only one aspect of his leadership. To all intents and purposes he was a supreme governor, of the type exemplified by Moses – appointed and equipped by the Lord to keep Israel in a right relationship with their Lord God, and depending upon his resources, in all their undertakings to live and work to his glory. It was a splendid vision, which Samuel was able to a degree to implement.

Samuel did not expect people always to come to him at Ramah, but travelled regularly to three centres: *Mizpah* (three miles [5 km] north) and *Bethel* (a further four miles [6½ km] north) and *Gilgal* (much further away in the Jordan valley, near the fords of Jordan, Jos. 4:19). These places were all on the border between Benjamin and Ephraim, to the south of Shiloh. The tribes which had settled in the extreme north and south of the country would not have had such regular visits.

[1] Gottwald, p. 418. He goes on to point out that David's success in incorporating the surviving old Canaanite city-states into his kingdom after the defeat of the Philistines must be seen in this context.

In these three instances *places* (Heb. *mᵉqômôt̠*) may mean 'sanctuaries'; the LXX has this meaning, and the mention that Samuel built an altar in Ramah would support this interpretation. Worship was central to all his activities, as it had been for Moses. But the writer is wanting to point the reader forward to an important development which will change the character of leadership in Israel.

c. The question of the kingship (8:1 – 12:25)

Writers who are accustomed to looking for sources underlying the text have found many signs that the material in 1 Samuel 8 – 12 is of diverse origin. This is indicated, for example, by differing views of the monarchy; Wellhausen distinguished source *a* (1 Sa. 9:1 – 10:16; 11:1–11), which was favourable to the monarchy, from source *b* (1 Sa. 8:1–22; 10:17–27), which regarded the monarchy as a rejection of Yahweh. (Source *b* is often identified with the Deuteronomic compiler.)

Once the material has been separated, it is possible to point to inconsistencies between the accounts: different places are named for king-making ceremonies (Gilgal, 1 Sa. 11:15; Mizpah, 1 Sa. 10:17); and while Samuel was the recognized leader of all Israel in 1 Samuel 8:4, Saul and his servant were only vaguely aware of his existence (1 Sa. 9:6–10).

It has to be conceded that the story of Saul and his servant, out to find his father's lost asses (1 Sa. 9:1 – 10:16), is in stark contrast to the Ramah speech of Samuel, in which he laid stress on the financial and social burdens a king would introduce (2 Sa. 8:11–18). Then, at Mizpah, Saul was chosen by the sacred lot and proved a reluctant candidate, about whose suitability for the kingship there was a division of opinion (1 Sa. 10:26–27), whereas after the battle of Jabesh-gilead all the men of Israel rejoiced greatly that Saul was their king. Samuel, who dominates the scene, appears to be first on one side and then on the other.

Despite the popularity over many years of the documentary source theory, different ways of explaining 1 Samuel 8 – 12 have gained favour. Childs, for example, starts with Wellhausen's sources *a* and *b*, and points out that they alternate thus: *b* (1 Sa. 8), *a* (1 Sa. 9:1 – 10:16), *b* (1 Sa. 10:17–27), *a* (1 Sa. 11), *b* (1 Sa. 12), drawing the conclusion that 'The editor suppresses neither of the traditions. Each is allowed its full integrity'.[1] Each viewpoint is seen to be important, but the dominant theme is Samuel's warning against apostasy. Robert Gordon presents the five sections as *tableaux*, each of which plays its part in completing the account of this far-reaching but highly controversial new development.[2] There is ample evidence that the biblical writers were not as concerned as we are about harmonization. They favoured 'multiple perspectives', in preference to 'a fusion of views in a single utterance', because they wanted to develop 'a literary form that might embrace the abiding complexity of their subjects'.[3] That being so, it is necessary to keep an open mind in order to notice the literary patterns and to appreciate the nuances of meaning they suggest.

1 Samuel 7 demonstrated Samuel's leadership at its best. At Mizpah he had brought the nation through religious reformation to repentance, while the stone called Ebenezer became a memorial to the fact that the Lord answered Samuel's intercessions and gave a signal victory over the Philistines. 'Hitherto the Lord has helped us' (1 Sa. 7:12) brought the triumphs of former days into the experience of the generation then living, and proclaimed his favour restored. While Samuel was judge all would be well.

But changes were pending. The attempt to set up a dynasty had first been made after Gideon's triumph over the Midianites, but he maintained Israel's theocratic tradition: 'I will not rule over you, and my son will not rule over you; the Lord will rule over you' (Jdg. 8:23). Ever since Moses had obeyed the Lord's call (Ex. 3:1–12), Israel's leaders had been divinely designated, and took their orders from God himself. The question of their setting up a dynasty did not arise until Abimelech, Gideon's son by a Canaanite concubine (Jdg. 8:31) tried the experiment, which was short-lived. Nevertheless the comment, 'In those days there was no king in Israel' (Jdg. 18:1; 19:1), and especially the added refrain in Judges 17:6 and 21:25, 'every man did what was right in his own eyes', indicates the writer's opinion that a king would have restrained lawlessness and established order.

Conflicting opinions are reflected in the narratives of 1 Samuel 8 – 12. Samuel, who took the request for a king as a

[1] Childs, *Introduction*, pp. 277–278.
[2] Gordon 1984, pp. 40–41, 49–50.
[3] Alter, p. 154.

personal attack on his leadership, never quite became reconciled to the new régime, despite the divine guidance he received to anoint a king. He valued the distinctive witness of Israel's traditions to the viability of depending on the leadership of the unseen God, and could see no good coming from the adoption of Canaanite models of kingship. Yet God instructed him to anoint Saul, and Samuel presided throughout the various stages of establishing Saul in office. In the light of pressure of public opinion, the Lord gave Israel the king they requested. Samuel issued appropriate warnings and exhortations. Despite Israel's apostasy in requesting a king, the Lord was positively at work to achieve his ultimate purpose.

i. The request for a king (8:1–22). 1–3. *When Samuel became old* marks a change of circumstances, recognized by Samuel himself as well as by the nation. He provided for the future by appointing his two sons, *Joel* and *Abijah*, who officiated at the sanctuary in *Beersheba*, to serve as judges for Israel. They evidently served as his deputies at this town in the extreme south of Israel's territory, well beyond Samuel's regular circuit (*cf.* 1 Sa. 7:16–17). These sons of Samuel disqualified themselves in advance because, like Eli's sons before them, they were more interested in lining their own purses than in maintaining justice.

4–6. *All the elders of Israel* were unanimous, and sufficiently in touch with one another to assemble at Ramah with the request that Samuel should appoint *a king to govern us like all the nations* (Heb. *gôyîm*, in the sense of 'gentiles'). The phrase is reminiscent of Deuteronomy 17:14–15 where the desire to emulate other nations is foreseen and permitted, rather than approved. Samuel thoroughly disapproved, but consulted the Lord nevertheless. Samuel's role as intermediary between the elders and the Lord, and between the Lord and the elders, is a feature of this chapter.

7–9. *Hearken to the voice of the people*: Israel's unanimous demand was to be granted, and twice the point is made (*cf.* v. 9). The Lord had his ideal for his people, but in this far-from-ideal world he adapted his purposes and acquiesced sufficiently to allow Israel a king, even incorporating the monarchy into his revelation of himself to Israel. Kingship was soon to be a major theme of the Old Testament, but so was the pattern, begun at the exodus, of refusal to obey the Lord's rule.

They have rejected me from being king over them: Samuel felt that he had been rejected, but basically this was because he was identified with the Lord's cause. As Hertzberg comments:

> Here one of the basic features of world history emerges: the struggle of man against God – already beginning in Gen. 3 – a struggle which, according to the general outline presented in the Bible, has its roots in the special position given to man in Gen. 1. Samuel experiences what Moses, the prophets, and even Jesus experienced: 'We do not want this man to reign over us' (Luke 19.14).[1]

There is no compulsion to accept the rule of God, yet ultimately there is no escaping it, for he appoints the king.

10–18. Even though the Lord sanctioned the monarchy, he gave advance warning of the price Israel would pay for this innovation. It is interesting and instructive to note the social ideals that had obtained in Israel up to this time. Each family had been autonomous, under the leadership of its elders. It had been beholden to no-one, whereas under a king military and agricultural conscription would restrict Israel's liberty. Nor would the women of the family escape, for as *perfumers and cooks and bakers* they would serve the royal house. Taxation, which had been unknown, would become increasingly oppressive, until the people were virtually slaves, and cried out for liberation. But having made a deliberate choice of this form of government, Israel would have to live with its restricting demands.

The ways of the king (*cf.* v. 9) could be translated 'the *justice* of the king' (Heb. *mišpat* has both meanings). There could be an element of satire in the word play, especially in the light of what follows. Yet the description of the requirements of the king is not exaggerated; indeed they are modest compared with the demands made by the modern state. While Israel was loosely organized under tribal leaders it was a threat to no-one, but once it had been organized as a monarchy it became part of the political map, a contestant in the power-struggle for domination, and in order to have an effective army

[1] Hertzberg, p. 72.

conscription was imposed.[1] All these developments took place as early as the reign of David (2 Sa. 6:1; 8:15–18), though it was under Solomon that the system became burdensome and oppressive (1 Ki. 12:4), and led to the rejection of Solomon's successor by the northern tribes.

His servants (vv. 14, 15) are 'ministers' of court, who, in acknowledgement of services rendered, are presented with the best land confiscated from others by the king. Monarchs in Ugarit (Ras Shamra), to the north, rewarded their personal retainers in property for their services to the king.[2] Such practices were already well established in association with the monarchy.

He will take . . . the best of your cattle (v. 16) is in the AV (following the Hebrew) 'your goodliest young men'. 'Cattle' is the reading in the LXX, representing the Hebrew *bāqār*, instead of *bāhûr*, and is generally preferred because the sense of the list seems to require it.

19–22. Nothing that Samuel could say had any influence with the elders of Israel, for their minds were made up. Did they expect one of their number to become the first king, and had they a proposal to put forward? If so, they were disappointed, for suggestions were not invited. Samuel's one concern was to consult Israel's Lord for direction, and since the Lord directed him to go ahead and *make them a king*, that was the end of the matter. The conference had completed its agenda, and the elders could return home.

From Israel's earliest days, God himself had directed his people, revealed his commands and given suitable leaders. Though the monarchy would introduce undesirable social changes, three considerations weighed with the people: i. they wanted to be *like all the nations*, to have influence and status;

---

[1] I. Mendelsohn, 'On Corvée Labor in Ancient Canaan and Israel', *BASOR* 167 (1962), pp. 31–35, shows that the corvée was prevalent in the ancient Near East from the eighteenth to the thirteenth century BC. It is not necessary to claim that the description given in 1 Sa. 8 has been written in the light of Israel's later experience of kingship, for it was already practised in the Canaanite city-states. *Cf.* I. Mendelsohn, 'Samuel's denunciation of the kingship in the light of the Akkadian documents from Ugarit', *BASOR* 143 (1956), pp. 17–22.

[2] *Cf.* P. C. Craigie, *Ugarit and the Old Testament* (Grand Rapids: Wm. B. Eerdmans, 1983), p. 33. The golden age of Ugarit was during the fourteenth and thirteenth centuries BC, some two hundred years before the time of Samuel.

ii. they desired *that our king may govern us*, so lifting responsibility from local leaders and providing a figure-head; iii. and they wanted someone to *go out before us and fight our battles*, a focal person, already accepted and therefore immediately prepared to lead the army against any invader. But what does the new divine directive say to us?

The collective decision of the community was taken seriously. There are 'movements' in society which need to work themselves out; here the people of God found themselves in tension between the traditional and the new, but in the case of the monarchy the new was not to be rejected. 'The time was ripe for the king, i.e. for the development of a state, even though the manifold dangers which could now cause theological chaos were seen all too well.'[1] This is the kind of dilemma in which Christians all too often find themselves. The ideal is not an option, because it would not find support, so another way has to be chosen which involves a compromise. The Lord, like a master chess-player, achieves his objective despite human plans and policies that temporarily impede what he wants to do.

ii. Saul's secret anointing (9:1 – 10:16).

Samuel had agreed to appoint a king, but had no idea who that would be. How long Samuel had to wait, we do not know, but we, the readers, are introduced to him before his identity is made known to Samuel.

1–2. *Kish*, the father of Saul, was *a man of wealth*. The last phrase hardly does justice to the Hebrew, *gibbôr hāyîl*, which implies much more: 'a mighty man of power' (AV). His long genealogy testifies to a family of importance in Benjamin, and his son Saul had the added advantage of unusually tall stature and extra good looks. He was outstandingly well endowed.

3. An untoward incident, the loss of valuable asses, took Saul away from home on a thankless errand to look for them. Animals could easily stray in the bare, limestone hills, where hedges were unknown and stone walls were forever needing repair. *The asses of Kish* should read 'some asses of Kish', the definite article in this construction identifying the particular asses about which the narrative tells.[2]

---

[1] Hertzberg, p. 73.   [2] McCarter 1980, p. 173.

4. The exact location of the districts mentioned is no longer certain, but *the hill country of Ephraim*, or Mount Ephraim, indicates the general direction, to the north of Gibeah, where Saul's home was (1 Sa. 10:26; 11:4). Saul and his servant made a circular tour, returning close to Ramah, though neither Samuel nor his city is named here. The reader knows Samuel came from the land of Zuph (1 Sa. 1:1), so he, unlike Saul, is aware that this journey has an importance that will take Saul by surprise. *The land of Benjamin* (the Hebrew lacks the 'ben') is almost certainly not the original reading. An area of Ephraim is required, and a less well-known place name has evidently been replaced by a familiar one.

5–6. One puzzling, often-noted feature of the story is Saul's ignorance of Samuel, but that may be to misinterpret the writer's intention. What he wants to convey is rather Saul's lack of awareness of the future. Just when Saul is ready to call off the whole venture, everything depends on his servant, who believes the *man of God* will give them the direction they need. A visit in time of need to a man of God was expected to change the whole situation, and on two counts this man was outstanding: he was esteemed by all who knew him, and his words were fulfilled (*cf.* 1 Sa. 3:19). Thus he passed the test of the true prophet (Dt. 18:22).

7–8. Saul wants to get home, and points out that they have nothing to give the man of God (an interesting sidelight on the funding of the prophets), but the servant 'happens' to have a silver quarter-shekel, which is considered adequate, so Saul's misgivings are overruled.

9. In a modern book this verse would be a footnote. It points out how the story of Saul's encounter with Samuel fits into Samuel's story thus far. He had been referred to as the 'prophet' (Heb. *nābî'*) in 1 Samuel 3:20, and the narrator considered this to be the appropriate word to describe Samuel, but Saul and his servant were wanting him to do them a favour by discerning where the lost asses were; this was the role of a diviner or 'seer' (from Heb. *rō'eh*, 'to see'). Later the two words were used interchangeably, for in 1 Chronicles Samuel is called a *rō'eh* without any sense of incongruity (1 Ch. 9:22; 26:28; 29:29).

10–14. In England it would be unusual nowadays to go *up the hill to the city*, though this would have happened in medieval times before the advent of canals and railways. In Israel even today the ancient hilltops are covered with dwellings, and strike the Western visitor as a distinctive feature of the landscape. The fact that springs and wells are usually below the city required daily water-carriers, a task that fell customarily to the *young maidens* (*cf.* Gn. 24:11). Though the seer was visiting their town, they could not omit their regular trip to the well. In any case, they had not been invited to the feast. The fact that Saul arrived just at the appropriate time to meet Samuel is another sign of providential overruling. This impression is strengthened when, as Saul and his servant enter the city gate, Samuel is just coming out. The *high place* was not within the city walls in this case, but on another height nearby; indeed the name Ramathaim (1 Sa. 1:1) has a dual ending, and implies two summits. Maybe Samuel had built this centre of worship (1 Sa. 7:17). This is the only mention in the Old Testament of blessing the sacrifice.

15–16. The day before, the Lord had 'uncovered Samuel's ear' to tell him to expect a man of Benjamin, whom he was to anoint *prince* (Heb. *nāgîd*) over Israel. The word 'king' is deliberately avoided because Yahweh was Israel's king. Samuel is to indicate the Lord's choice of prince-designate by a private anointing. This ceremony symbolized the imparting of divine gifts for the fulfilment of the task to which he was being called, and made the recipient the *māšîaḥ*, or 'anointed one'. In particular, he was to lead Israel against the Philistine oppressors.

17. 'When Samuel caught sight of Saul' (NIV) he had the Lord's confirmation that this was the man who would 'govern' Israel. Again the obvious verb, 'rule' (despite the RSV), is avoided, and a verb which usually means 'restrain' (Heb. *ʿāṣar*) is used instead, indicating a special form of rule, under the kingship of the Lord.

18–19. How extraordinary that when Saul needed directions to the seer's house he should unwittingly have approached Samuel. *I am the seer* was a surprising answer, but more surprisingly still the seer had a message for Saul. He was invited to the sacrifice and to the feast that followed; but as for explanations, he would have to wait till the next morning.

20–21. Saul could forget about the *asses*; they were found. His journey had taken on a new and mysterious dimension. Honours were coming to him and his family, but he did not understand why that should be, and protested that his tribe was small (it had been decimated in a punitive battle, Jdg. 20:46, and Benjamin was the youngest of Jacob's twelve sons) and his family undistinguished (but *cf.* v. 1). Like Gideon before him (Jdg. 6:15), he felt unworthy of the honour, whatever it was, and not a little scared by the sudden new development in his life. It may also have been considered good manners to play down one's social standing, especially in the presence of God's prophet or messenger, but in Saul's case there seems to have been a modesty that was combined with a shy temperament (*cf.* 1 Sa. 10:22).

22–24. Shy or not, Saul and his servant were ushered into the feast and seated at the head of the table, where places had been kept. They were honoured guests! The leg of meat that the cook had set aside was the portion allotted to the priests, 'And you shall consecrate . . . the thigh of the priests' portion . . .' (Ex. 29:27). Saul must have been mystified that not only was he expected, but he was also treated as though he were a priest. He did not yet know that he was the Lord's choice for Israel's first king, and so, as the Lord's anointed, entitled to the special privileges, including the apportioned joint of meat.

25–27. Having returned to the city, and spent the night in the cool of the roof-top, Saul was wakened early. The RSV's *a bed was spread for Saul* follows the LXX here, while the AV and NIV keep to the Hebrew, 'he [Samuel], talked with Saul', which makes good sense. Outside the city, Samuel wanted a private word with Saul, hence the request that the servant should go on ahead.

10:1. The time had not yet come for a public proclamation of Israel's first king, and from Saul's point of view it was merciful that he should be given time to adjust to the sudden disclosure that he was God's chosen. Saul received the anointing that set him apart from all his contemporaries and symbolized the Lord's endowment of him to fulfil the role of *prince* (Heb. *nāgîd*) over *his people Israel*. The RSV has again followed the LXX; the Hebrew has instead of *people*, 'inheritance', which more usually refers to the land of Canaan, but nevertheless is also used of God's people (*e.g.* 1 Ki. 8:53; 2 Ki. 21:14; Is. 19:25). The remainder of verse 1 is taken from the LXX, and does not appear in the Hebrew text, hence its omission in the AV, RV and NIV (though the NIV includes the longer text in the margin). The addition makes a better transition to verse 2, and the signs to Saul that follow.

2. The first sign will be a meeting with two men who will assure him that his father's asses have been found. They will in turn reassure his father about Saul's safety.

The place *Zelzah* is unknown, but *Rachel's tomb*, somewhere between Bethel and Bethlehem (Gn. 35:16–21), was near the border between Ephraim and Benjamin; Jeremiah suggests that it was in Ramah (Je. 31:15). The present-day 'Rachel's tomb', just north of Bethlehem, erected by the Crusaders, is not in keeping with the biblical evidence.

3–4. The second sign, at the *oak of Tabor*, a landmark on the road to Bethel, will involve three travellers to the shrine there. The things they are carrying are sacrificial offerings, but Saul is to accept the *two loaves* they offer him, even though he is not a priest. As the Lord's anointed he is a sacred person, and qualifies to eat 'holy' bread, as did David (1 Sa. 21:6). Moreover, he and his servant see their needs being met.

5–7. The third sign occurs at *Gibeathelohim*, where there was another 'high place' (*cf.* 1 Sa. 9:12, 14). The name means 'hill of God', and may indicate Gibeah, Saul's own city. Mention of the Philistine presence there gives a reminder of the threat that Saul is to remove, but he needs to be empowered by the Spirit of God. This empowering happened, not through the instrumentality of Samuel, but through a group of prophets who prophesied to the accompaniment of music. The *spirit of the Lord* would cause Saul to prophesy, and he would *be turned into another man* (lit. 'overturned', transformed'). These signs will be proof that the Lord is with him, but he for his part must fulfil all that the Lord directs him to do. In the context, this appears to be the meaning of the idiom *whatever your hand finds to do*.

8. *You shall go down before me to Gilgal*, the important shrine near Jericho, in Benjamite territory. Since it was situated in the rift valley, a thousand feet below sea-level, the traveller literally 'went down'. Once there, Saul was to wait for Samuel seven days, so that Samuel could offer sacrifices. The instruction appears to have been given more than once (*cf.* 1 Sa. 13:8).

9–13. Saul was all set to be obedient, and as he left Samuel *God gave him another heart* (lit. 'turned to him'; *cf.* v. 6). A change took place in him because God was at work in him. All the signs were fulfilled, but only one is related. When he was with the prophets Saul also prophesied, and the people of the place, who evidently knew Saul well (evidence that supports Gibeah as the location), made disapproving comments. The *son of Kish* should know better than to get mixed up in such company. *Who is their father?* implies scorn for illegitimate prophets, who, in social terms, were nobodies. Yet before long Saul would be opposing the prophet Samuel, hence the irony behind the remark, *Is Saul also among the prophets?*, which became proverbial for an incongruous alliance. Indeed he was not a prophet, though his ecstatic state suggested that he might be. The people of the time, familiar with religious ecstasy in Canaanite rites (*cf.* 1 Ki. 18:26–29), did not regard uncritically the implications of such behaviour. The experience could have been of God, without necessarily indicating that Saul had the prophetic calling; time would tell, and there were objective tests (Dt. 18:22), just as there are for the church (1 John 4:1–3). For Saul the important point was that Samuel's predicted signs had been fulfilled, and he could therefore be sure that the Lord was with him. There is no evidence that he ever prophesied again (except in his rejection and humiliation, 1 Sa. 19:23–24).

He came to the high place: the definite article indicates the one mentioned in verse 5, close to his home.

14–16. Direct questions elicit from Saul nothing more than the barest outline of events. There is more here than natural reticence, for Samuel had been careful to commune secretly with Saul (1 Sa. 9:27), and Saul knows that he has to say nothing about the anointing. News that Samuel had honoured Saul had probably reached Gibeah, where curiosity would have been aroused. The narrator at last uses the word *kingdom* (Heb. *hammᵉlûkâ*). The king has indeed been chosen, but his identity has yet to be disclosed.

iii. Saul elected and proclaimed king (10:17–27). 17.

Samuel, who had sent the people to their homes (1 Sa. 8:22), now assembles them at Mizpah, the very place where he had interceded, and close to which he had set up the victory stone (1 Sa. 7:5–12). Where Samuel's prophetic leadership had been most clearly vindicated, he was to inaugurate the new era the people had demanded.

18–19. Samuel takes as his text words of the Lord that

echo the first words of Decalogue (Ex. 20:2; Dt. 5:6), the foundation for Israel's covenant commitment. The Lord's saving acts had continued to their own day, but despite the deliverances they had seen, including that at Mizpah, there was popular clamour for a king. Though Samuel saw this clamour as rejection of Yahweh, he still called the people to present themselves before the Lord, who had evidently not given them up, *by your tribes and by your thousands*. This interesting reference to the social organization of Israel at the time shows that the basic unit, the tribe, was subdivided into 'thousands' (Heb. *ªlāp̄îm*), the equivalent of 'families' in verse 21. The word that later meant 'a thousand' had at this early date a less precise meaning.[1] For that reason, numbers based on this sub-unit cannot be used to compute the size of the population, nor indeed of the army.

20. *The tribe of Benjamin was taken by lot*: the casting of lots was a common practice throughout the ancient world, and provision was made in Israel for the Lord's guidance to be given in this way. The land of Canaan was allocated by lot (Jos. 18:10); lots decided the fate of the two goats on the day of atonement (Lv. 16:8–10); and the culprit responsible for the defeat at Ai was discovered by the same method (Jos. 7:16–18). Decisions thus reached were accepted as final (Pr. 18:18), because the Lord was directing the outcome (Pr. 16:33). The last recorded use of the lot in Scripture is in Acts 1:26.

21. Selection was then made between the main subdivisions of Benjamin, the great families descended from the 'fathers'. The name *Matrites* is not mentioned elsewhere in the Old Testament, but there is no textual warrant for substituting 'Bichrites', from the name Becher in 1 Chronicles 7:6, where the sons of Benjamin are named (and *cf.* 2 Sa. 20:1, 'Sheba, the son of Bichri').[2] By a process of elimination Saul was finally designated God's choice.

---

[1] Gottwald goes into this whole subject in great detail, and argues that even the military unit in old Israel 'did not contain one thousand men, nor indeed any fixed number, but rather a very much smaller but variable number of men actually mustered by a *mishpāhah* [family] in order to supply a round number of troops from the *shevet* [tribe] for all-Israelite wars' (p. 271). *Cf.* Clark, 'Large Numbers of the OT', pp. 82–92.

[2] The genealogy of Saul's father, Kish (1 Sa. 9:1) made no reference to anyone called Matri, whereas Becorath might conceivably be connected with Bichri. The subject is explored by Gottwald, pp. 259–260.

22–23. The fact that Saul is missing puts everyone in a quandary. Has the lot failed to give the right answer? *Is there yet a man to come hither?* (RSV mg., which gives the meaning of the Hebrew, while the text follows the LXX) implies that Samuel may have missed someone in operating the selection process. But the word of the Lord led the leaders to Saul's hiding-place. Why did he hide? He had had time to prepare himself for this moment, but seems not to have been able to see himself in the role of king, though he had now had the assurance of the prophetic anointing confirmed by the lot. Reluctantly he revealed himself to be of outstanding physique, and therefore acceptable to the people as their leader, but he did not want to be king.

24. The secret is out, Saul is accepted as king and publicly acclaimed, using an expression common in the ancient Near East that became traditional (1 Ki. 1:25, 31, 34, 39; 2 Ki. 11:12; 2 Ch. 23:11) and is today exactly parallelled, for example, in the French, 'Vive le roi!' The matter was taken out of Saul's hands, *all the people* were of one mind, and their decision was binding; Saul had no opportunity to protest. Moreover, Samuel had staged the epoch-making event in a covenant setting, bringing home to the people the accusation that they had rejected the kingship of Yahweh (v. 19), and then presenting them with their new leader. Just as the ark had been acclaimed with a great shout (1 Sa. 4:5), so now Saul is similarly acclaimed. By popular demand a king had been appointed, but if Israel thought that he would solve all their problems by leading them to conquests without reference to God's law, they were quite wrong.

25. The ceremony has one important additional feature: the monarchy Israel had embraced was not like that of the nations, for it was circumscribed with *rights and duties* (Heb. *mišpaṭ* requires both words to convey its meaning), which were designed to prevent the oppressive style of rule described in 1 Samuel 8:11–18, and to ensure a constitutional monarchy. Moreover, it is clear that these stipulations that govern the monarchy are laid down by the prophet of the Lord; if the hope had been to distance Israel's politics from the terms of the covenant, that hope was not fulfilled, for, like the laws of the Sinai covenant, the rights and duties of the kingship were written *in a book* and laid *up before the Lord* (*i.e.* in the sanctuary; *cf.* Dt. 31:26; Jos. 24:26). The covenant was merely extended to cover the monarch, and to keep him from taking liberties with his people, or from exercising despotic power over them. Samuel then ordered the assembly to disperse.

26-27. Saul led the way in obedience to Samuel, and returned home; at the same time he discovered he had a following who supported his style of kingship as it had been defined by Samuel. These were *men of valour* (Heb. *haḥayîl*, lit. the 'force'), people prepared to fight under Saul's captaincy and enforce his leadership. These were men *whose hearts God had touched*, as he had also touched Saul and changed him (v. 6); but others had not wanted this kind of theocratic king, and made no secret of their contempt for Saul, even to withholding the customary tribute. It may be to Saul's credit that he turned a deaf ear, but the reader feels unsure how this new king is going to deal with the opposition, and pioneer a style of kingship in accord with Samuel's charter. As yet he still has to prove in action that he has what it takes to lead Israel into battle, and an opportunity to do so quickly presents itself.

At this point in our Bible, at the break between 1 Samuel 10 and 11, there is a sudden transition from Saul to a new character, Nahash the Ammonite, and to a new location, Jabesh-gilead, away to the east of Jordan. In the Qumran manuscript 4QSamᵃ, however, an extra paragraph introduces this next incident, and Josephus reveals that it was part of the text he used.[1] It appears to have been omitted from the LXX and MT by accident. It explains that Nahash had been oppressing the tribes of Reuben and Gad, putting out the right eyes of all the men they captured, but that seven thousand had taken refuge in the city of Jabesh-gilead. The last words of 1 Samuel 10:27 (RSV) are transformed by a slight change in the Hebrew to the meaning 'About a month later', as in the LXX and Josephus, so giving an indication of the passing of time between the two incidents.[2] As translated by McCarter (p. 198), the addition reads:

Now Nahash, the king of the Ammonites, had been oppressing the Gadites and the Reubenites grievously,

[1] Josephus, *Antiquities*, 6.5.1.
[2] The 4QSamᵃ text here has been reconstructed by F. M. Cross, who argues for its superiority in 'New Directions in Dead Sea Scroll Research: II. Original Biblical Text Reconstructed from Newly Found Fragments', *Bible Review* 1/3 (1985), pp. 26-35.

gouging out the right eye of each of them and allowing Israel no deliverer. No men of the Israelites who were across the Jordan remained whose right eye Nahash, king of the Ammonites, had not gouged out. But seven thousand men had escaped from the Ammonites and entered into Jabesh-gilead.

It may be that this additional material will one day be incorporated into the texts of our Bibles. If so, though it will not add substantially to the meaning of the text (*cf.* the commentary on 1 Sa. 12:12–13), it will supply a helpful introduction to the Ammonite incident.

iv. Saul confirmed as king (11:1–15). Unwittingly, the Ammonites provided just the opportunity Saul needed to take an initiative, and to prove to himself as well as to Israel at large that he could 'save' his people from oppressors. The Ammonites were related to Israel (Gn. 19:38; Dt. 2:19), but they were characteristically aggressive, harassing the tribes east of Jordan from their territory further to the east (Jdg. 3:13; 11; *cf.* Dt. 23:3–6). They claimed that the east bank of the Jordan belonged to them (Jdg. 11:12–13). It is clear in the Jephthah episode that in the initial battle Jephthah led troops from the Transjordan tribes only. The rallying-point was at Mizpah in Gilead (Jdg. 11:29), the place from which Jephthah came, and no help was forthcoming at the crucial moment from the Ephraimites west of the Jordan (Jdg. 12:2). For their part, the inhabitants of Jabesh-gilead had not gone to the disciplinary action against Benjamin (Jdg. 21:8). There was little precedent, therefore, to give hope that in the current threat there would be help forthcoming for Jabesh-gilead from the western tribes.

1. *Nahash*, the Ammonite king, is mentioned later as an ally of David (2 Sa. 10:1–2), but here his policy of maiming Israelites by putting out their right eyes, so incapacitating them from taking aim in battle, was inhuman and cruel.[1]

Jabesh-gilead is probably the modern Tell abu Kharaz, on the wadi Yabis, which retains the name (Heb. *yābēš* = Eng. Jabesh). It was only about two miles (3 km.) from the Jordan,

---

[1] Another example of inhuman cruelty on the part of Ammon was cited by Amos some three hundred years later; such crimes against humanity inevitably called down judgment (Am. 1:13–15).

and easily accessible from the west. Intermarriage between the Benjamites and Jabesh would have established a bond between the two, which forms part of the background to Saul's reign.

So desperate was the situation of Jabesh that the inhabitants judged they could only surrender and accept terms; they were at the mercy of the Ammonites.

2–4. So confident was Nahash in his command of the situation that he made unreasonable demands, and even permitted Jabesh to seek help from other parts of Israel's territory. In his estimation, help was unlikely to be forthcoming. *Seven days* was barely time enough for messengers to reach the whole land, and return. When they come to *Gibeah* there is much concern, even weeping, for the plight of Jabesh, but no plan of action.

5–6. Saul, who is absent when the messengers arrive, 'happens' to drive home his oxen when the weeping is at its height. When he hears the reason *the spirit of God* seizes him, arouses his indignation, and moves him to action, as happened in the time of the judges to those endowed for leadership.

7. Saul's action was carefully calculated to be a reminder of the incident recorded in Judges 19. The Levite from Ephraim had spent the night at Gibeah, where his concubine had been killed. He brought the crime before all Israel for judicial decision, and it was his method of rallying the tribes that Saul consciously imitated when he cut his oxen in pieces and threatened with a similar fate the oxen of any who failed to respond to his call to arms. Saul's inclusion of Samuel implies that he expects the prophet to accompany him into battle in view of the fact that Saul is responding to the Spirit of God. The support of Israel's fighting men is immediate and united: Saul's strong lead ensures the co-operation of all the tribes (contrast Jdg. 5:16–17).

8. *Bezek* (modern Khirbet Ibziq) was a well-chosen rallying point in Ephraim, opposite Jabesh-gilead, which was only about ten miles (16 km.) away on the other side of the Jordan. The number of men who rallied should probably be interpreted as military units rather than 'thousands' (Heb. *'alāpîm*), as in 1 Samuel 10:19.

9–10. The messengers were thus able to return with positive news of military aid, which enabled the leaders of the besieged Jabesh to inform the Ammonites that *tomorrow* would be the decisive day. *We will give ourselves up to you* is the obvious meaning, but the Hebrew verb *yāṣā'* (lit. 'go or come out') can have military implications (as in 1 Sa. 18:13, 'he went out . . . before the people' [as their commander]), so that the message contained a clever ambiguity, while giving the impression that surrender was intended.

11. Saul adopted well-tried tactics when he divided his army into three companies so as to surround the enemy. Gideon and Abimelech had done the same (Jdg. 7:16; 9:36–37). He also used the surprise of a dawn attack, and by midday had completely routed the enemy.

12–13. In the light of Saul's victory there is public demand for the death of the men who had questioned Saul's ability to save Israel. He had promised deliverance (v. 9) and now *the Lord has wrought deliverance*, so vindicating Saul before the whole army and the population of Jabesh. In the flush of new confidence, Saul will have no-one put to death; at this point he does not put a foot wrong.

14–15. At Mizpah, Saul had been chosen and proclaimed king, but he was not supported by all (1 Sa. 10:27); having now proved himself in action, he will be established by *all the people*, and so the words of Samuel, *let us . . . renew the kingdom*, imply unanimous support for Saul. The ceremony at Gilgal 'renews' the kingdom in the sense that opposition is no more, peace offerings imply reconciliation, and 'all the people' make Saul king.

Gilgal was the place where the Israelites under Joshua first set foot on the soil of Canaan, and acknowledged the Lord's great power exercised on their behalf, as well as the fact that they belonged to him (Jos. 4:23–24; 5:2–7). At this ancient sanctuary, accessible for the tribes east of Jordan, *they made Saul king before the Lord*. Any suggestion of a secular style of kingship was thereby repudiated, and Saul was acknowledged as leading Israel under the kingly authority of the Lord. The theocracy had not after all been rejected, and the feasting that followed the sacrifice of peace offerings was marked by great rejoicing. 'The men of Israel are happy to have such a king, Saul is happy to be such a king, and Yahweh has installed the type of king who maintains the relative positions of himself and Israel: he as their God and they as his people.'[1] Within

---

[1] Eslinger, p. 381.

this understanding of the monarchy the conflicting viewpoints and interests could be resolved, but the implications of the situation had still to be spelt out.

v. Samuel hands over to Saul (12:1-25). Now that all Israel has accepted Saul as king, Samuel has to withdraw as the theocratic leader, though he continues to exercise his prophetic ministry – albeit restricted to some extent, in so far as the monarch may choose to ignore his advice and instructions. But first he wants to set the record straight, and point out that under his leadership Israel had had just and effective administration, in keeping with the covenant, without any undue demands being made to restrict personal liberty.

1-2. In accordance with the Lord's instructions (1 Sa. 8:7), Samuel had complied with popular demand for a king, who from this time on *walks before* them as Samuel had done. The expression in this context means 'fulfils the function of leader', living in the public eye, under constant scrutiny. Samuel has done this all his life, and he mentions his sons to reinforce the fact that his ministry has covered the generations.

3-5. Samuel is seeking vindication not only of his own integrity but also of the style of rule he represented. He had in no way attempted to enrich himself, or boost his own importance. (Did Samuel wonder whether he would have been better appreciated if he had been self-assertive and acquisitive?) In his capacity as judge he had been entirely just, never favouring the rich and powerful by taking *a bribe*. His strict uprightness is established before the Lord and before *his anointed* (Heb. *mᵉšîḥô*, echoing perhaps 1 Sa. 2:10). By using this title Samuel was laying stress on the king's responsibility to represent aright the Lord whom Samuel had served. Samuel is acquitted of any possible accusation against himself.

6-11. Samuel goes on to proclaim the God whom Israel has come to know in experience, through their history as a people. Speaking as a judge and prophet, he sets forth a Deuteronomistic understanding of Israel's history. The events of the exodus, Sinai and the entry into Canaan became a kind of 'creed', recited and commented upon on formal occasions of national assembly such as this. Many, if not all, of those listening to Samuel would have known the outline of events he recounted, but Samuel is calling each person to identify himself by faith with past generations who experienced the

Lord's deliverance; the saving deeds of the Lord were firstly *for you* and secondly *for your fathers*. Each new generation entered into the covenant commitment, with its obligations and privileges, but every act of obedience, and every act of apostasy, had repercussions that influenced the future. In order to understand their own situation in relation to their covenant God, those of Saul's generation needed to see how they had been brought to their land, and had experienced both defeat and victory, depending on their loyalty to the Lord. Even in the times of apostasy, once they turned to the Lord in repentance, he had sent deliverers.

Samuel sums up the basic sin of Israel in the words, *they forgot the Lord their God*. It is an indictment worth pondering. Having forgotten him they forsook him, and put in his place the seductive local cults connected with the *Baals and the Ashtaroth* (see the commentary on 1 Sa. 7:3–4). The sermon is making the important point that, despite the despicable depths to which Israel fell, the Lord did not abandon them. Instead, he put them under pressure from enemies so as to cause them to seek him. Among the deliverers, Samuel names *Jerubbaal* (Jdg. 6:32), better known as Gideon, *Barak* (the Hebrew has 'Bedan', who is not mentioned in Judges; the rsv has followed the lxx), Jephthah (Jdg. 11 – 12:7), and finally he includes himself, for he was reckoned among the judges (1 Sa. 7:15–16) and brought their era to an end. Thanks to these deliverers, Israel *dwelt in safety*; Samuel had had a crucial role to play, which all his hearers acknowledged. The sermon now touches each one personally.

12–13. When the question of a king was first raised with Samuel (1 Sa. 8:4–22), no mention was made of the Ammonite threat, which Samuel now says caused the request. The events of 1 Samuel 8 – 12, however, cover a relatively short period, and it could well have been known already at that time that Nahash was oppressing the tribes east of Jordan. According to the extra material from 4QSamᵃ, it is evident that the Ammonite raids had been going on over months. The request for a king, first made after Gideon's victory (Jdg. 8:22), became more insistent when society gave evidence of moral breakdown (*cf.* Jdg. 18:1; 19:1; 21:25; 1 Sa. 8:3). Fear of social chaos seems to have been second only to fear of external enemies; the latter called for immediate action when the Ammonites became aggressive. Expectation was high that a king would deal effectively with both dangers; but Samuel continued to drive home the enormity of preferring a human ruler, by asking the people to look at the king they had chosen.

14–15. Yet prosperity would still be a possibility, on condition they and their king gave full allegiance to the Lord and his commandments. The monarch in Israel was subject, like everyone else, to the Lord God.

16–18. Samuel wants to make sure his words are taken with all the solemnity they deserve. By calling for a thunderstorm at *wheat harvest* (*i.e.* in May and June, when the rains of spring were over), Samuel was asking for 'a sign', a demonstration of the Lord's support for his servant, whom the people would ignore at their peril. Despite the establishment of the monarchy, the Lord would continue to speak through his servants the prophets.

19–25. The words of Samuel, reinforced by the storm, brought the assembly to repentance. This enabled the prophet to bring reassurance: *Fear not*. The *you* that follows is emphatic, as is the *I* in verse 23. Israel had done wrong; Samuel had his part to play, but what mattered most was the affirmation that *the Lord will not cast away his people, for his great name's sake*. What the Lord has undertaken to do, he will complete, because he is God and will not allow his purposes to be thwarted. This truth stands despite the apparent contradiction of it in verse 25. In the long term the threat was carried out, but, as Paul argues, God did not cast off his people (Rom. 9 – 11; *cf.* esp. Rom. 11:1).

Samuel had the ongoing task of intercession, which he had no intention of neglecting, together with that of instruction and counselling. His immediate exhortation to fear and serve the Lord he supported with the practical advice to *consider what great things he has done for you*. Nothing is likely to prove a more effective incentive to faithful service.

Saul appears to have overcome his reluctance to accept his God-given calling. He was now fully installed as king of the tribes of Israel, who had by implication agreed to give him their allegiance. Any theorizing as to his role had to give way to practical considerations, for enemy incursions continued and required urgent military action. In this sphere, Saul had begun to gain a reputation; would he be able to keep it up? The ominous last words of Samuel's sermon were not

encouraging, speaking as they did of the possibility of both
the people and their king being swept away.

In relation to Samuel, it is obvious that Saul had a problem.
On the one hand he owed his appointment to Samuel, but on
the other hand he was taking over Samuel's position as Israel's
leader. Samuel spoke frequently of the wickedness of the
people in requesting a king, apparently implying that he, Saul,
should not really be in office. Yet Saul had not sought to be
king, and would have preferred, at least at first, to have been
left in obscurity, but he had not been offered any option. Too
many signs had been given that he was the person of God's
appointment, and prayers for deliverance from the Ammonites
had been marvellously answered. He was king by divine
anointing, by God's overruling of the sacred lot, and by united
popular demand. He had caught the imagination of the
people, who wanted a hero, and against all odds he was
expected to pass muster.

Had he realized it, Saul could have gained much by the
presence of a seasoned prophet like Samuel alongside him,
ready to give guidance, instruction and, if necessary, rebuke.
Above all, Samuel was an intercessor who knew the Lord's
mind, and saw prayer answered. Samuel would indicate the
right way, and all Saul had to do was follow. He could have
leant hard on Samuel and he would have found reassurance.
In the event, this was exactly what Saul could not bring
himself to do.

II. SAUL: THE FIRST KING (1 Samuel 13:1 – 31:13)

a. Key incidents in the reign of Saul (13:1 – 15:35)

i. Jonathan attacks the Philistine garrison (13:1–23). 1.
Now that the account of Saul's reign is about to begin, the
formula that accompanies the record of each of the kings in
the books of Samuel and Kings (*e.g.* 2 Sa. 5:4–5; 2 Ki. 11:21;
12:1) is inserted, but without the figures needed, as the RSV
mg. indicates. It seems likely that that information was
missing from the start, or that it was misunderstood and
therefore omitted by later scribes who thought the numbers

given could not be right.[1]

2. Saul's first act as king is to set up a standing army made up of picked troops, on whose professional competence he hopes to rely. He himself commands two divisions ('thousands') and Jonathan one. Jonathan has authority to take action and Saul identifies with him.

3. Jonathan precipitated a crisis by defeating the Philistine *garrison* at *Geba*. The similarity of the name to Gibeah, where a garrison of Philistines had already been located (1 Sa. 10:5), and where Jonathan and his troops were stationed, has given rise to the suggestion that Gibeah should stand in the text here also. The two towns were only about four miles (6½ km.) apart, and *Michmash* was another two miles (about 3 km.) beyond Geba, in a northerly direction; though the rugged terrain involved extra exertion, it also provided excellent conditions for guerrilla warfare. Saul wanted to make the most of Jonathan's victory by alerting everyone with the trumpet blast: *Let the Hebrews hear*. Or maybe it was a Philistine cry, 'The Hebrews have rebelled!' (*cf.* the NEB's rendering, based on the LXX).

Who are meant by 'the Hebrews' (Heb. *'ibrîm*) in this context? The term was not normally used by Israelites of their own people, and a third party is assumed by the words that follow in verse 4, 'And all Israel heard it said . . .' – which prompts us to ask 'By whom?' The fact was that Canaanite inhabitants remained in the land, some of whom occupied strategic cities like Jerusalem, and they as well as the Israelites were threatened by the Philistine incursions. In addition, there were the unenslaved fighters of the hills, who were ready to serve as mercenaries. From the Philistine point of view, all these sections of the population were viewed as subordinates who owed allegiance to the Philistine overlords, whose

---

[1] The MT has 'Saul was "son of a year" ', *i.e.* a year old; two Greek MSS have 'thirty years old', but since Jonathan is already a warrior even this is not convincing. Some other Greek MSS omit the verse. E. Robertson, 'Samuel and Saul', *BJRL* 28/1 (1944), pp. 175ff., argues for fifty-two years on the grounds that a tabular list had used the Hebrew letters *bêt nûn* as numerals. As for the length of his reign, the 'two years' of the MT (cf. AV, RV) are considered by most commentators to be too short a time. Acts 13:21 has 'forty years'; so too does Josephus (*Antiquities* 6.14.9), though later (*Antiquities* 10.8.4) he reckons twenty years. Both these periods are thought to be too long. They may have been based on the twenty years mentioned in 1 Sa. 7:2, or they may have incorporated the combined rule of Samuel and Saul.

superior organization and technology earned them dominion and influence. All the inhabitants of the hill country of Canaan were potential slaves, producing food and serving as paid labourers or mercenaries. According to Gottwald, this was the meaning of 'Hebrew', a social group distinguished by socio-political rather than by ethnic or economic factors.[1] Others, however, argue that the term has an ethnic connotation; it represents the descendants of Eber (Gn. 11:16), so designating a group wider than the sons of Abraham, Isaac and Jacob, but nevertheless including them.[2] This makes good sense here, because many of Saul's men had deserted, and now were desperately needed. On hearing the trumpet call, these troops would return to rejoin the battle lines.

4. Saul is generally hailed as a hero, and there is considerable support for him as he mobilizes the resulting forces at *Gilgal*, where he had been made king (1 Sa. 11:14).

5–7. The overwhelmingly superior forces of the Philistines – superior both in equipment and in numbers – took up their positions in the very area Saul had occupied, and commanded the hills east of Bethel (an alternative name for *Beth-aven*; *cf.* Ho. 4:15). Saul's troops were so intimidated that they took to their heels and hid in the many caves and other holes in the rocks.

Or crossed the fords of the Jordan is a correction (*cf.* RSV mg.); the AV's 'And some of the Hebrews went over Jordan . . .' follows the Hebrew text. If, as we have argued, these 'Hebrews' are the uncommitted recruits whom Saul had attracted to himself, it is understandable that they should be singled out for separate action. The text needs no emendation. The hirelings fled.

8–10. *He waited seven days, the time appointed by Samuel*: the reference can hardly be to 1 Samuel 10:8, but presupposes a similar instruction given for this occasion also; maybe Samuel undertook always to come within seven days in any time of crisis. Jonathan had not been bound by any such commitment when he raided Geba, perhaps because that was not full-scale war.

Saul knows he must soon make a move if the whole army is not to desert, and he is on edge as he impatiently waits

[1] Gottwald, p. 401.
[2] *Cf. IBD* 2, 'Hebrews', pp. 626, 627; McCarter 1980, pp. 240–241.

for Samuel to offer the sacrifices that preceded battle, and demonstrated Israel's dependence on the Lord. It was a test case. When Samuel did not appear, Saul took matters into his own hands and offered the burnt offering. No sooner had he done so than Samuel arrived, only to be greeted by Saul as if nothing had happened. Either Saul was insensitive on spiritual issues, or he was bold-faced, for, by his disobedience, he was challenging Samuel's spiritual authority and therefore that of the Lord, whose prophet Samuel was.

11–12. Saul condemns himself in his answer to Samuel's question. True, he was in a dilemma from which he could see no escape, so he took matters into his own hands and, ironically, says he had not *entreated the favour of the Lord*; he could have done so privately of course, as Hannah did, without intruding into the prerogatives of Samuel. Doubtless he would then have found relief from his anxiety and renewal for his faith, but the correct ritual was important to him.

13–15a. *You have done foolishly* is a stronger condemnation than we might suppose, for in Scripture the fool is morally and spiritually blameworthy, not merely lacking in intellect. Saul had seen the Lord undertake for him in the Ammonite battle; he had heard the Lord's word of assurance through Samuel (1 Sa. 12:14), but at the first moment of strain he has failed to be obedient to the Lord his God. The penalty is severe, *your kingdom shall not continue*; that is, Saul will not set up a dynasty. It was a stern judgment, and we might be tempted to think that Samuel over-reacted, having subjected Saul to an unnecessarily long period of waiting, only to condemn him.[1] What Samuel is at pains to establish once and for all is the essential difference between Israel's monarchy and that of the nations. In Israel the Lord is king, and obedience to him must be paramount. It follows that any sign of a desire for independence of action becomes a disqualification: it is the equivalent of rebellion against the Lord. Already the Lord has selected Saul's successor, who will be *a man after his own heart*, prepared to let the Lord's will, as spoken by his prophet, be the guide of his life.

Samuel's departure was symbolic of the breach between himself and Saul, who was abandoned without any guidance for the defeat of the Philistines, and, with the sacrificial

[1] So Gunn 1980, p. 66.

offerings only half-completed, was left to his own devices.

15b–18. By the time Saul had taken up his position again in the hill country near Geba, where Jonathan and his men were stationed, their total forces numbered only *six hundred*. A deep ravine acted as a barrier between them and the Philistines on the other side of the valley at *Michmash*, but from nearby vantage-points it would be easy to keep track of every movement of the enemy. Philistine bands went out raiding in three directions: northwards towards *Ophrah*, westwards to *Beth-horon* and their own territory, and south-eastwards to *Zeboim*, near the Dead Sea (Gn. 14:2–3). This last route followed the precipitous ravine through the hills.

19–22. These verses depict the superiority of the Philistines in technical knowledge of the latest weaponry and its maintenance, knowledge which they were careful to monopolize for as long as possible. The Israelites were still in the Bronze Age, while their enemies, who had come from the Aegean region of the Mediterranean, had access to the latest developments in iron from the Hittites after their monopoly was broken in the twelfth century BC. It is clear that the Philistines kept all maintenance and servicing of weapons and implements in their own hands, so forcing the Israelites and other inhabitants of the hill country to be dependent on them. The *pim*, mentioned only here in Scripture, weighed ¼ oz. or 7.8 gm. (weights have been discovered with the word inscribed on them), about two-thirds of a shekel. The shekel was used to weigh gold and silver, which was handed over as payment before money came into use in the sixth century BC. Since the customer had no other option, a high price could be asked. The consequence was that only Saul and Jonathan were armed with sword and spear, and the enemy knew exactly how little equipment their army had.

23. The Philistines further threatened Israel by setting a garrison at *the pass of Michmash*, beside the ravine that separated the armies, and tension in the story mounts.

ii. Jonathan's second initiative (14:1–23). This vivid and attractive account of Jonathan the prince, and his bold sortie against the enemy, provides a detailed picture of the king who would have been Saul's successor, had Saul 'obeyed the commandment of the Lord'. The word of the Lord to Samuel when the identity of Israel's first king was being revealed was,

'He shall save my people from the hand of the Philistines' (1 Sa. 9:16), and Jonathan took that word with all seriousness.

1. The strain of Saul's indecision was more than his son could bear, hence his decision to survey the enemy garrison at close quarters. Secrecy was essential to success.

2–3. His father, deprived of Samuel's support, had turned to *Ahijah*, the great-grandson of Eli and therefore by right of heredity, chief priest, to give him the guidance he needed. The representative of the Shiloh traditions and guardianship of the ark of the covenant reappeared on the scene, despite the prophetic judgment pronounced on Eli's family (1 Sa. 2:27–36), and endorsed through the young Samuel (1 Sa. 3:11–14).

If Saul was in *Gibeah*, he had withdrawn somewhat from his original position; it may be that the text should read Geba (*cf.* 1 Sa. 13:16), or that *the pomegranate tree* was in that region (though in Is. 10:28 *Migron* is north of Michmash; the name means 'precipice', and could have applied to more than one location). Some disarray in Saul's camp is indicated.

4–5. The ravine which Jonathan and his companion had to negotiate was precipitous and involved skilful rock climbing. So noted were these cliffs that they had names: the south-facing cliff on the north side was *Bozez*, 'shining', because it was in the full sun; the shadowed north-facing cliff which they had to descend was *Seneh* (meaning 'thorny', or perhaps 'blackberry-covered'). This was the last route anyone in their right mind would choose to take, hence the surprise Jonathan managed to spring on the enemy.

6–10. Jonathan's motivation now becomes plain. He regards the Philistines as incompatible with Israel because they are *uncircumcised*, whereas Israel was committed by circumcision to the living God (Gn. 17:1–8). Since the time of Abraham there had been numerous examples of God's saving power, and Jonathan was convinced that the significant factor had always been the power of God and not the size of the army. It followed that, if the Lord God was with the two of them, he could give them victory, for *nothing can hinder the Lord from saving by many or by few*. Such an appreciation of Israel's Lord contrasted with his father's indecision (v. 2). The fact that his armour-bearer was of one mind with Jonathan indicates that Israel still had a core of true believers. The RSV makes sense of the Hebrew text here in verse 7 by correcting from the LXX, as the margin indicates; the NIV accepts this, and translates idiomatically, 'Do all that you have in mind . . . Go ahead; I am with you heart and soul.'

Jonathan was not foolhardy, however, but allowed for the possibility of a mistake on his part. The way the Philistines responded to their approach would be taken as a sign from the Lord: a challenge to *Come up* would indicate potential victory.

11–12. When the Philistines saw them, they responded with contempt, calling them *'ibrîm, Hebrews*, a derogatory term here, almost 'cavemen'. By taunting the two men to *Come up* the Philistines imply that the rock face is too steep for anyone to climb. If they do manage it, the Philistines will 'teach [them] a lesson' (NIV).

13–15. This was evidently not the first time Jonathan had been rock climbing. He not only scaled the cliff, but also had energy enough to attack the garrison and kill twenty men *within as it were half a furrow's length in an acre of land* (Heb. 'a yoke of land', *i.e.* the area ploughed by a yoke of oxen in a day), 'in an area of about half an acre' (NIV). The panic caused by this surprise offensive was increased when the earth itself began to quake and *even the raiders trembled*. The Lord himself had intervened!

16–17. Some of Saul's men on lookout duty reported troop activity in the distance. Saul must have guessed that someone from his camp had been responsible, for he orders a roll call, and discovers who is missing.

18–19. At this crisis Saul refers to his new adviser, Ahijah, who has brought the *ark of God* into battle (*cf.* 1 Sa. 4:3, and its disastrous sequel). It seems that Saul was still expecting explicit divine orders to be given, but in the event he did not wait for them, even if they would have been forthcoming, because the escalating noise from the Philistine camp demanded his attention. Saul had been sitting waiting for a lead when he should have been on the attack, and now he was on the attack when he needed to listen to the advice he had presumably requested.

20–23. There was nothing orderly about the ensuing battle. The *Hebrews* are clearly distinguished from the Israelites here, and the author has in mind uncommitted 'outlaws', who, on assessing that the Israelites have the upper hand, switch their allegiance to them from the Philistines. Similarly, those who had fled to hide in the hills of Ephraim heard rumours of the turn of events and rallied to Saul and Jonathan, so as to share in the victory. For *the Lord delivered Israel that day*; he had done his saving work and the Philistines fled westwards in panic, and so were defeated.

iii. Saul's rash oath (14:24–46). The mopping-up operations after a rout were all-important if the maximum benefit from the victory was to be reaped, but pursuit of the enemy involved an exhausting, unremitting journey over steep hills for hours on end.

24. Before going into battle, Saul was so determined to get the better of the Philistines that he imposed a ban on food for the day, evidently in an effort to gain the Lord's favour after hurrying away from Ahijah and the ark. No wonder the men were *distressed*; they were suffering from exhaustion, aggravated by fasting. This incident is one of a number of examples in Scripture of rash vows and oaths that are better avoided (*cf.* Jdg. 11:31–40; Ec. 5:4–5; Mt. 5:33–37). It also illustrates Saul's knack of getting the wrong end of the stick in things spiritual.

25–30. The text is obscure in verse 25, but the general sense concerns the finding of honey, dripping on to the ground from honeycombs of wild bees, in the trees of the forest into which the army had come. Jonathan, not knowing anything about his father's imposed fast, took advantage of the providential supply of energy-giving food, and was revived. When he heard of his father's oath and saw that the people were faint, he expressed open criticism: *my father has troubled the land.* The word 'troubled' (Heb. *'ākar*) is bound up with an attempt to deceive in Joshua 7:24–26, and with an unwise oath in Judges 11:35. There was in each case a death involved, and death threatens in this incident also. Yet there was food to hand which would have renewed the strength of all, so that they could have established their victory in the Philistine's own land.

31–35. As it was, the Israelites pursued them as far as *Aijalon*, on the border of the Philistine plain, within six miles from Gezer, capturing spoil which they proceeded to eat *with the blood.* Concerned to fulfil the ritual requirements, Saul made use of a rock, so that when the animals were killed their blood was drained and poured into the soil (*cf.* Gn. 9:4;

Dt. 12:23–24), and so kept separate from profane use.[1] And Saul *built an altar to the Lord*, still trying in his own way to gain the Lord's favour once more.

36–37. Evening had already come, and that is why Saul's oath had no longer been binding, and everyone had eaten. Now Saul envisaged renewed pursuit of the Philistines during the night. The priest's suggestion to seek the Lord's guidance seemed good, but when no answer was forthcoming to his questions, Saul assumed that someone's sin was responsible.

38–42. These verses tell us almost all we know about the way the sacred lot operated. Two possible answers, 'yes' and 'no', could be given by the two counters, which, as verse 37 shows, could also indicate 'no answer'. The counters were kept in the breastplate of judgment worn by the high priest, which was attached to the ephod (Ex. 28:30), and were named Urim and Thummim. The initials of the two words were the first and last letters of the Hebrew alphabet, which may have been written on the counters to distinguish them. Another suggestion is that two colours represented the 'yes' and 'no'; when these failed to coincide on the two counters the lot gave no reply. Such conjectures are helpful, though they cannot at present be verified.

At the beginning of his search for the culprit, Saul and Jonathan were set over against all the people, and Saul prayed, *If this guilt is in me or in Jonathan my son . . . give Urim, but if this guilt is in thy people Israel, give Thummim*. The text of the RSV has reconstructed the Hebrew using the LXX, but the NIV follows the Hebrew: 'Then Saul prayed to the Lord, the God of Israel, "Give me the right answer" ' (Heb. *tāmîm*, 'perfect things'; 'Thummim' is Heb. *tummîm*). In this instance there is too little reason to adopt the LXX, which could well reflect later practice, and we do not know how the lot operated at the time of Saul. It did, however, give the correct answer. It was Jonathan who had offended.

43–46. So eager was Saul to set himself in the right and gain God's favour that he determined to have even Jonathan put to death. The irony was that without Jonathan's heroic

[1] Interestingly, this incident demonstrates that in the early monarchy non-sacrificial slaughter was practised. 'The implication of this for Dt. 12:15ff. is that it can no longer confidently be seen as an attempt to institute a non-sacrificial kind of slaughter in the later monarchy,' J. G. McConville, *Law and Theology in Deuteronomy* (Sheffield: JSOT Press 1984), p. 47.

lead there would have been no victory in the first place, and the rank and file, who had by their silence protected Jonathan (v. 39), now took matters into their own hands and saved the life of (Heb. *yipdû*, 'ransomed') the one who had wrought salvation (Heb. *yšûʿâ*) that day. *He has wrought with God*, they say, so acknowledging that the whole episode had been a divine rather than a human deliverance. The outcome did nothing to reassure Saul, who was virtually given a vote of 'no confidence'; as for the Philistines, they escaped further pursuit that night. Saul was left in an agony of doubt as to his relationship with the Lord, and therefore his confidence in his ability to rule was further undermined. So far as outward observance of religious ritual was concerned, he had done the right thing, but he had failed to appreciate the crucial importance of submitting his will to that of the Lord God of Israel.

iv. A survey of Saul's reign (14:47–52). This short summary indicates that much more could have been written about the reign of Saul, and that the incidents related in detail have been selected with a purpose. A similar summary of David's reign is given in 2 Samuel 8.

47–48. *When Saul had taken the kingship* is an unusual turn of phrase, marking the fact that there had been internal opposition to overcome (1 Sa. 10:27), while simultaneously he was engaged in defeating surrounding peoples, uneasy at Israel's new status as a kingdom. *Moab* had not previously been mentioned, but the *Ammonite* threat had played an important part in Saul's acceptance as king (1 Sa. 11:12–15). *Edom*, south of Moab, completes the campaigns to the east and south-east, while *Zobah* was a region to the north-east, north of Damascus. The *Philistines* to the west had played a central part in the story. This total list of campaigns, however, puts Saul in a new light. Israel's king had won the allegiance of his men to the extent that they had followed him and fought off enemies far and near. Never before had Israel got the better of such a succession of potential invaders, and Saul *did valiantly*, winning high esteem. He was yet to undertake war against the *Amalekites*, at the express orders of Samuel. *He . . . delivered Israel out of the hands of those who plundered them* sums up the satisfaction felt by many, no doubt, who had hoped for just such security when they agitated for a king. Saul became their 'beloved captain'.[1]

49–51. The names of Saul's sons appear again in 1 Samuel 31:2 (and 1 Ch. 10:2) as *Jonathan*, *Abinadab* and *Malchishua* (*cf.* also 1 Ch. 8:33; 9:39, where the order is changed and Eshbaal is added). *Ishvi* and Eshbaal (or Ishbosheth, 2 Sa. 2 – 4) may be alternative forms of the same name, the former, a corruption of Ishiah, 'the Lord's man', avoiding the ambiguous word 'baal' (which meant 'lord', but was also a male Canaanite deity). Saul's daughters come into the story of David (1 Sa. 18:17–19), but his wife and father-in-law are not otherwise mentioned. It is interesting to discover that Saul's general, Abner, was his cousin. The simplicity of Saul's family life is in marked contrast with that of David, and even more so with that of Solomon.

52. The most persistent enemies of all were the Philistines, against whose incursions Saul built up a standing army of picked troops. This was the one development he made in the organization of the kingdom.

v. Samuel's final confrontation with Saul (15:1–35). It was an ancient injustice, not a recent one, that Saul was sent to avenge. The Amalekites were nomadic raiders, inhabiting the desert between the southern borders of Judah, south of Beersheba, and Egypt, but extending south into the Sinai peninsula. It was in this last region that they had tried to prevent Israel from reaching Sinai after their miraculous crossing of the Red Sea, and for this opposition to God's saving purpose the Amalekites were doomed to destruction (Ex. 17:14–16; *cf.* Nu. 24:20; Dt. 25:17–19). It falls to Saul to carry out the sentence of God, and this makes the incident quite different from all the other battles of Saul. He is here engaged in 'holy war', as opposed to a war of aggression or of self-defence. It is war at God's command, carried out as his judgment and on his behalf. The victory is the Lord's so there is no material advantage for the army; all the spoils of war belong to the Lord and are therefore holy. People and property alike are put under a ban for this reason. No-one may take possession of them. It is easy to understand the viewpoint of the soldiers who would be tempted to complain

---

[1] See the chapter on Saul in A. Dale, *The Winding Quest* (Oxford: Oxford University Press, 1972).

that they had put themselves in danger, yet had no benefit from the battle. Nevertheless the principle was well understood, for it had operated in the battles against Jericho and Ai, and underlay the conquest of Canaan. Here were cities that had been dedicated to other gods. The Lord claimed them for his people, 'gave them into their hand', but the city of Jericho, for example, its inhabitants and its possessions, had to be 'devoted to the Lord for destruction' (Jos. 6:17), the only exception being Rahab, who, by hiding the spies of Israel, had shown herself to be on Israel's side.

So it came about that the sinful nation of Israel became the agent of God in defeating another sinful nation. It was a necessary stage in the on-going purpose of God to bring about the salvation of mankind, and we need to see it in that light, not forgetting that Israel's unfaithfulness met a similar, though less total, destruction at the hands of the Assyrians and Babylonians. The incident is a reminder that it is a fearful thing to oppose the living God.

1–3. When Samuel appeared suddenly to Saul, it was to point out to him that he was king, not primarily by popular acclaim, but by the Lord's appointment. His duty, therefore, was to carry out the commands of the Lord, and in particular the command, *go and smite Amalek, and utterly destroy all that they have*. The verb *heh⁽rîm*, 'utterly destroy', is used seven times in this account, as though laying stress by repetition on this special act of consecration to the Lord of hosts, who directed and gave victory to Israel's armies.

4–7. Saul made an immediate response by rallying the fighting men at *Telaim*. A place called Telem is listed among southern border cities of Judah in Joshua 15:24, but the site has not been identified, though somewhere in the Negeb is required by the geography of the campaign, and Telem belonged to Judah. The tribe of Judah was mentioned specially among the forces that rallied to Saul: they comprised ten contingents (*thousand*) of the total of two hundred contingents, or maybe in addition to them. *The city of Amalek* is strangely vague, and no city of that name is known, but it is not impossible that this tribe of desert-dwellers had settled and built a centre for their king and court.

The Kenites had been closely connected with Israel since the time of Moses, and had settled in the Negeb of Judah (Jdg. 1:16; *cf.* Ex. 2:15b–22; 3:1; 4:18–20; 18:1–5; Nu.

10:29–32). Though they were independent, they were allies of Israel, hence Saul's reluctance to involve them inadvertently when he attacked Amalek. They appear to have been experts in metal work (the name means 'smith'), and to have settled down among other peoples as craft specialists; but, heeding Saul's warnings, they moved away from the Amalekites and avoided defeat in battle.

Saul's defeat of Amalek was effective from *Havilah* to *Shur*. Havilah, mentioned in Genesis 25:18, was an area of Africa hundreds of miles away, beside the southern end of the Red Sea; unless there was another Havilah in the Negeb, the name has been changed in the process of transmission. One possible original is 'from the valley' (*cf.* v. 5; Heb. *mnhl*, which may have been assimilated to the Hebrew name in Gn. 25:18). Shur was on the eastern border of Egypt.

8–9. In the aftermath of the battle, Saul interpreted in his own way the instruction of Samuel. Though the population as a whole was destroyed in accordance with the decree to devote them to the Lord, *Saul and the people spared Agag and the best of the sheep*; there is a clear hint that Saul wanted to keep on the right side of popular opinion. The Amalekite people were dispensable, but it was a pity to destroy excellent stock!

10–12. The Lord's word, *I repent that I have made Saul king*, seems to be contradicted later by Samuel (v. 29). The Lord does not change his mind in the sense that his purposes change, but he could no longer use Saul. Saul himself was fully responsible for his attitudes and action. The sovereign God is so fully in control that he takes in his stride the actions of human beings and adjusts his plans when necessary, but achieves his ultimate aims. What exactly was it that caused Samuel to be so *angry* ('grieved', AV; 'troubled', NIV) that he spent the whole night agonizing in prayer? In the first place, Samuel's theology was being put in question. Against his better judgment he had co-operated in king-making, announcing that Saul was the one whom the Lord had chosen (1 Sa. 10:1, 24; 11:15). Now it appeared that the Lord, who 'will not lie or repent' (v. 29), had changed his mind, and Samuel could not come to terms with this challenge to God's sovereignty. In the second place, what was to become of the leadership of Israel? The country was in a worse plight than ever. Last but not least, Samuel was torn within himself by the divine word, and needed to settle his own turmoil before the Lord. The personal cost of ministry is seen in the life of Samuel, and in this passage in particular.

Expecting that Saul would still be in the Negeb, Samuel set off southwards, only to find that he had gone in the wrong direction. Saul had already returned from fighting the Amalekites, and had celebrated his victory by setting up a commemorative monument in Carmel (*cf.* 1 Sa. 25:2), a place about ten miles south of Hebron and not to be confused with Mount Carmel. Thanks to Israel's 'bush telegraph', Samuel was saved a long fruitless journey, and found Saul comparatively close at hand in Gilgal, where Saul's kingship had been confirmed (1 Sa. 11:14–15).

13–16. This was to be the final confrontation between Samuel and Saul, but Saul, in the full flush of his victory, greeted Samuel with enthusiasm, in the misplaced confidence that he had done what had been asked of him. In answer to Samuel's enquiry about the noise of penned-up animals, Saul was still unconcerned. *They . . . the people* had spared the best animals for *sacrifice to the Lord your God*. The little word 'your' speaks volumes about Saul, who does not speak of 'our God'. One suspects that there were more selfish motives at work than the desire to sacrifice when the decision was made not to kill the best of the stock, but Saul knows how to put the case to best advantage. *The rest we have utterly destroyed* betrays a totally inadequate appreciation of all that was meant by the *ḥerem*, with its dedication of everything to the Lord, including the 'perks' from the battle and the enemy king.

17–21. Saul's attempt to put the blame on the people now recoils on his own head. Is he not king? Then he is responsible. The Lord, to whose election he owed his kingship, had given him a mission to fulfil. How could he do something else? But Saul continued to stand by his interpretation of events.

22–23. In a memorable prophetic utterance, Samuel pronounces for all time the futility of attempting to rely on ritual sacrifice when what is required is obedience. No ceremonial can make up for a rebellious attitude to God and his commandments, because obstinate resistance to God exalts self-will to the place of authority, which belongs only to God. That is why it is as bad as *divination* (by evil spirits), and tantamount to *idolatry*, for another god, self, has usurped his place. The parallel statements of the last two lines (five words altogether in the Hebrew) bring out the justice of the

115

condemnation. Saul has disqualified himself for kingship in Israel. He has refused to defer to the divine king.

24–26. At last Saul admits that he is in the wrong, but he does not take with full seriousness the condemnation pronounced by Samuel. Surely in the circumstances he can be forgiven and continue in office? In his admission, *I have transgressed* (Heb. *'ābartî*) *the commandment*, 'transgressed' renders an ordinary word which means literally 'to pass over' (we should say, 'I overlooked'), though put in this way the contradiction in terms becomes obvious. Saul had felt the need of popular support, and had not been able to resist the temptation to curry favour by permitting some material gain from the victory. Samuel repeats his statement of Saul's rejection, which cannot be repealed. Saul must live with the results of his own decisions.

27–31. By this time Saul was thoroughly awake to the implications of his rejection, and when Samuel turned to leave him Saul grabbed and tore the prophet's robe in an attempt to salvage some shred of his reputation. Samuel's torn garment provided a vivid picture of the kingdom torn from Saul, and to be given to a neighbour more worthy of it. Though Saul continued to be king, this day became the decisive one in the history of his reign, because, in the words of Balaam, who tried to reverse the Lord's blessing on Israel, 'God is not man, that he should lie, or a son of man, that he should repent' (Nu. 23:19). Indeed not. But neither could the Lord overlook persistent, deliberate rejection of his will, for that would negate his sovereignty. *Honour me now before the elders of my people and before Israel*, pleads Saul, who is unwilling to lose face and wants Samuel's presence in order to make it appear as if nothing has happened. Samuel relents and accompanies Saul as he worships.

32–33. Samuel has not quite fulfilled his prophetic tasks. Though he is old (1 Sa. 8:1) and so far as we know has never killed anyone in his life, he needs to complete what Saul has left undone, and devote Agag, the Amalekite king, to the Lord by putting him to death. (*Hewed . . . in pieces* follows the Vulgate; the Hebrew verb occurs only here and its meaning is uncertain.) Thus Samuel fulfils the orders he himself had given (v. 3), shows that he is willing and able to perform what he tells others to do, and above all that he obeys the commands of the Lord.

34–35. The final separation now took place: *Gibeah* and *Ramah* were less than ten miles apart, but Samuel was never to confront Saul again.

Samuel grieved over Saul: having known Saul from his youth, Samuel had grown fond of him, and he suffered deeply over their severed relationship. Even the Lord 'was grieved' (NIV) that he had made Saul king over Israel.

Saul's home in Gibeah (Tell el-Ful) is generally agreed to have been uncovered by excavation, though whether he built it or took it over from the Philistines is a matter of dispute. It was a large rectangular structure, fortified by a tower at the one corner which has survived.[1] Compared with the palace which David was to have built (2 Sa. 5:11), not to mention the palace of Solomon (1 Ki. 7:1–12), Saul's citadel was a very simple structure, designed for defence rather than for prestige. His restraint may have been due to the influence of Samuel, who was known to oppose the self-aggrandizement commonly associated with monarchy (1 Sa. 8:10–18); neither of Saul's immediate successors lived under the shadow of such a towering prophet as Samuel, and neither of them hesitated to enhance his own importance by elaborate building programmes.

Did Samuel continue to administer justice from his home in Ramah, while Saul ruled as king in Gibeah (*cf.* 1 Sa. 7:15–17)?[2] It is easy to see that anyone in Saul's position would need extraordinary humility, grace and wisdom to succeed in holding the allegiance of the people and in giving due authority to the older leader and prophet of the Lord.

The biblical text appears to give differing evaluations of Saul as a man and as king. In the first place he is proclaimed

---

[1] W. F. Albright's reconstruction of the ground plan of the citadel is reproduced in his book *The Archaeology of Palestine* (Harmondsworth: Penguin Books, 1949), p. 121, and in *IDB* 2, art. 'Gibeah', pp. 390–391. For a recent assessment of excavation at the site, see *IBD* 1, art. 'Gibeah', pp. 557–558. It is not possible to decide who built the fortress.

[2] One of the basic functions of the monarchy in Israel was the administration of justice, and both David and Solomon are depicted as fulfilling this role (2 Sa. 8:15; 1 Ki. 3:9, 28). As K. Whitelam shows in chapter 1 of his *The Just King* (Sheffield: JSOT Press, 1979), entitled 'The Ideal', the judicial responsibility of the monarchy was regarded very highly in the ancient Near East. Saul may well have felt that, deprived of his role as judge, he was less than king of Israel.

as the Lord's anointed (1 Sa. 10:1), equipped by God's Spirit (1 Sa. 10:9) and acclaimed as the Lord's choice by the people (1 Sa. 10:24). He soon proves that he is equipped to win the battles of the Lord's people (1 Sa. 11:5–11) and is solemnly installed as king (1 Sa. 11:12–15). He is generous towards his enemies on this occasion, refusing to execute those who had opposed him, and at the same time he is modest, even diffident, about his own claim to honour (1 Sa. 9:21; 10:22). Yet he looks the part, for he is tall and impressive (1 Sa. 9:2; 10:23), and a popular choice. How then are we to explain what goes wrong?

Saul starts at a disadvantage because Israel's traditions, which had developed in the egalitarian society of Moses' time and the wilderness journey, had opposed the idea of a human king. The Lord was king. Thus when Gideon was invited to set up a hereditary monarchy, he knew the right answer (Jdg. 8:22–23). Abimelech, the 'bramble among the trees', succeeded in setting himself up as king, but soon came to grief (Jdg. 9:1–57). Samuel firmly stood by the traditions, and it was evidently with reluctance that he agreed to the innovation (1 Sa. 8:6–9). Yet Samuel was in no doubt about the Lord's choice of Saul, and there is evidence that Samuel came to love him.

Samuel, of course, stood for the sovereign Lord God, whose word had to be paramount. He was the bearer of the Lord's instructions, and it was his task to see that those instructions were precisely carried out. There was no other culture in which the king had to bow in this way before the human representative of the deity, and it put Saul to the test. Saul undoubtedly wanted to do the right thing; he waited seven days for Samuel (1 Sa. 13:8), but was not patient for quite long enough. He was careful to seek the Lord's guidance in opposing the Philistine encroachment (1 Sa. 14:2–3, 18), and was meticulous in fulfilling the oath he had made, even to his own disadvantage (1 Sa. 14:24, 38–45), and he would not permit any transgression of the ritual law, even though the circumstances were exceptional (1 Sa. 14:33–35). Despite his concern to keep the law, however, Saul found Samuel looming over him in condemnation, telling him on two occasions that his kingdom would not continue, and that he would be replaced by a man after the Lord's own heart (1 Sa. 13:14; *cf.* 15:28).

There is something tragic about the person of Saul, the hero-king of Israel. He is in the process of discovering his kingly powers within the theocracy of Israel, and immediately confronts Samuel's criticisms. The conflict between church and state, so familiar from later periods of history, was already operative. As one recent writer has commented, 'The story of King Saul is, I believe, one of the Bible's "uncomfortable" stories.'[1] One never feels quite satisfied that it has been properly understood, for David, who from the start seems to be in favour, committed appalling sins, of which Saul was never guilty. Why therefore is Saul so harshly judged? David, after all his wrong-doing, found forgiveness and kept Bethsheba as his wife, yet Saul seemed to be doomed to fail right from the beginning of his reign.

The idea of a dark fate hanging over Saul has been taken up and examined in detail by David Gunn. He poses the question, 'Does Saul fail as king because of his own inner inadequacy as a human being, or because he is brought low essentially by external forces or circumstances?'[2] In the story thus far (for though Saul's rejection is final, his reign is far from over), the king has had to face many a dilemma: Jonathan had precipitated the battle of Michmash, and Saul, watching the army melt away, had felt forced to fulfil the ritual requirements that Samuel had not appeared to perform; again Jonathan took the initiative and, by his astonishing success, involved his father and all the army in a full-scale pursuit of the Philistines; Saul imposed a vow on his army to make clear their commitment to the Lord, but the vow trapped Jonathan and deprived the soldiers of much-needed sustenance; finally, in the Amalekite incident, Saul admitted to having 'feared the people and obeyed their voice', as opposed to the supreme command of the Lord through Samuel. Does all this amount to an opposing 'fate', the 'dark side' of God's dealings with mankind?

Certainly Saul appeared to be cumbered with inhibitions that hindered him from taking a lead, and in some respects he was undoubtedly to blame, but it is hard to know who would have had the maturity and spiritual insight to succeed where Saul failed. This first king of Israel, like Ananias and Sapphira in the early days of the church, seems to have been

[1] Gunn 1980, p. 9.   [2] *Ibid.*, p. 115.

judged by the highest possible ideals and allowed no margin of error. At the same time, no account is taken of the many sins associated with kingship which Samuel had listed (1 Sa. 8:10–18), but which Saul had avoided.

There is a sense in which Saul might have done better if he had been less conscientious in his desire for the Lord's guidance (sitting waiting for instructions instead of expecting guidance as he moved forward), and less dependent on reassurance that he was in favour, whether with God or man. 'His honest, yet anxious, concern to be on a right footing with the Lord is a practical hindrance to his exploiting the victory to the full' is one writer's comment on 1 Samuel 14:36,[1] and on several occasions Saul is characterized by an anxious uncertainty that makes him unable to act. In itself this is a character fault, a disqualification for leadership, for a king is expected to be a policy maker. Samuel would not have seen Saul's indecision in that light, but rather as the result of an obstinacy pitted against himself, and therefore against the word of the Lord. A later prophet warns against walking in the light of one's own torch, and advises: 'Let him who walks in the dark, who has no light, trust in the name of the Lord and rely on his God' (Is. 50:10–11, NIV). This was what Saul found impossible to do: hence much of the torment of the remainder of his life, as well as the tragedy of his reign thus far. Saul may have felt that he could have done much better as king without Samuel; if so, he was to have opportunity to prove that from this point on. He had a loyal following and he was a great warrior, but something vital was missing from his life.

In retrospect then, the 'key incidents' selected for inclusion in the acccount of Saul's reign underline his rejection, and show Jonathan in a favourable light. He led Israel in battle and won great victories, which made him so popular that his father could not do him any harm. Jonathan 'receives such marks of divine approval, and such acclaim of the people, as befits a king, and does so in the very context of his father's rejection'.[2] Thus the scene is set for the rise of the neighbour

---

[1] Hertzberg, p. 116.

[2] Jobling, p. 8. He goes on to point out that in the narrative thus far there is identification of role between Saul and Jonathan, but also separation. The meaning of Jonathan's exaltation, he thinks, 'is undoubtedly to be sought in the mediary role which Jonathan is later to play in the transition from Saul's kingship to David's'.

who is better than Saul (1 Sa. 15:28), and all the tensions his appearance will cause.

b. David comes into prominence (16:1 – 19:17)

i. David's secret anointing (16:1–13).

Samuel was not permitted to continue dwelling on regrets over the failure of Saul. The Lord had directed him to Israel's first king, and now he was being sent once more with a secret errand to the family chosen to provide the enduring dynasty. Despite the great significance of this new development, the incident is related in restrained terms, with attractive simplicity. Samuel, revered and honoured as he was, is seen clearly to be the messenger of the Lord, discerning what the Lord was saying and doing accordingly. His greatness lay, not in the originality of his ideas or in the initiatives he took, but in carrying out the instruction of the Lord: what mattered was simple obedience.

1. *Jesse the Bethlehemite* was grandson of Ruth and Boaz (Ru. 4:17, 22), and it has been suggested that this account of Samuel's visit to Bethlehem may have been part of a collection of treasured records handed down in that place. It has all the directness of a first-hand account. Samuel was to take his horn of sacred oil for the ceremony of anointing, but the significance of the ritual, which had been carried out only once before, and then in secret (1 Sa. 10:1), would have indicated only to Saul that a new king had been designated. *I have provided for myself a king* contrasts with 'make them [the people] a king' in the case of Saul (1 Sa. 8:22).

2–3. On this occasion Samuel fears that obedience will cost him his life. Already Saul has given Samuel reason to suspect that his hatred could flare up into murderous attack, but under cover of offering a sacrifice Samuel can carry out his task.

4–5. The fear with which the elders met Samuel is an indication of the prophet's reputation and of the loneliness of his position. Since the elders as well as Jesse and his household were invited to the sacrifice, a considerable number of people witnessed the anointing of David, and someone could have passed the information to Saul.

6–10. The eldest son, Eliab, impresses Samuel as a suitable candidate, but his appearance is deceptive, as Saul's had been.

The Lord sees not as man sees becomes an important maxim (*cf.* 1 Ch. 28:9), which illuminated the prophetic vision of the servant of the Lord, 'marred beyond human semblance', 'despised and rejected by men' but declared to be supremely great (Is. 52:14; 53:3). There is a corrective here to merely superficial judgment. Elihu, appointed ruler of Judah by David (1 Ch. 27:18), is probably Eliab. *Shammah* is variously called Shimeah (2 Sa. 13:3), and Shimea (1 Ch. 2:13; 20:7). *Seven of his sons*, according to 1 Chronicles 2:13–15, included David, but one may have died young. When Samuel failed to find the man of God's choice, he checked first for human error.

11–13. The youngest, considered so unlikely that it had not been deemed necessary to call him from the sheep, is the one of the Lord's choice (*cf.* 1 Cor. 1:27). The Lord has a way of choosing the person people think the least likely, but nevertheless David was good-looking; *ruddy* implied light-skinned by comparison with his compatriots, and therefore striking in appearance. His selection, however, was entirely the Lord's doing, and as time went on David came to see that he had been kept safe from his birth onwards (Ps. 22:9–10), to fulfil a special purpose. His anointing is unexplained, but the onrush of *the Spirit of the Lord* ensured that he was also being divinely equipped, whatever the future might hold. Samuel withdrew to Ramah, his mission fulfilled, and the family of Jesse continued as before.

ii. Saul needs a musician (16:14–23). Meanwhile, events were taking place which would bring about changes for David.

14. *The Spirit of the Lord departed from Saul*, as he had done from Samson (Jdg. 16:20), and with equally tragic consequences, for Saul became troubled by *an evil spirit from the Lord*. Though 'evil' should be read in the sense of 'injurious' here (so NIV mg.), the statement remains problematic to the modern reader, who finds it incompatible with the goodness of God. The writer of the book of Job made the point, 'Shall we accept good from God, and not trouble?' (Jb. 2:10, NIV), while at the same time indicating in the remainder of his book how costly such acceptance can become. On a national level, invasion and defeat by a ruthless enemy had also to be accepted from the Lord, whose sovereign direction of history involved the discipline of his people: 'I am the Lord, and there is no other. I form light and create darkness, I bring prosperity and create disaster; I, the Lord, do all these things' (Is. 45:6–7, NIV). As a philosophical problem, the origin of suffering continues to be baffling, but the people of God are encouraged in Scripture to take adversity of all kinds direct from the Lord's hand (*cf.* Jn. 9:3; 11:4; 2 Cor. 12:7–10), and through such acceptance God is glorified.

In the case of King Saul, it is important to note that signs of mental illness began to occur only after the confrontation with Samuel over the question of obedience to the divine command. This suggests that his illness was due to his rebellion against God; certainly he was held responsible for his actions, and regarded himself as responsible (1 Sa. 24:16–21; 26:21).[1]

15–18. Profoundly disturbed by his loss of Samuel's support, Saul needed help. At this stage he suffered from intermittent bouts of mental disturbance, for which the recognized 'treatment' was evidently music. Interestingly, music is still a recognized form of therapy, often prescribed to restore troubled states of mind. Saul's servants knew a suitable musician, whose qualities would grace Saul's court, a son of Jesse of Bethlehem. The hand of God in this development of the story needs no emphasis. David's *lyre* (Heb. *kinnôr*) was evidently portable, whereas illustrations from antiquity suggest that the harp was a larger instrument, less easily carried around.[2] It is the earliest stringed instrument mentioned in the Bible (Gn. 4:21), and the only one referred to in the Pentateuch.

19–23. The royal message constituted a command, and required immediate obedience (in contrast to Saul's reluctant compliance with God's orders to him). Moreover, no-one appeared before the king empty-handed, so Jesse gave not only his son, but also some of the produce of his farm.

Saul loved him greatly: David must have been a lovable character, and the affection Saul had for him would have

---

[1] The text does not suggest that Saul had already been constitutionally prone to some severe depressive illness, which might have mitigated his responsibility for his behaviour.

[2] *Cf.* the Sumerian lyre, illustrated in *IBD* 2, p. 1033, with the harps (pp. 1036–1037). Nevertheless, the identification of the various instruments is rarely certain.

helped towards Saul's healing, while the therapeutic charm of David's music calmed and refreshed him in times of disturbance. Unwittingly, Saul was becoming dependent on the one designated to succeed him.

iii. Saul needs a warrior to fight Goliath (17:1 – 18:5).
This gripping story of David's youthful faith and courage is one of the world's classic narratives, and one of the best-known of the Bible. It provides an outstanding example of the Lord's power to give victory against dramatically overwhelming odds in response to faith and courage. It does present difficulties in relation to the previous chapter, from which it appears to be entirely independent. It need not surprise us that David's anointing is not mentioned, because that was in any case private, and its purpose undisclosed, but, if the events of 1 Samuel 16 preceded those of this chapter, the obvious question is: why did Saul not recognize David as the one who had served him at court as both musician and armour-bearer? It is, of course, possible to conjecture that in the meantime David had returned to his father's house, and had matured into a bearded adult who looked very different from the youth of 1 Samuel 16; probably the compiler was drawing on different sources, but the fact remains that there is no attempt in the text to reconcile the two accounts.[1] If 1 Samuel 16 originated in Bethlehem, 1 Samuel 17 would appear to belong with military records, emphasizing as it does the defeat of the Philistines, and the disposal of Goliath's sword.

1–3. The ongoing war with the Philistines was about to enter a new phase, to be fought, not this time in the central hills from which the enemy had been chased westwards, but nearer their territory on the borders of Judah. The emphatic *Socoh, which belongs to Judah,* shows the Philistines encroaching nevertheless. The names Socoh and *Azekeh* are preserved in the names of present-day villages in the foothills due west from Bethlehem, and *the valley of Elah,* in which both were

---

[1] The Vaticanus MS of the LXX omits large portions of the chapter (1 Sa. 17:12–31; 17:55 – 18:5), including some of the passages which highlight the discrepancies. However, the Hebrew text is consistent and shows every indication of being an entity; it is less likely to have been expanded than the Greek version is to have been abbreviated, perhaps in the interests of harmonization.

situated, drains the water from the hills into the Mediterranean during the rainy season.

4–7. *A champion* (Heb. *'îš-habbēnayîm*) *named Goliath*: the word translated 'champion' occurs only here in the Old Testament, but is used frequently in the Qumran 'War Scroll', where it means simply 'soldier', 'infantryman'. The fact that he is selected to represent the Philistines in single combat implies a claim to the title 'champion' here. Goliath is a name which has affinities with Asia Minor. *Gath*, the Philistine city, was a little further west in the valley of Elah. This local champion was chosen for his powerful stature, his height (*six cubits and a span*) being 'over nine feet' (NEB; NIV),[1] but since Saul was head and shoulders taller than any of the people (1 Sa. 10:23), he could have been expected to respond to Goliath's challenge.

Single combat as a means of settling the outcome of war between two armies is not well attested in the ancient Near East. According to Roland de Vaux, Mesopotamian historical texts provide no examples, though the motif is used in conflicts between the gods.[2] Under David, however, individual soldiers were rewarded for personal acts of bravery with the title *gibbôr* (2 Sa. 23:8–39). Whenever detail is provided, it is always the Philistine who issues the challenge to fight. 'The natural question therefore is to ask apropos of 1 Sa. 17, whether single combat was not a Western custom imported by the Philistines.'[3] This would seem likely.

Great interest is shown in Goliath's armour: the *helmet of bronze* might have been expected to cover the temples, in the way that the gold helmet, found at Ur, would have done.[4] For some reason this was not the case. The *coat of mail*, weighing *five thousand shekels of bronze*, that is, about 126 pounds (or 57 kg.), was a scale armour, known from fifteenth century Nuzi.

[1] Two MSS of the LXX have the variant 'four cubits and a span', a reading supported by 4QSamᵃ, hence the 'six and a half feet tall' of the NAB. *Cf. IDBS* art. 'Goliath', p. 370.

[2] R. de Vaux, *The Bible and the Ancient Near East* (London: Darton, Longman and Todd, 1972), p. 13.

[3] *Ibid.*, p. 127.

[4] On the armour mentioned here, see *IBD* 1, art. 'armour'. The word for 'helmet', *kôbaʿ* (v. 5) and spelt *qôbaʿ* (v. 38), first used in this chapter, may be cognate with a Hittite word *kupahi*, 'head dress', introduced into Canaan by the Philistines. *Cf.* T. C. Mitchell, *AOTS*, p. 415; J. P. Brown, 'Peace Symbolism in Ancient Military Vocabulary', *VT* 21 (1971), p. 3.

Hundreds of metal scales were attached with thread to cloth or leather. *Greaves* to protect his legs completed his armour, the expense of which makes it likely that only he among the soldiers would be so equipped. As for his weapons, the *javelin* (Heb. *kîdôn*), which should probably be translated 'sword', had a flat, curved blade like a sickle, but with the outer edge the cutting edge; the *spear* (Heb. *ḥanit*) was more like a javelin, with an iron point and a shaft *like a weaver's beam*, that is, equipped for use like a sling.[1] His shield (Heb. *ṣinnâ*), carried by an armour-bearer, was a large rectangular one, affording maximum protection.

8–11. Confident in the superiority of his equipment, as well as in his great natural strength, the giant defies Israel to find his match in single combat. So certain is he of winning the fight that he commits his fellow countrymen to slavery if he fails, though when the unexpected happened, and Israel triumphed, the Philistines did not serve Israel.

12–18. Mention of David's name requires an explanation of his circumstances at the time. His *Ephrathite* father (*cf.* 1 Ch. 4:4; Ephrathah was mother of Hur, who was 'father', maybe the civic leader, of Bethlehem), was already too old for military service, but his three eldest sons were in Saul's army at the front line, and needing supplies of food. David, the youngest, had the responsibility of fulfilling this errand in addition to looking after his sheep.

While Saul was fully occupied with military manoeuvres he would not need his minstrel, so David was back home for a while. The need to keep the army fed took David to the front and introduced him to the Philistine challenger.

19–23. The details – David's early start, his arrival just as the fighting men moved to confront their opposing army, and his disposal of his load at the camp – all lend vividness to the developing climax.

24–27. The close-up view of Goliath caused panic among Israel's troops, to the astonishment of David, who, as he was approaching, caught only half the story. David is indignant that anyone, no matter how powerful, should presume to insult the people of Israel, and therefore, by implication, Israel's

---

[1] Such a javelin in use is portrayed on a ceramic plate from Greece (B.M. e380) dated fifth century BC. It shows a cord wound round the shaft to give extra distance and spin, see Y. Yadin, *The Art of Warfare in Biblical Lands* (London: Weidenfeld and Nicolson, 1963), p. 355.

God. The *uncircumcised Philistine*, who worships man-made gods, knows nothing of the living God, in whom David declares his trust. In answer to his question, David learns of the threefold prize which will go to the one who will kill Goliath, including, along with riches and a royal bride, *free* status for his family in Israel. This last privilege, exempting the victor's family from service to the king at court, was tantamount to bestowing equality with the king.[1]

28–30. Eliab's resentment against the 'boy from back home' who shows up his elders is understandable. Eliab is angry with his youngest brother because he presumes to enter their military world, and implies that he may supersede them.

31–40. The fact that there may be a volunteer to face the challenger is reported to Saul, and David reassures the king that he is capable of killing Goliath, despite his comparative youth and inexperience of warfare. The Philistine has sealed his own fate by pitting himself against *the armies of the living God*, who has already given David deliverance from a lion and a bear;[2] and because he is living he is always at hand to save. Therefore David can assert, *The Lord . . . will deliver me from the hand of this Philistine*.

We now learn that King Saul had armour, for he urged David to use it, but David preferred to fight in the way he knew, free from encumbrance and using only his sling and selected stones from the brook Elah.

41–47. There could hardly have been a greater contrast than that between the heavily armed Goliath, with all his protective gear, and David, who looked entirely vulnerable and so easy to defeat that Goliath took the selection of the youth as an insult. David is not intimidated by the Philistine

[1] A. F. Rainey, in L. R. Fisher (ed.), *Ras Shamra Parallels* 2 (1975), p. 104. 'Free' (Heb. *ḥopšî*) in 1 Sa. usually means 'freedom from slavery', but Ugarit provides a parallel for its use here: 'and the king has exempted him [a man who has accomplished a brave deed] from service to the palace' (*RS* 16.269:14–16).

[2] G. S. Cansdale, *Animals of Bible Lands* (Exeter: Paternoster Press, 1970), pp. 105–111, 116–119, confirms that both lions and bears were widespread in Palestine and adjacent countries throughout Old Testament times, and bears survived in the Hermon range into this century. Both animals, but especially in practice the bear, could knock out a victim with a paw, hence mention of the 'paw' in v. 37: 'in general a lion is more predictable and therefore safer; a bear hides its intentions. This is also suggested in 1 Sam. 17:37, "the lion . . . the bear . . . this Philistine", where the three are listed in order of increasing danger' (pp. 118–119).

who *cursed David by his gods*, and threatened to make him food for the wildlife of the area. David claims to be on the side of the *Lord of hosts* ('Lord Almighty', NIV), and proof that his claim is honoured will be victory over both Goliath and the Philistine army. When David is victorious the result will be that *all the earth may know that there is a God in Israel . . . and that the Lord saves not with sword and spear.* This was no ordinary battle, but one in which God's honour was at stake, and in this circumstance David's exposure to danger permitted God's honour to be more clearly acknowledged than if David had more obviously been a match for the Philistine. At no point did David take any credit for the successful outcome, which he confidently expected. By using his sling, David could operate beyond the range of Goliath's weapons.

48–49. The Philistine had scarcely had time to move towards David when he was felled by David's one stone, slung with deadly accuracy so that it penetrated the one vulnerable spot in Goliath's elaborate armour. The combat was over in a moment.

50–54. Though the battle had been won without a sword blow being struck, David did not scorn to take possession of Goliath's sword in order to finish his work. The stone had stunned the giant, and now the sword must kill him. The Philistines retreated with all speed, and the Israelite army pursued them, driving them back to their own towns, and afterwards plundering their camp, so enjoying the spoils.

It is surprising to read that David *took the head of the Philistine and brought it to Jerusalem*, in view of the fact that this city was still in Jebusite hands, until David captured it (2 Sa. 5:6–10), but little is on record to give information about the status of the city just before that event. The city had been taken by Judah and destroyed (Jdg. 1:8), but it soon recovered (Jdg. 1:21; *cf.* Jos. 15:63), though no king is subsequently mentioned in the city. Friendly relations between Israel and Jerusalem obtained during the judges period (Jdg. 19:10–12), or at least a state of neutrality; the city was surrounded by Israelite settlements on all sides except the west, which was semi-desert, and, in company with the remainder of the Canaanite population, was indebted to Israel for protection against the invaders. Was David already becoming the strategist, giving this important city reason to recognize Israel's dominance?

He put his armour in his tent, keeping it as a trophy of battle, though when it is next mentioned it is in the tabernacle, under priestly care at Nob (1 Sa. 21:9).[1]

55—58. Having promised his daughter to the champion of Israel, Saul is personally concerned to know the family of a likely son-in-law. The reader, privileged to have a specially selected amount of information, wonders why neither Saul nor *Abner* remembers who the champion is. After the event, the family would not easily be forgotten.

18:1—5. David was immediately given status by his relationship with the royal family. Jonathan, the crown prince, recognized in David a kindred spirit, and struck up a deep friendship with him, while Saul decided that he needed David's presence beside him, and so gave him a home in the palace.

Jonathan made a covenant with David, apparently on the spur of the moment, in the glow of David's victory; but it was a lasting commitment that both men were to honour, and which they never regretted. Jonathan's action in stripping off his royal insignia, and his royal armour and weapons, only to give them all to David, was more than spontaneous generosity, to meet the need of his new-found friend. It was a recognition of David's worth, for which Jonathan was willing to give his all, even his right to the throne, for 'he loved him as himself' (v. 3, NIV). In our political world, where power plays such an important role, what would be thought of a prince who voluntarily renounced his throne in favour of a friend whose character and godly faith he admired? It is an unusual theme, unique, maybe. What did Jonathan's contemporaries think, and in particular his father?

Evidently David won hearts everywhere he went, and when Saul made him his general, sending him instead of Jonathan to fight his battles, the appointment met with universal approval. That was one side of the picture.

iv. Saul's jealousy and fear of David (18:6–30). 6–9.
Joyous dancing and singing, accompanied by instrumental

---

[1] 'The passing of arms from the lesser to the greater so carefully described by the narrator, seems to have had political implications in the Ancient Near East', J. A. Thompson, 'The Significance of the verb *love* in the David-Jonathan Narratives in 1 Samuel', *VT* 24 (1974), p. 335. A footnote refers to [2]*ANET*, pp. 276, 281. *Cf.* 2 Ki. 11:10; 2 Sa. 8:7, 11–12. David received in turn the armour of Saul, Goliath and Jonathan.

music, welcomed the victorious army home, as the women expressed their appreciation of the heroes of the battle. Not surprisingly, David was hailed as the paragon, while Saul was put in second place, a judgment which he had not the maturity and security to accept and endorse, but which rankled and festered into incurable jealousy. The jingle was not meant to be derogatory to Saul in the process of celebrating the outstanding bravery of David, but, in the light of Samuel's rejection of Saul, the words seemed to point to David as his replacement. The suspicion that he had made the right deduction poisoned his relationship with David from that point onwards.

10–11. The second stage in Saul's angry reaction well illustrates the close connection between jealousy and murder (*cf.* Mt. 5:21–22). Given the chance, it will express itself in an attempt to kill. That Saul *raved within his house* could have been translated, 'Saul prophesied within his house', for the verb (Heb. *nābā'*) regularly means 'to prophesy', and links this episode with his experience of ecstasy among the prophets (*cf.* 1 Sa. 10:10). Outwardly the two experiences were similar, though in this case the spirit that seized him was *evil*, and required the ministration of David to calm him. Before the music had had its effect, Saul had twice made an attempt on David's life.

12–16. Saul knew deep down why everything was going wrong for him and right for David: it had to do with enjoying the Lord's covenant favour, and he, Saul, had alienated himself from the Lord, hence his fear of David. He therefore gave David an army commission, which kept him out of his sight, but also at the same time kept him in the public eye. David's success and popularity went hand in hand, *for the Lord was with him*. The writer lays great stress (*cf.* v. 12) on this fact; looks and natural abilities alone did not account for David's prestige; *all Israel and Judah loved David* (even Saul's own son). Whatever move Saul made to minimize David's influence failed, and had the opposite effect.

17–19. There remained the matter of David's marriage to the royal princess, *Merab*, which appears to have been delayed. *Be valiant for me and fight the Lord's battles*, says Saul, implying that David still needs to win his spurs, and hoping, according to the compiler, that he will be killed in battle. David's courteous refusal to claim any right to the king's daughter is taken at its face value, and Saul gives her to *Adriel the Meholathite*, from Abel-meholah, east of Jordan. Their sons were to meet a tragic end (2 Sa. 21:8–9).

20–30. Saul had deliberately avoided making David his son-in-law, but when he learnt that his daughter *Michal* was in love with him, Saul devised a means of taking advantage of the fact. His courtiers approached David, pointing out the additional support this marriage would give to his already considerable status. This time David's reply specifically stated *I am a poor man*, suggesting that he would never be able to raise the bride price for such a wife. It was the reply Saul wanted, for the price he named would involve a high degree of risk to David's life: however, to David and his men it was all in a day's work to kill not merely one hundred, but two hundred Philistines. Thus he qualified to marry into the royal family, and this time was given his bride, Michal.

The rise of David from shepherd lad to royal family, though less meteoric than that of Saul, was characterized by divine approval (*the Lord was with David* is the comment once more, v. 28). It was also characterized by popular approval, *all Israel loved him*; already following his lead in war, all the tribes gladly gave him loyal allegiance. Such solidarity behind David increased Saul's feeling of isolation, and intensified his fear and insecurity. David had more to fear from Saul than from the Philistines, against whom he was outstandingly successful; far from losing his life, he kept gaining honours.

v. Jonathan and Michal save David's life (19:1–17).
1–7. Saul's next move was to enlist the help of Jonathan, so endeavouring to drive a wedge between him and David. Despite the pressure of family loyalty, Jonathan remained true to his covenant friendship with David, undertaking at this stage to act as a go-between in order to reconcile his father to David. But first Jonathan warns David to go into hiding because Saul intends to kill him: *take heed to yourself* means 'be on your guard' (v. 2, NIV). In the morning Jonathan would bring his father within reach of David's hiding-place, and let David know the outcome of his conversation with Saul.

The conspiracy was well planned, and Jonathan had thought out carefully what he would say about David in order to touch the right cord and evoke his father's good will, as they took their walk that morning. Passing over the recent frustrations Saul had experienced with regard to David, Jonathan went back to the *good service* David had given to Saul when he slew the Philistine, and *the Lord wrought a great victory*. These last words echoed Saul's own declaration when he triumphed at Jabesh-gilead, and was confirmed in the kingship (1 Sa. 11:12–15). At that time he had generously refused to punish his detractors, and the memory of all the associated emotions brought him to the same mind again: *As the Lord lives, he shall not be put to death*. In those days he had been right with the Lord, and in certain moods Saul wanted that relationship renewed. Consequently David was able to return to the court.

8–10. It was a temporary reconciliation, however, for when further military triumphs again put David in the limelight, Saul's jealousy returned (*cf.* 1 Sa. 18:8–11). He would have transfixed David with his spear but for the quick evasive action taken by David. This time he *fled*, never to return. Flight and escape were to be the facts of David's life while Saul lived, and the word 'fled' becomes a recurring motif in the subsequent narrative.

11–17. Though Michal was Saul's daughter, she was also David's wife, and her first allegiance was to David. With the house under surveillance, she nevertheless enabled him to make his escape through a window, and delayed discovery of his departure by putting *an image* (Heb. *ṭerāp̄îm*; translated 'household gods' in Gn. 31:19) in his bed, and saying he was sick. Saul resented her disloyalty in deceiving him, and might have transferred to her his murderous intentions but for her further lie that David had threatened her with death. The involvement of Saul's children in the conflict between him and David intensifies the love-hate relationship, 'and the story, inasmuch as it may be considered a mirror of the human condition, gains immeasurably in intensity and sophistication'.[1] As a study of the conflicting emotions that have the power to turn a person into a murderer, this section could hardly be surpassed. The victim incites his rival to jealousy simply by being the person he is, and in the end complete separation of the two people involved is the only remedy.

[1] Gunn 1980, pp. 79–80.

c. David the outlaw (19:18 – 26:25)

i. David takes refuge with Samuel (19:18–24).

David's first thought in his time of emergency was the prophet who had from the beginning been his trusted guide, and whose home was less than an hour's walk from Gibeah. The incident discloses the fact that, far from being a lone figure, Samuel presided over a centre where prophets engaged in worship. Whether this gathering was in the nature of a short convention, or whether it was on a more permanent basis, we have no means of knowing.

18. It would appear that David went first to Samuel's home, and from there to *Naioth*, which means 'dwellings' or 'tents', where David would be able to take advantage of the opportunity for spiritual help and fellowship, as well as of the safety of numbers. It was in *Ramah* that Saul had had his providential encounter with Samuel, and had been secretly anointed; now Samuel was protecting David, in that very place.

19–22. Even Saul's attempt to arrest David was thwarted, because his envoys were caught up in the fervour of the worship, and *prophesied*. There was an infectious enthusiasm which so gripped them that they forgot their errand, and Saul in desperation finally had to go in person. But he was on an unworthy errand, and the spirit of prophecy, which had originally confirmed his calling (1 Sa. 10:9–13), would now block his way. At first Saul could not find the right place, despite his knowledge of the region; mention of *the great well* and of other details suggests an account contemporaneous with the events.

23–24. *The Spirit of God came upon him also*, rendering him helpless, lest he should commit some dreadful crime against the one of God's choice. So intense was Saul's experience of ecstasy that for twenty-four hours he was unconscious, lying stripped and naked, yet *he prophesied*. There could be no clearer proof of the ambiguity of the gift of prophecy. It could result in mere 'raving' (*cf.* 1 Sa. 18:10, and see the commentary on 18:10–11), and uselessness, hence the need to be discerning (1 Jn. 4:1). The question, *Is Saul also among the prophets?* emphasizes the link between this incident and Saul's first experience of prophesying (1 Sa. 10:12), while at the same time calling attention to the mystery connected with the phenomenon. Far from being a doublet of 1 Samuel 10:12, as has been suggested, the incident becomes an ironic comment on Saul's life story.

ii. David and Jonathan make a pact (20:1–42). The fact that Saul was out of action gave David the opportunity to seek out Jonathan, who had already acted successfully as mediator between Saul and David, and who might be able to do so again.[1]

1–4. David, breathless, plunges directly into his urgent questions, so protesting his innocence. Jonathan, apparently unaware of the reason for David's agitation, refuses to believe that his father wants to kill David. David needs the matter settled once and for all. He will leave Saul's service only if that is unavoidable, and if Saul's family and court recognize it to be so. Above all, Jonathan must be convinced that David's assessment of his father's intentions is justified.

5–11. David has devised a test for the next day, when it would be *the new moon*, a rest-day each month for which special sacrifices were prescribed (Nu. 28:11–15), and Saul had a three-day festival (v. 12) when his close associates were expected to be present. His reaction to David's absence, purportedly at a family celebration, would be indicative of his intentions. David pleads by their sacred covenant that Jonathan will *deal kindly with [his] servant*. Jonathan as crown prince had initiated the covenant between them (1 Sa. 18:1–5), and David was dependent on Jonathan's good will (Heb. *ḥesed*, 'covenant love', v. 8), as well as being a 'minister' of Saul, hence 'servant'. Jonathan is under no obligation, however, if David is guilty of some disloyalty to King Saul. David's own innocence of such a charge must be established.

Jonathan, clinging to his father's declaration on oath that David should not die (1 Sa. 19:6), still naïvely supposes that David is in no danger.

12–17. Out in 'the field', the open hillsides outside the city, Jonathan swears to keep David informed of his father's mood,

---

[1] Some think that originally this incident did not follow immediately upon the Ramah episode. Hertzberg, for example, would put it after 1 Sa. 19:8–10, for, 'Here there would be room for an investigation of the king's intentions' (p. 172). This would also account for Jonathan's ignorance of what had happened. McCarter also puts this event after David's escape through the window (McCarter 1980, p. 343). But, as Gunn points out (Gunn 1980, p. 151 n. 15), it is in keeping with the last scene involving them both (1 Sa. 19:6–7).

and for his part takes the opportunity to make an appeal to David, whom he recognizes as the future king. *If I am still alive, show me the loyal love* (Heb. *ḥeseḏ*) *of the Lord*: when David is in power, it would be expected that all the family and supporters of the previous régime would be put to death. The king's son is fully aware that he has renounced his throne in favour of David, and that he stood to be in an ambiguous position if he survived the installation of the new king. David was to remember his oath to Jonathan at a later date by honouring his son (2 Sa. 9:7), and by sparing him from death (2 Sa. 21:7). It was the least David could do to fulfil his commitment to Jonathan, who *loved him as he loved his own soul*, and such was the binding nature of a covenant that David could do no less. Genuine love, person to person, sealed by a covenant, such as there was between David and Jonathan, provides a most telling model of an unbreakable relationship. It is the basis of a marriage relationship; above all it is the picture the Lord himself chooses to enshrine his own unchangeable commitment to love and redeem his people (Dt. 7:7–9).

That was not all, however, for Jonathan was swearing loyalty to David at a cost. He was surrendering his right to the throne so that David could be pre-eminent. The context in which this kind of commitment was expected and given was after subjugation by a great power, when the conquered had to 'love the new king as themselves'.[1] The voluntary commitment to sacrificial love is rare and deeply moving. In Jonathan's case it was accompanied by a naïveté regarding his own father. 'He fails to see that David represents any threat to his father and is accordingly reluctant to acknowledge that Saul actually intends David harm (20:1–7) – hence the facility with which he is prepared to aid his friend and, as the reader may see it, betray his father.'[2] When he invokes the Lord's *vengeance on David's enemies*, he is unaware of involving his father, who had said to Michal, 'Why have you . . . let my enemy go?' (1 Sa. 19:17; *cf.* 18:29).

18–23. *You will be missed*: 'Saul's rightful place in the royal lineage . . . should normally have taken precedence over

[1] W. L. Moran, 'The Ancient Near Eastern Background of the Love of God in Deuteronomy', *CBQ* 25 (1963), p. 80.

[2] Gunn 1980, p. 84. He points out that Jonathan's speech here is full of awful irony.

David's personal annual remembrance of his own ancestral line (verses 6, 29).'[1] David's absence was undoubtedly provocative.

You will be greatly missed: in this and in several other places the RSV follows the LXX, as the marginal references show, but here and in verse 16 and at the end of verse 19 NIV makes good sense of the Hebrew text.

The stone Ezel (RSV mg., NIV) means 'stone of departure'; the Targum explained this as a 'sign-stone', a 'cairn'. It was an unmistakable place where the sign of the arrows could safely be enacted. There is no connection here with belomancy, or divining by means of arrows (*cf.* Ezk. 21:21).

The Lord is between you and me for ever, reminiscent of the oath between Laban and Jacob (Gn. 31:48–53), means that the Lord himself, no less, will avenge any breach of the covenant to which he has been witness.

24–29. Saul's *seat by the wall* will have been the central place, opposite the entrance; the details suggest an eye-witness account.

He is not clean: ceremonial uncleanness disqualified anyone from taking part in a religious festival (Lv. 7:20–21); it is to Saul's credit that he began by making out a case for David's absence. Jonathan, by giving David leave to absent himself, has put to the test his father's relationship with himself.

30–34. Instantly Jonathan experiences, perhaps for the first time ever, the flashing anger of Saul. *You son of a perverse, rebellious woman* means in Hebrew idiom 'you perverse rebel'. It is Jonathan's deep attachment to David that arouses Saul's resentment, very understandably. Jonathan's naïve questions put to his father at this juncture could have been calculated to provoke Saul further because they betrayed what he would see as Jonathan's utter stupidity. In a frenzy of exasperation, Saul casts his spear at Jonathan, who has identified himself with David and so, in Saul's mind, has taken his place. In attempting to kill David, Saul now aims to kill his own son. After this it is Jonathan's turn to experience *fierce anger*, not because he has narrowly escaped death at the hand of his father, but because Saul has treated David so shamefully as to accuse him of treason (v. 31). The tension for Jonathan had

---

[1] D. J. Wiseman, *EOPN*, p. 152; he shows that family descent was widely associated with the legitimacy of the ruler in the ancient Near East.

become unbearable; he left the feast, and all its guests, who had witnessed the scene.

35–42. The parting of David and Jonathan is vividly depicted. A little boy goes out with Jonathan to run and fetch his arrows, not knowing that they fulfil a sign. His carefree return to the city of Gibeah contrasts with that of Jonathan (v. 42), with his insoluble relationship problems. For the moment, Jonathan judges that it is safe for him and David to have a few minutes together before they finally part company. Pent-up emotion finds relief, first in tears and then in remembrance of their mutual commitment before the Lord. The dependability of the Lord who guarantees their covenant provides firm ground for the future, insecure though each was at the time.

iii. Ahimelech the priest helps David (21:1–9).

In his emergency David had quickly to decide the people he could count on as allies. Food and shelter were his immediate needs, but he was also unarmed. He made first for *Nob*, which had taken the place of Shiloh as the city of the priests (1 Sa. 22:19), and was close at hand, about two miles (3 km.) in the direction of Jerusalem (*cf.* Is. 10:32).

1–3. *Ahimelech* was the brother of Ahijah, who had joined Saul as his spiritual adviser after Samuel withdrew his services (1 Sa. 14:3; *cf.* 22:9). For that reason David was unsure whether to trust Ahimelech, and decided to make up a plausible story to account for the fact that he was on his own. Even so, Ahimelech must have been suspicious, in view of the certainty that a royal ambassador would always have royal provisions, and a bodyguard. Nevertheless Ahimelech makes no demur, accepts the need for secrecy, and a planned rendezvous with associates, and the request for *loaves of bread*.

4–6. The *holy bread*, or *bread of the Presence*, which was set out on a table in the holy place of the tabernacle (Lv. 24:5–9), was all that Ahimelech had available. Twelve large loaves symbolized the twelve tribes with whom the Lord had entered into covenant.[1] When they had been replaced the discarded loaves were not for ordinary use, but had to be eaten by the priests, yet such was David's plight that Ahimelech made an

[1] Wenham, *Leviticus*, p. 310 n. 6, points out that each loaf contained 'about 3 liters or 3 ½ lbs. of flour'. These were not the little pancakes sometimes indicated by 'bread' in the Bible.

exception and gave him the five loaves he wanted, on the assurance of David that he and his men were ritually 'clean', by the criteria laid down in Leviticus 15. Jesus was to endorse the judgment of Ahimelech in putting mercy before ceremonial law (Mt. 12:3–7).

The strictness with which 'holy war' discipline was accepted on an expedition is illustrated by the behaviour of Uriah the Hittite (2 Sa. 11:8–13). It was based, not on any ascetic view of marriage, which is totally alien to the Bible, but on united and total commitment to the cause of the Lord, in whose name the battle was being fought.

7. The information slipped in at this verse is significant for later developments in the story (1 Sa. 22:9). Saul had fought Edom (1 Sa. 14:47), and had taken *Doeg the Edomite* into his service, perhaps after his victory. *The chief of Saul's herdsmen* remains the preferred reading, despite the suggested emendation to 'runners', in the light of the relatively frequent mention of men to run before the king's chariot (1 Sa. 8:11; 2 Sa. 15:1) or as messengers (1 Sa. 4:12; 10:23). The word translated 'chief' (Heb. *'abbîr*) means 'mighty', but is also used to mean 'violent' and 'obstinate'; the presence of this man was ominous, especially as he was *detained before the Lord* perhaps against his will, or at least as some kind of punishment. David later reveals that he had been uneasy at the presence of the Edomite at Nob (1 Sa. 22:22).

8–9. *The king's business required haste* was a clever way of explaining why David was unarmed, and at the same time suggested that he was on a royal mission. The *sword of Goliath* had already served David well (1 Sa. 17:51); David presumably knew that it was in safe keeping at Nob. First David had been assisted by the great prophet Samuel, and now he has successfully appealed for food and a sword from the established priests at the sanctuary. But having accomplished his errand he dare not linger.

iv. David in danger at Gath (21:10–15). Needing to get clear of Saul, David's next destination, some thirty miles (50 km.) to the south-west, was in Philistine territory. He was bold to attempt acceptance in enemy country (carrying Goliath's sword!), but such was his extremity that he hoped to be unrecognized, and to be taken on as one of the servants of *Achish*, the king. He had been over-optimistic: he was too well known to go incognito in the palace, and David had the presence of mind to feign insanity in order to extricate himself from danger.[1] He rightly conjectured that Achish would not want to retain an imbecile at court, and so escaped.

The courtiers of Achish called David *king of the land*; on the basis of his acclaim after the Goliath episode they surmised that this was his potential (if not yet his actual) status. Later on David was to come this way again in very different circumstances and find a welcome, so successfully did he impress Achish that he was an ally in opposing Israel (1 Sa. 27:2–12). On his first visit, however, a lone fugitive with no-one he could trust to stand by him, he was probably at his lowest ebb. But though he was in 'the valley of the shadow of death' he discovered that the Lord was with him, enabling him to devise plans and survive danger. The title of Psalm 34 identifies its contents with this episode, and its opening words are an invitation to 'bless the Lord at all times', even in deep trouble, such as David dreaded from the Gittites, the inhabitants of Gath (see 2 Sam. 15:18). He universalized his testimony: as the familiar hymn paraphrases the psalm, 'Deliverance he affords to all who on his succour trust' (*cf.* Ps. 34:17).[2] It is at one and the same time a declaration of God's grace and an encouragement to live by faith in his word.

v. David at Adullam and in Moab (22:1–5). Escaping from enemy territory, David made for the area he knew: *Adullam* (the name means 'refuge') in Judah, half way between Gath and Bethlehem. It was a Canaanite city in patriarchal times (Gn. 38:1), and was captured by Joshua in the course of his occupation of the land (Jos. 12:15). Close by was a hill which was both fortified and known for its caves, which provided a natural shelter for the homeless David, though his movements did not go unnoticed. *His brothers and all his father's house*, under threat from King Saul because of their relationship to David, took advantage of the opportunity to escape

---

[1] The Heb. root translated 'mad' (*šg'*) is rare (*cf.* Dt. 28:24, 28; 2 Ki. 9:20; Zc. 12:4). D. J. Wiseman, ' "Is it peace?" – Covenant and Diplomacy', *VT* 32 (1982), pp. 320–321, questions whether *šg'* 'may describe some unfavourable attitude of heart and mind other than "madness" . . . The Akkadian *šegû* is used of an attitude . . . which may best be described as "highly aggressive" – the opposite of peaceful'. This nuance would imply that David was a danger to society.

[2] N. Tate and N. Brady, 'Through all the changing scenes of life'.

from Bethlehem, which was too close for comfort to Gibeah. Others who resorted to him were men *in distress* (Heb. *māṣôq* suggests 'oppressed'), *in debt* and *discontented* or, more literally, 'embittered', and therefore passionate for change. It was from such raw material that David trained a loyal army, with its 'mighty men' who would do anything for him (*cf.* 2 Sa. 23:8–39). Thus his abilities as a leader were developed as he and his 'underground' force of *four hundred men* prepared for action. Not much later he was commanding six hundred men (1 Sa. 25:13). He appears to have accepted all comers.

David's parents needed a safe place in which to make their home, hence the journey to Moab, outside the territory of Saul, and suggested by family ties through Ruth, the Moabitess grandmother of Jesse (Ru. 4:17). *Mizpeh*, evidently a royal city of Moab, is not otherwise known. Having settled his father and mother in Moab, David took refuge in his *stronghold* (Heb. *mᵉṣûdâ*), which was apparently not in Judah, but cannot now be identified. The same is true of the *forest of Hereth. The prophet Gad* was already identifying himself with the cause of David, and would eventually be one of the chroniclers of David's reign (1 Ch. 29:29). He lived to see the Temple in use, and played his part in regulating its worship (2 Ch. 29:25).

vi. The price of helping David (22:6–23). 6. The scene changes to *Gibeah*, where Saul is holding court at the top of the hill, under *the tamarisk tree*, evidently a landmark, which provided shade.[1] Inaction enables him to brood over the disloyalty he suspects among his retainers.

7–10. Carefully avoiding use of the name David, Saul nevertheless shows that he is obsessed with thoughts of his rival, and longs for reassurance that he still commands the full support of his army and its leaders, whose silence worries him. The tribe of Benjamin had been honoured by Saul with gifts of land and positions of leadership. He implies that the son of Jesse of Judah will have no such attachment to Benjamin. It is impossible not to feel sympathy for Saul in his isolation, yet it is of his own making. Neither his son nor David, whom he still regards as *his servant*, would have deserted him had Saul himself not driven them away by his attempts

---

[1] A similar open-air court scene is depicted in 1 Ki. 22:10 (*cf.* 1 Sa. 14:2), and was a familiar feature of early Near Eastern literature.

to murder them. Now he imagines that David is lying *in wait* to kill Saul, so attributing to David the motivation he himself would have had in similar circumstances.

One of the company will 'talk'; Doeg echoes the king's tone with all the art of the traitor, omitting all reference to Ahimelech's trembling and cautious questioning (1 Sa. 21:1),[1] and Ahimilech is incriminated.

11–15. Ahimelech appears not to have been alarmed by the summons of the king to appear with all his fellow priests at the court in Gibeah. His conscience is clear and he speaks up for David, whom he has always respected, laying stress on David's reliability, his honoured position in the royal family and at court, and David's habit of consulting him in order to know the Lord's guidance.

16–19. To Saul, Ahimelech's straightforward statement of his point of view was tantamount to a confession of treason. He had aided and abetted David, the enemy of Saul; and he had failed to inform the king of David's movements; therefore he deserved to die, together with his fellow priests. *The servants of the king* faced *the priests of the Lord*; no mere man, though he be king, should touch the anointed of the Lord, hence the united refusal of Saul's servants to obey his command to kill them. Only the Edomite would carry out such an order, and the king who had begun so well by acknowledging the Lord's deliverance (1 Sa. 11:13) now put the Lord's servants to death, including, presumably, Ahijah (1 Sa. 14:3). The priestly family was almost wiped out, including women and children and even their animals. The contrast with Saul's reluctance to carry out the ban on the Amalekites is pointed (1 Sa. 15:9). It is as if Samuel's rebuke to him on that occasion still rankled and gave rise to retaliatory action.[2] Saul has power, but he uses it to destroy the priests of the Lord.

20–23. In the providence of God, Abiathar, one of the sons of Ahimelech, escaped the massacre, rescued the ephod (1 Sa. 23:6), and fled to join David, who thus had access to the

[1] Doeg the Edomite is now said to have 'stood by (Heb. *niṣṣāḇ ʿal*) the servants of Saul'. This is the same verb as was used of Samuel in 1 Sa. 19:20, translated 'standing as head over them'. It would seem that Doeg had already been favoured by the king and preferred before Benjamites.

[2] D. M. Gunn draws attention to signs of Samuel's judgment against him in Saul's behaviour here: 'The episode thus (rather like chapter 14) parodies the scenes of Saul's rejection, especially chapter 15 . . . the question is increasingly one of who has the real "power" ' (Gunn 1980, pp. 87–88).

priestly oracle, while Saul deprived himself of all such help.
The only surviving priest and the king-designate are together
driven into hiding, each a support for the other, and their
friendship continued right through David's reign (but *cf.* 1
Ki. 2:26–27). David became the protector of the priesthood.

vii. Saul hunts David (23:1–29). While Saul was occupied
in seeking David's life, the Philistines were able to continue
their aggression unmolested. David was conscious of their
incursions, the latest of which was directed at *Keilah*, which
belonged to Judah but was well behind the enemy lines at the
time of this attack. The site is Tell Qila, south of the ancient
Adullam.

1–5. This was an occasion when David depended on the
direction of Abiathar through the ephod in order to know the
mind of the Lord. The danger involved put fear into the hearts
of even David's troops: they could easily be surrounded and
their retreat blocked, hence David's double check on the guidance he received. Reassured, his men successfully fought the
Philistines and *brought away their cattle*; what the Philistine
troops were doing with cattle is not clear. It may have been
booty from earlier skirmishes, or 'transport' for their baggage.
The city of Keilah was liberated by David, who might have
expected loyal support in return.

6–13. King Saul, however, was still in power, and he knew
of David's whereabouts, just as David knew that Saul was
planning to capture him there. The general call-up pointed to
a huge army ready to besiege the city. Having already
occasioned the death of the priests, David was anxious not to
incur further bloodshed. His prayer reveals his thoughts, *Saul
seeks . . . to destroy the city on my account*. The ephod gives affirmative answers to both David's questions: Saul is coming, and
the people of Keilah will surrender David. It would be the
obvious way to avoid the destruction of their city.

David had the signal he needed. While the way was open,
he and his six hundred men made their exit from the city
and Saul called off his *expedition*. The incident illustrates the
contingent nature of the information given by the oracle: of
necessity it is limited by the questions asked, but permits
actions which can change the outcome of events for the one
who requests help. Saul, on the other hand, deprived of super-
natural guidance through the priesthood, has his plans

thwarted. Any hopes David may have had of making Keilah his headquarters were abandoned.

14. Under constant pressure from Saul, David and his men were forced to hide in the inhospitable and little-frequented areas of the mountains of Judah, to the south and south-east of Hebron. *Ziph* was on the crest of hills some five miles south-east from Hebron. The fugitives were apparently at the mercy of Saul, *but God did not give [them] into his hand*. The protection of God was over David.

15–18. *David was afraid*. His fear drove him to exercise greater faith in God, who alone could protect him, but faith did not prevent the return of fear, and the courageous visit of Jonathan *strengthened his hand in God*. It was not only the warmth of human friendship that strengthened David, but much more Jonathan's certainty as to God's purpose for the future. Jonathan had come to see that his father's hope of ridding himself of David and of reinstating his own dynasty was a forlorn one. The hand of Saul would not succeed, because God had another plan which his hand was bringing to pass; *Saul . . . also knows this*. But Saul continued his stubborn resistance. Jonathan in this last brief meeting with David confirmed his resolve to renounce in David's favour his right to the throne, while cherishing the hope that he would be his second-in-command. This idealism apart, Jonathan is aware now of the situation: the extent of his father's jealousy, and the lengths to which he is prepared to go. But, far from being downcast, he remains optimistic about the outcome because he is so sure that the Lord is bringing about a new era, with David at the helm.

Ziph, like Keilah, belonged to Judah, but its inhabitants remained loyal to Saul, despite the fact that David was of their tribe. No doubt they hoped to profit in some way from their betrayal of David's position. David's assessment of them is that they are insolent and ruthless, men who 'do not set God before them' (Ps. 54:3; *cf.* the heading of the psalm). He for his part could say 'God is my helper', and in that confidence he made his request for God's vindication.

19–24. The geographical details, meaningful to the inhabitants of those bleak hills but not to Saul, put the Ziphites in a strong position as the king's route finders. Though the places cannot now be identified, David was gradually retreating further into the precipitous, deserted hills to the south and east of Hebron. Saul has no wish to be on a wild goose chase in country like that, hence his insistence that David's whereabouts be thoroughly checked so that any double-dealing is discovered.

25–29. Saul eventually tracked David down on a particular hill, identified by rocks that made it a landmark, and was closing in to capture David. At the eleventh hour David finds that his trust in God has not been misplaced. A Philistine raid demands Saul's attention; his personal feud must give way before the threat to national security, so David is given a respite.

That place was called the Rock of Escape: the verb from which the name derives (Heb. *ḥālaq*) usually means 'divide', hence 'rock of parting' (NIV mg.). The rocks became a lasting memorial to the God who delivered David, and so vindicated him. Making for the region of the Dead Sea, David settled for a while in the hot, isolated precipices of the hills above the oasis of *Engedi*, where water at least was available.

viii. David spares Saul (24:1 – 25:1a). David had been well aware that he had only a temporary respite from Saul's pursuit, which began again once the Philistine threat had been dealt with.

1–7. Saul with his three crack battalions should have been more than a match for the fugitive, and the king was closer than he realized to capturing him; but this time David had the upper hand, and the roles of the two men are reversed. That Saul should have chosen the very cave where David and his men had taken up occupation was a striking coincidence that had its funny side. But it was also an unexpected opportunity for David to snatch the initiative. So far as his men were concerned, this was his chance to kill the king, and David moved silently towards his victim as if to do so, but instead he *cut off the skirt* (Heb. *kānāp̄*) *of Saul's robe*, a very tricky manoeuvre to accomplish without detection, and one which would take his men by surprise.[1] David's explanation cleverly

---

[1] The word *kānāp̄* means literally 'wing', 'extremity'; David probably cut off just a corner of the hem of Saul's robe. In the second millennium this was taken as a symbol of disloyalty and rebellion, whereas 'to seize the hem of a garment' was a symbol of faith, loyalty and covenant-making (*cf.* Mt. 9:20–21), D. J. Wiseman, 'Abban and Alalah', *JCS*, 12 (1958), pp. 128–129.

drew the sting of his men's aggression; his repentance for having taken advantage of the king's exposure made impossible any attempt on his life.

8–15. At long last David had an opportunity to remonstrate with Saul, who had gone on his way unsuspecting. Holding in his hand a piece of Saul's robe, David brought home to Saul how close he had been to losing his life. If David had really wanted to kill Saul, he would certainly have done so in the cave. Instead, here was David bowing before Saul, having spared his life, and calling him *my father* (v. 11), a good example of the flexible meaning of the word, which is used to imply a covenant relationship (*cf.* 1 Sa. 26:25).[1] David was also tactful in suggesting that others put into Saul's mind the idea that David sought his hurt, whereas he knew very well that murderous thoughts arose from Saul's own jealousy. Having now proved his innocence beyond doubt, David points out to Saul that, in seeking to kill him, Saul is the one who is in the wrong. *May the Lord judge between me and you*, says David, because for his part he will do nothing to avenge himself. The saying, *Out of the wicked comes forth wickedness*, reminiscent in its form of Samson's riddle (Jdg. 14:14), is part of David's motivation. He will not do wrong for whatever reason; he has no need to do so because he has a vindicator in the Lord.

A dead dog! . . . a flea!: The point is that there is nothing Saul can gain by all his searching and contriving. Indeed, if these phrases are punctuated with question marks, as is equally possible, 'there is a hint of threat; as if to say "You have taken on more than you imagine!" '[2] David's argument is that ultimately Saul has taken on the Lord, who will show David to be in the right.

16–22. Saul, deeply moved, is temporarily back on his original footing with David, whom he calls *my son* (*cf.* v. 11). He acknowledges that what David has said is true, and that David has repaid evil with good. He even goes so far as to admit openly that David will become king and establish his dynasty. Such a statement was almost in the nature of a confession, for it was the rejection of his own kingship that had caused Saul's bitter resentment and irrational brooding

[1] J. M. Munn-Rankin, 'Diplomacy in Western Asia in the Early Second Millennium BC', *Iraq* 18 (1956), pp. 68–110.
[2] Gunn 1980, pp. 154 n. 6.

over murdering David. But while he is in touch with David, Saul takes the opportunity to exact from David an oath that he *will not cut off* Saul's *descendants* (Heb. 'seed'), though, as Saul sees it, David has already 'cut off' Jonathan from him. Saul no longer has any illusions as to the future of his house, but he will do all he can to protect the family from the slaughter that was expected on a change of dynasty. Neither Saul nor David expects the reconciliation to restore the lost relationship; each goes his own way.

The verb 'cut off' forms something of a recurring theme, a *leit-motiv*, in 1 Samuel 20 – 24. Jonathan had reiterated it when he and David exchanged oaths of loyalty (1 Sa. 20:14–17). 'When the Lord cuts off every one of the enemies of David', Jonathan asks not to be among their number. In the present chapter David cuts off the corner of Saul's robe, and symbolically makes a bid for his status as king, for the royal robe stood for the royal office, and already the robe-tearing had been interpreted by Samuel as a symbol of the cutting off of Saul's dynasty (1 Sa. 15:28). Now David had 'grasped at' the kingship of Israel by cutting away part of Saul's robe, and by calling the king his 'father' he was preparing the way for a legitimate claim to the throne after Saul's death.

25:1a. There is an appropriateness about the death of Samuel just at the point when Saul had been willing to accept the implications of Samuel's judgment on him, and to let it be known publicly that David is to be his successor. For Israel Samuel's death marked the end of an era, but his burial under the floor of his house at Ramah would discourage any tendency to venerate his tomb.

ix. David wins Abigail (25:1b–44). This episode takes place in the vicinity of Maon, mentioned in 1 Samuel 23:24–26 as 'the wilderness'. David and his men are in need of a square meal, but their hopes are slim unless a farmer of substance can be cajoled into sharing with them some of his produce. On the surface this account tells how David obtained not only food but also a wife! It would be all too easy to dismiss it at that level, for the intention of the narrator is not spelt out. Some recent commentators have pointed out themes which connect this story with other wilderness events. There is, for example, the motif of reward for good or evil, which features in 1 Samuel 20 and 24; the words 'good' and 'evil' each occur seven times in 1 Samuel 25.[1] But there are subtle overtones in the way these adjectives are applied, and it will be profitable to explore these in the course of studying the chapter. Another connection between this episode and those on either side of it is summed up in the term 'narrative analogy':

> a device whereby the narrator can provide an internal commentary on the action which he is describing, usually by means of cross-reference to an earlier action or speech. Thus narratives are made to interact in ways which may not be immediately apparent; ironic parallelism abounds wherever this technique is applied.[2]

Though Nabal is the subject of the opening verses, there may be ways in which Nabal resembles Saul, whom we are perhaps meant to see reflected in Nabal.

1b–2. Though the area of Maon is described as 'wilderness' or semi-desert, it was, and still is, sheep-rearing country. *The wilderness of Paran* was in the Sinai peninsula, and cannot have been intended here; some LXX manuscripts have 'Maon', and this more likely reading is adopted in the NIV. A conical hill about seven miles (11 km.) south of Hebron still preserves the name (*Tell Ma'in*). *Carmel* was a village in the same area (*cf.* 1 Sa. 15:12, and see the commentary on 1 Sa. 15:10–12).

A man . . . the man: the narrator's art captures interest in this very rich farmer and his sheep-shearing before either disclosing his name or telling us what sort of a person he was. Sheep-shearing was traditionally celebrated by feasting, with enough and to spare.

3. *The name of the man was Nabal*, meaning 'foolish', an unlikely name for a mother to give her son, and probably a popular distortion of his real name. Nabal fulfils to a letter the biblical meaning of the word (*e.g.* Ps. 14:1; Pr. 18:2, 7); *the man was churlish* (Heb. *qāšeh*, 'hard'; *cf.* Mt. 25:24) *and ill-behaved* (lit. 'evil in his doings', AV, RV). The name and the description of the man form a kind of bracket round details of his attractive wife, *Abigail*, whose name means 'my father is joy[ous]', and whose beauty is more than skin deep. While he is evil (Heb. *ra'*), she is *of good* (Heb. *tôb*) *understanding*. The contrast is such that the pair are totally mismatched.

[1] Gunn 1980, pp. 96, 154 n. 7.
[2] R. P. Gordon, 'David's Rise and Saul's Demise', *TynB* 31 (1980), pp. 42–43.

A Calebite: a descendant of Joshua's companion at the time of Moses, who had recommended entering the land of Canaan (Nu. 13:30). As a reward Caleb eventually inherited the hill country around Hebron (Jos. 14:6–15).

4–8. David's *ten young men* take David's salutations, wishing *peace* and prosperity (Heb. *šālôm*) to Nabal's house and to all he has. It was a conventional greeting through the centuries (*cf.* Mt. 10:12–13), but it was often more than that. David had protected Nabal's men, and the messengers ask for a favourable reply, together with a token gift for his 'son' David. 'This would seem to be an instance of negotiation with an invitation to Nabal to enter into a regulated covenant with David.'[1] Nabal can, after all, afford to be generous, and Eastern hospitality, as well as the Israelite law, traditionally extended to the poor, the outcast, those 'for whom nothing is prepared' (Ne. 8:10; *cf.* Est. 9:19). David does not count himself among these, however, but rather calls attention to the protection he and his men have provided for Nabal's flocks, when they could easily have helped themselves to the animals they needed for food. The inference has been drawn that David was running a protection racket.[2] Certainly, the way David reacts when his polite request is refused supports that suggestion; on the other hand, David was looking further ahead than the immediate present, and such a policy would hardly have endeared him to the population of Judah unless he limited himself to their oppressors. In that case he would increase his support in Judah, and that is what he seems to have done. Nabal was a prime target because he was virtually 'lord' of the district, with plenty of this world's goods, and was unloved even by his servants.

We come on a feast day (Heb. *yôm ṭôb*, 'a "good" day'), is in keeping with the 'good/evil' theme of the chapter. *Your son David*, implying that Nabal was the great man and David his humble servant, was perhaps at the same time over-familiar, but this was the language of negotiation.

9–13. Nabal's delayed reaction to David's message leaves his servants in no doubt about the hostile nature of their reception. Nabal has no intention of 'adopting' the *son of Jesse*: he knows perfectly well who David is and what game David

[1] Wiseman, 'Is it peace?', p. 318.
[2] J. D. Levenson, '1 Samuel 25 as Literature and as History', *CBQ* 40 (1978), p. 19.

is playing, but he has no time for runaway servants. (Ironically, his own servants are none too loyal, v. 14.) Nabal gives away his own lofty self-centredness by reiterating *my bread and my water and my meat . . . my shearers*, as if he had produced them all by his own power. He is certainly not going to share his hard-won produce with the riff-raff commanded by David.[1] Nabal stubbornly refuses to see what his own servants had accepted, namely that David was on the way to becoming king.

Without a moment's hesitation, David gives his orders and the word *sword* reverberates round the camp, as *four hundred men* armed for battle set out to attack Nabal.

14–17. Guessing David's reaction to Nabal's rebuff, the shepherds feared the expected onslaught. Since it was hopeless to attempt to talk to Nabal, a messenger went to his wife in the hope that she would intervene. Abigail hears a report slanted in David's favour.

David sent . . . to salute (Heb. *lᵉbārēk*) *our master*: 'salute' is not the same word in Hebrew as that in verses 5 or 6, but means 'to bless'; David sought the good of Nabal but received insults in return. David's help to Nabal's shepherds is put in more positive terms than David had used: his men *were very good to us* (once more the word 'good'), and *a wall* (Heb. *hômah*) *to us*, that is, a protection, just as the sea had been a protection to the Israelites escaping from Egypt (Ex. 14:22, where the word *hômah*, 'wall', is also used). Now, thanks to Nabal's ill-will, *evil is determined against* him and *all his house*.

Just below the surface lie questions of motivation. Is Nabal the only Calebite to oppose David, and if so, what does he hope to gain by being so churlish? 'Are Nabal's servants really recalling a genuine favour or merely dressing up a racket in the interests of practical survival?'[2] Either way, the reader discerns a power struggle between the two men, in which Nabal's shepherds expect David to gain the upper hand.

18–22. The practical Abigail realizes what is at stake and loses no time in putting together provisions such as six hundred men would need for a satisfying meal. No doubt

[1] Gunn 1980, p. 97, sees Nabal's scathing dismissal of David as strongly reminiscent of Saul's sarcastic outburst against David in 1 Sa. 22:7–8. And it is one of the points R. P. Gordon, 'David's Rise and Saul's Demise', p. 45, makes in likening Nabal to 'a diminutive Saul'.

[2] Gunn 1980, p. 98.

preparations were already completed for the feast, from which she takes what she needs, without noticeably depriving the shearers of their ample fare, for Nabal knows nothing and suspects nothing of his wife's initiative. Meanwhile David – musing on the injustice, *he has returned me evil for good* – is on his way to avenge the insult by wiping out Nabal and all his men. Though he had spared Saul and had repaid him good for evil (1 Sa. 24:17), David on this occasion has no second thought about incurring blood-guilt. The meeting of Abigail and David is therefore full of dramatic tension: at least a woman from Nabal's house may survive the sword!

23–26. It would be unusual to see a caravan of laden asses on these mountain slopes, and astonishing to find the lady of the land prostrated on her face in obeisance to David, so much so that the army was stopped in its tracks. From her lowly place at David's feet, Abigail addressed him as *my lord* (Heb. *ªdōnî*) and referred to herself as his *handmaid* (Heb. *'āmāh*); both terms recur with increasing impact as she continues, and seeks to reverse her husband's evil attitude and response to David. *Upon me . . . be the guilt*, she says, so putting David in the impossible position of wreaking his vengeance on a beautiful and discerning woman. It is easy to see in Abigail how a woman's gifts may effectively be used in negotiation and in defusing a dangerous situation. She did not hesitate to dissociate herself from her husband's foolish behaviour, calling him *ill-natured* (lit. 'a man of Belial', meaning 'wicked', 'godless', so living up [or down] to his name, in what he says and in his motivation, for the fool in the Bible is godless, Ps. 14:1; Is. 32:6). David she perceives to be very different: *As the Lord lives, and as your soul lives*, she says all in one breath, implying that David and the Lord are at one, and she goes on to assume that through her intervention the Lord has restrained David from the blood-guilt towards which he was heading. Her bold suggestion that David will do as she asks is followed by an imprecation which anticipates the fall of Nabal and of all David's enemies, of whom the chief was Saul.[1]

27. Casually, in the middle of her masterly presentation of her case, Abigail makes passing reference to *this present* (Heb.

[1] Hertzberg sees a prophetic role for Abigail here: 'In this section Abigail represents the prophetic voice' (p. 203). But it would seem that most of Nabal's household were of her opinion with regard to David's future.

bᵉrāḵā, 'blessing'; *cf.* v. 14), which she had sent on ahead of her to 'disarm' David. Though she speaks as a 'handmaid' to her *lord*, Abigail is master of the situation.

28–31. *Pray forgive the trespass*: she does not dare to imply that David is dependent on her gift, and fears lest he be offended and refuse to accept it even for his men. Such need as he has is merely temporary, for Abigail is convinced that the Lord will make him *a sure house*. The word 'sure' (Heb. *neʼᵉmān*) bears an unmistakable likeness to her husband's name, and must have evoked a smile and even a knowing nod as the account was later recited.

Evil shall not be found in you: resorting now to flattery, Abigail goes on to contrast the murderous intent of *men* (Heb. *ʼāḏām*, 'mankind') with *the care of the Lord your God*. Whereas the ultimate fate of David's enemies is described in terms of a sling stone flung out of the Lord's presence (*cf.* 1 Sa. 17:49), the *life* (Heb. *nepeš*, 'self') of David will be *bound in the bundle of the living*, and so protected from harm, like Isaiah's teaching given to his disciples (Is. 8:16).[1] Abigail is evidently well aware that the Lord has made promises to David, though she could have conjectured that this was the case without knowing exactly what had been said, except that he will be *prince* (Heb. *nāḡîḏ*) *over Israel*, the one designated for leadership (*cf.* 1 Sa. 9:16). Her intention is that David should avoid taking violent action to avenge an insult, because that would involve him in guilt. Rather, he should expect the Lord to work out a just outcome, as David had consistently done in the face of Saul's aggression, but had failed to do when provoked by Nabal's stubborn meanness. Her parting shot, *remember your handmaid*, requests something which David was to be quick to grant, given the subsequent turn of events.

32–35. Thanks to Abigail's intervention, David had been reminded of his commitment to live by faith in the Lord God, and not by his own impulses, hence his acknowledgment, *Blessed be the Lord, the God of Israel, who sent you this day*, and thus saved many from death and David *from bloodguilt*. It was a major lesson in David's training for kingship, and one that he was going to need to keep before him at future crises. The

---

[1] It is possible that 'bundle' (Heb. *ṣᵉrôr*) should be translated 'document' here, in which case the meaning would be 'the book of the living', as in Ps. 29:28. N. H. Tur-Sinai, *The Book of Job: A New Commentary* (Jerusalem: Kiryath Sepher, ²1967), pp. 240–241.

implication is that violence breeds violence, whereas restraint makes way for a peaceful solution. This he knows with his head, but he may fail to remember it when his blood is roused. This time Abigail has saved the situation: *Go up in peace* is more than a conventional salutation, for Abigail has won her case and has changed the course of events.

36–38. Abigail returned to witness the feast, *like the feast of a king*. Mean towards others' needs, Nabal indulged himself to such an extent that he was unapproachable that night; if he was virtually 'king' of the hill country of Judah, his gluttony soon disqualified him. In the morning, on hearing his wife's news, *his heart died within him*: he suffered a stroke from which he did not recover, and his death was regarded as the Lord's judgment upon him.

39–42. David recognized that the Lord had thus vindicated him, so setting his seal on the rightness of refusing to vindicate oneself (Pr. 20:22). While David's wooing of Abigail is not unexpected, surely it is going too far to suggest that David picked a quarrel with Nabal with just such a marriage in mind![1] His first concern had to be to feed his troops, and it was in that connection that the incident occurred. Nevertheless, the chapter does provide 'a proleptic glimpse, within David's ascent, of his fall from grace' (see 2 Sa. 11).[2] He could be very susceptible to feminine charms. His passionate nature had great potential, both for good and for evil, and this incident should have been a warning for his life as king.

Eastern wedding customs do not seem to have changed through the ages. David sent his *servants*, 'friends of the bridegroom', to fetch his bride, who took her *five maidens* and went to the marriage feast (*cf.* Mt. 25:10). Traditional weddings still feature a similar order of events, the bride going to her husband when he fetches or sends for her. Abigail is clearly more than glad to be marrying a man she can respect, one with whom she has much in common. In her enthusiasm she prostrates herself even before the servants of David, and volunteers to do for them the service of a slave.

Through his marriage to Abigail, David acquired more than a good wife. There is evidence in the biblical text that at this period to marry the wife or concubine of a ruler was to make

[1] So Levenson, '1 Samuel 25 as Literature', p. 27.
[2] *Ibid.*, p. 23.

a bid for his status and power (2 Sa. 3:6–11; 16:21–23; 1 Ki. 2:21–22). David, by the same principle, had a right to the estates of Nabal to which his new wife entitled him, though at this juncture he was not in any position to settle down anywhere on account of Saul.[1] After Saul's death, however, he would have some claim to territory in southern Judah.

43–44. A general note about David's marital position is slipped in while the subject is in mind.

Saul had given Michal his daughter, David's wife, to Palti: his enmity towards David caused Saul to regret having made David a member of the family, and he took advantage of David's absence to contract another marriage for Michal. *Ahinoam* was the name of Saul's wife (1 Sa. 14:50); though the name occurs only there and in this verse, it is inconceivable that they are one and the same person. Since Ahinoam is always mentioned before Abigail (1 Sa. 27:3; 30:5) and bore David's first son (2 Sa. 3:2), it is likely that David had married her already.[2]

It is hard to imagine how these ladies, at least one of whom was accustomed to some luxury, endured the constant pressure of life on the run, some detail of which is given in the next few chapters. Michal also had a hard time, being used as a pawn in her father's political game, but the narrator is not concerned about the royal women, except in so far as they had a part to play in the future of David.

Had Abigail, with all her beauty and intelligence, worked towards marrying David, and had he, brilliant strategist that he was, thought from the start of his quarrel with Nabal that he would ultimately possess all Nabal's assets, including his wife? Surely not. As David testified, the hand of the Lord, the God of Israel, was over these events (1 Sa. 25:32), including the human initiatives. A lesser man than David would have scorned the pleas of Abigail and persevered with his own preconceived course of action. David recognized the God-given wisdom of her words, and never regretted acting on her

---

[1] *Cf.* M. Tsevat, 'Marriage and Monarchical Legitimacy in Ugarit and Israel', *JSS* 3 (1958), p. 241; R. de Vaux, *Ancient Israel: Its life and institutions* (London: Darton, Longman & Todd, ²1965), p. 116.

[2] Levenson's suggestion, '1 Samuel 25 as Literature', p. 27, that David married Saul's wife during Saul's lifetime, so making a bid for the throne, is hardly credible. The supporting evidence, Nathan's word in 2 Sa. 12:8, is too slight for so monstrous a deed.

advice. There was more here than a political struggle, and the text points strongly to the living Lord who had bound David, despite all his failings, 'in the bundle of the living' (v. 29), kept him from murderous revenge, and prepared him for the throne of Israel.

x. David spares Saul a second time (26:1–25). The *Ziphites*, who had already betrayed David's whereabouts to Saul (1 Sa. 23:19), and who would have brought about his downfall but for the Philistine raid that called for Saul's intervention to the west, made another attempt to assist Saul. All David's movements were carefully monitored.

1–5. Saul still has his three 'thousands' of picked troops with which to pursue David (*cf.* 1 Sa. 24:2), while David has a mere six hundred in his army. Nevertheless, David is not afraid to reconnoitre on his own, so that he knows at first hand the enemy camp. His own base, by the time Saul arrives, is *in the wilderness*, but he does not wait for Saul to find him; instead he takes the initiative, and notes from a distant vantage point how well protected Saul is, with *Abner*, his cousin, as his bodyguard, and the army encamped all round.

6. Far from being put off by the impregnable camp of Saul, David works out an intrepid plot for which he needs a companion. *Ahimelech the Hittite* is not to be confused with either of the other Ahimelechs who come into David's life (1 Sa. 21:1; 2 Sa. 8:17). *Abishai the son of Zeruiah* was a nephew of David's (1 Ch. 2:13–16). His sister Zeruiah had three sons (her husband is never named), all of them valiant in David's entourage. Abishai is positively eager to accompany David on his dangerous mission.

7–9. With great daring, the two picked their way between the sleeping troops to the central point where Saul was sleeping. The royal *spear* at his head was meant to be for his protection, but it very nearly became the offensive weapon that in the hands of Abishai would have killed him. Abishai prided himself on his professionalism as a soldier: *I will not strike him twice.* As always in the presence of Saul, David is unhesitating in his reaction: *who can put forth his hand against the Lord's anointed, and be guiltless?* The person of the king is sacrosanct.

10–12. Encouraged by his memory of Nabal's death, David became convinced that Saul would come to an untimely end without any intervention on David's part. No-one would be able to accuse David of having murdered Saul in order to set himself on the throne. Abishai has to be content to take Saul's spear and waterpot as trophies; *a deep sleep from the Lord* upon Saul and his men ensures that he and David escape undetected. David counts on the Lord's overruling and is not disappointed.

13–16. At a safe distance, yet positioned so that his voice was audible on the opposite hill, David called Abner by name, taunting him that he had failed to keep watch over his lord, *the Lord's anointed* (Heb. *mᵉšîaḥ*; *cf.* vv. 9, 11), and therefore deserved to die. Understandably, Abner had nothing to say.

17–20. Saul's response gave David the opportunity to plead the irrationality of Saul's continuing pursuit by asking what guilt David had incurred. On this occasion David made no concession to the fact that Saul had addressed him affectionately as *my son David*, and continued to do so (vv. 21, 25); David addressed Saul as *my lord* and *king*, whereas in 1 Samuel 24:11 he had addressed him as 'my father'. David is becoming both more certain of his future role and more desperate to escape his pursuer.

If it is the Lord . . . but if it is men: David is not really in doubt that Saul's motivation comes from within himself, but he tactfully suggests otherwise. By driving David beyond the boundaries of Israel's land, Saul is virtually forcing him to *serve other gods* and break the first commandment. (He hints here that he will go beyond Saul's reach, as he was when he took refuge among the Philistines [*cf.* 1 Sa. 21:10–15; 27:1].) Thus Saul will force David out of reach of worship, which in that time took place only in the Lord's land, where *the presence of the Lord* was known. David appeals to Saul's compassion: *let not my blood fall to the earth away from the presence of the Lord*, implying that Saul will succeed in taking his *life*. The RSV follows the LXX in reading 'my life', but the Hebrew 'a flea' is more picturesque (*cf.* AV, RV, NIV), as in 1 Samuel 24:14. The less obvious expression is more likely to be original.

A partridge in the mountains: David takes up Abner's question (v. 14, 'Who are you that calls [Heb. *qārā'tā*]?') by referring to himself as a partridge (Heb. *haqqorē'*, 'the caller-bird'), mercilessly pursued by hunters. David implies that Saul's search, whether for a flea or a partridge, is beneath his dignity.

21–25. Saul had learnt by this time to admit to his faults

(1 Sa. 15:24–25; 24:17), but never before had he gone so far as to say, *I have played the fool, and have erred exceedingly*. In this contrite frame of mind, Saul wants David to return, but David ignores this request. He has given up all hope of being able to trust Saul's gestures towards reconciliation, so he submits Saul to the indignity of having to send a soldier to fetch his spear, and commits himself to the Lord, rather than to Saul, for protection and deliverance. Unlike Nabal, Saul had not collapsed on hearing that he might have lost his life at David's hand, but he is a sorry figure, nonetheless, as he pronounces his blessing on David and foresees his many successes, which presuppose Saul's death. These last words to David were worthy of Saul, and such as David could cherish in his memory of 'the Lord's anointed' in days to come. Apart from that, nothing had changed. David continued his wanderings, and Saul went back to his court. We are not told whether he recovered his spear, the symbol of his kingship.

d. David resorts to the Philistines (27:1 – 31:13)

i. With Achish, king of Gath (27:1 – 28:2). It is a measure of the desperation David felt that he was prepared to consider approaching the very enemies he had successfully fought on Israel's behalf, and offer them his services. Not that he had any intention of turning traitor to his beloved Judah, but he would have to appear to do so in order to reassure his Philistine allies. This was not David's first attempt to enlist Philistine protection (*cf.* 1 Sa. 21:10–15), an episode which would not have helped him on this second approach to Achish), but this time the situation was very different.

1–4. *I shall now perish one day by the hand of Saul* expressed the human fear David had, living like a hunted animal. Though he knew that he had been anointed to be king, and had seen the Lord's providential ordering of his life, he could not bear indefinitely the hide-and-seek existence in Judah's barren wilderness, especially now that he had his wives to provide for. The hospitality of Achish at Gath, in welcoming not only an army of six hundred but also wives and children, was remarkable, and demonstrates David's power to charm even an enemy king. David's ruse succeeded and Saul *sought for him no more*.

5–8. From every point of view it was good that David

should move away from Achish's capital, but especially because he needed freedom to operate his own independent policy without being observed too closely. Achish, in his role as king of a city-state with dependencies, had the feudal right to bestow land, and his choice of *Ziklag* for David was particularly suitable. In the first place it was a border-town in the foothills between Philistine and Simeonite territory; though allocated to Simeon (Jos. 19:5; 1 Ch. 4:30), in Joshua 15:31 it is listed among Judah's towns, but either it was never occupied or it was reconquered by the Philistines. From the time of Achish's gift, Ziklag belonged to the kings of Judah (v. 6). From David's point of view Ziklag had the advantage of being well away from Saul's territory and isolated from the Philistine pentapolis. Its main disadvantage was that it tended to be the target of marauding bands from the desert, *Amalekites* particularly. *Geshurites*, mentioned in Joshua 13:2, lived between southern Philistia and Egypt, and need to be distinguished from people of the same name in northern Transjordan (2 Sa. 15:8). *Girzites* are not otherwise known.

Achish stood to gain from having David's army to protect his southern territory; he may also have hoped to have won the support of Judah against Saul, which might have enabled him to take the whole land, as he very nearly did in the battle of Mount Gilboa (1 Sa. 31:7). *A year and four months* gives a helpful indication of the time-scale. David was sufficiently long in Ziklag to build up relationships with Israelites living in the far south (*cf.* 1 Sa. 30:26–31).

9–12. David directed his attacks against the plunderers who despoiled Judean as well as Philistine towns. His policy of extermination protected him from informers who might have told Achish that David was playing a double game. David would report that he had fought against Judah or Judah's allies, the *Jerahmeelites* (1 Ch. 2:9), whom David had protected together with the *Kenites* (1 Sa. 30:29). The latter tribe had entered the wilderness of Judah near Arad, to the east of Beersheba, and settled in that region. In fact he fought only against their common enemies, but *Achish trusted David*, believing that David was alienating himself from his own people out of loyalty to the Philistines, whose vassal he appeared to be: *my servant always* (*cf.* Dt. 15:17).

28:1–2. This was the situation when Achish was preparing for war to gain supremacy over Israel. David found himself in a tight corner when Achish committed his army to fighting against Saul, and David to becoming chief *bodyguard* to Achish. David's answer, designed to avoid a straight reply, satisfied Achish but left David wondering how he would escape this dilemma.

ii. Saul consults a medium (28:3–25). When this episode opens, the battle lines are already being drawn, but Saul has no heart for the battle. He desperately needs someone on whom to lean for advice and encouragement, but finds himself totally isolated.

3–7. The repeated mention of Samuel's death and burial (*cf.* 1 Sa. 25:1) shows Saul deprived of the great prophet's guidance, which in any case he had earlier disregarded. The illicit substitutes for prophets – *mediums* (Heb. *'ōḇôt*), who consulted the dead, and *wizards* (Heb. *yiddᵉ'ōnîm*), 'who chirp and mutter' (Is. 8:19) as they speak on behalf of the dead – Saul had banned from Israel. By his own action in obedience to the law (Lv. 19:31; 20:6; Dt. 18:10–11), Saul had rightly cut himself off from the resort of those who did not know the Lord. The fact that he now regrets this indicates how far he has departed from his early commitment (*e.g.* 1 Sa. 11:13). He had the worst of both worlds.

Shunem, in the Valley of Jezreel, was about twenty miles (32 km.) north of Aphek, the most northerly Philistine city. The fact that the Philistines had penetrated thus far gives an indication of their dominance over Saul's kingdom, and of their intention to press further east to the Jordan. Hence Saul's choice of Mount Gilboa, a vantage-point from which to observe the movements of the enemy on the western slopes of the Hill of Moreh across the valley. Saul *was afraid* with the kind of fear that gnaws physically and incapacitates a person for action. *The Lord did not answer him* by any of the permitted means that remained: dreams, which could have given him direct guidance, *Urim*, the priestly oracle, of which he had deprived himself when he killed the priests at Nob (1 Sa. 22:17–19), or by *prophets*, trained in Samuel's school (1 Sa. 19:20). Despite Saul's legislation against mediums, the king's own servants were well aware that they still practised their trade. *Endor* was only a short distance away, on the north of the Hill of Moreh, and accessible despite the Philistine forces close by.

8–10. *So Saul disguised himself... and went ... by night*, furtively, like a criminal, with just two companions, in an attempt to escape from the dread fate which was closing in upon him. Despite the finality of Saul's last confrontation with Samuel (1 Sa. 15:10–35), Saul still longed for the word of the Lord which he had received through the prophet who first anointed him and proclaimed him king. He must have hoped that Samuel would somehow reverse the judgment which he had pronounced, in much the same way as some of our contemporaries refuse to take seriously the dark side of the word of God. *Divine for me by a spirit*, he says, so indicating the nature of the claim made by the 'medium' (v. 7), for he wants the woman to conjure up someone from the dead. She is appalled, because she suspects a trap and fears the death penalty. Inconsistently, Saul swears, *As the Lord lives*, that she will be safe, while he himself endeavours to reverse the word of the same living Lord, pronounced against himself.

11–12. The indication is that the woman was taken by surprise when Samuel appeared to her. It was a moment of revelation, hence her crying out *with a loud voice*, and her realization that the person who was consulting her was Saul, the king.[1] The incident does not tell us anything about the veracity of claims to consult the dead on the part of mediums, because the indications are that this was an extraordinary event for her, and a frightening one because she was not in control.

13–14. *I see a god [Heb. ʾᵉlōhîm] coming up out of the earth*: the word *ʾᵉlōhîm*, used with plurals, means 'judges', authority figures, in addition to 'gods' (see the commentary on 1 Sa. 2:22–25); the appearance of Samuel clearly impressed upon her his authority and dignity. Saul did not see Samuel, but was dependent on the woman's description. *An old man . . . wrapped in a robe* is a vague description, from which we might think it would be impossible to identify anyone, but the key word may be *robe*, the prophetic robe, the tearing of which had become the symbol of Saul's downfall as king (1 Sa. 15:27–28). Moreover, Saul knew intuitively that his request had been granted, and he prostrated himself before Samuel as if before the Lord.

---

[1] *Cf.* W. A. M. Beuken, '1 Samuel 28: The Prophet as "Hammer of Witches" ', *JSOT* 6 (1978), p. 8.

15. *Why have you disturbed me?*: these words of Samuel suggest that Saul has interrupted a life of restfulness which Samuel had been enjoying and had been reluctant to leave. The short answer to his question was that Saul was utterly desperate: *God has turned away from me and answers me no more*. Saul is asking for guidance when his course of action is obvious: he has to fight the Philistines. What he really wants is reassurance that all will be well and that he will win the battle. Is this not the whole purpose of prophets and counsellors, to give a reassuring message?

16–19. Samuel, however, does not in any way change the message he had spoken to Saul when he lived at Ramah. He is still the prophet of the Lord, and he speaks in the name of the Lord, reiterating that name seven times over in these four verses. Whereas Saul had said, '*God* has turned away from me', Samuel uses the covenant name, '*the Lord* has turned from you'. Far from reversing that judgment, Samuel can only reinforce it, for the word he had spoken (1 Sa. 15:28) is about to be fulfilled, and the name of the neighbour who will inherit the kingdom can now be given. The message of 1 Samuel 15:18–19 has not been repealed, but is still in force *this day*. The Philistines, who in Saul's early days as king had defied the armies of Israel and had terrified Saul, are about to defeat Saul and *his sons*, who will *tomorrow* be with Samuel, in the mysterious world beyond the grave. *The Lord will give the army of Israel also into the hand of the Philistines*, for the people and their army are bound up with their king, and they too will suffer defeat as the result of Saul's disobedience.

20. Saul, who had not seen the divine vision, but had heard only too plainly the prophet's words, was as good as finished already. The fatal truth overwhelmed him with deep fear, so that he fell prostrate, for *there was no strength in him*. The Hebrew is emphatic: he was 'all in'. Why *he had eaten nothing* is unexplained. Some commentators suggest that he needed to go fasting to the medium, others that the exigencies of the war demanded it because food was not easily obtained, but most people in peril of their lives lose their appetite!

21–22. *And the woman came to Saul*, evidently not having been present while Saul received Samuel's message. It seems likely that she had an inner sanctum where she practised her secret

rites, perhaps an inner cave.[1] One look at Saul, and she knew
at once that he was *terrified* (Heb. *nibhal*), totally exhausted
and paralysed with fright. 'The root of the verb *bhl* [terrified]
can indeed refer to the fright . . . in which the grip of death
on man becomes visible (cf. Ex. 15:15; Lev. 26:16; Is. 13:8;
21:3; 65:23; Ps. 30:8 (EVV, 7); 78:33; 90:7; 104:29).'[2] Her good
sense tells her that what the king needs is a good meal; perhaps
then he will feel better able to face the coming battle. Whether
she appreciated the seriousness of the situation in the light of
the word of the prophet, we cannot know; most likely she was
thinking in human terms of some way to boost the morale of
the king. Though she could not save him from his fate, she
could give him temporary help and comfort to strengthen his
fainting spirits. But she was astute enough to realize that Saul
was in no mood to eat, hence her reasoned argument that,
since she had risked her life for him, he should be willing to
do something for her.

> But unwittingly she herself has disclosed to him the deepest
> meaning of her invitation: 'Hearken to me as I have heark-
> ened to you' (vv. 21f). In a grieving manner she amplifies
> the accusation of Samuel: 'Because you did not hearken to
> YHWH . . . therefore YHWH has done this thing to you
> this day' (v. 18). Saul realizes he has landed in a situation
> which resembles a covenant with the medium instead of
> with YHWH.[3]

All this was the outcome of Saul's willingness to compromise
with evil in order to escape the word of the Lord. It is hard
to envisage a more terrible situation in which to find oneself.

23–25. Saul at first refuses to eat. Without doubt he lacked
any appetite. More importantly, it was inappropriate to
participate in a festive meal, especially one from the hand of
a necromancer, on the eve of what he knew would be the day
of his death. But eventually he was persuaded. In the middle
of the night, in the dwelling of a woman who consulted the
dead, Saul got up from the earth floor, sat on the bed, and
watched all the familiar homely processes of preparing a meal,

---

[1] This is the suggestion of R. A. S. Macalister, *Bible Side-Lights from the
Mound of Gezer* (London: Hodder & Stoughton, 1906), p. 70. Such a double
cave was found at Gezer (fig. 16).
[2] Beuken, 'Hammer of Witches', p. 12.
[3] *Ibid.*, p. 13.

from the killing of the calf to the kneading of dough for baking (*cf.* Gn. 18:6–8). If the meal and its preparation were conducive to a feeling of normality (for it was a dinner fit for a king), that in itself was sinister, because Saul was soon – in a matter of hours – to be king no longer.[1] Saul and his two servants disappeared once more into the night.

Saul had begun well, but early on he had shown signs of stubborn resistance to the requirement of Samuel that the king should be the Lord's obedient servant, ready to carry out to the letter the commands of the Lord's prophet. In the key battle against the Philistines, Saul had not waited for Samuel to perform the pre-battle ritual at Gilgal. As king he reserved the right to take initiatives himself, regardless of Samuel's orders, and already he had earned the Lord's condemnation, and the sentence, 'But now your kingdom shall not continue' (1 Sa. 13:14).

In recent literature a good deal of sympathy has been expressed for Saul. In connection with Samuel's late arrival (1 Sa. 13:10), 'He appears here starkly as the plaything of fate . . . Saul's explanation of his action is brushed aside without even cursory consideration . . . Nor is the king given any opportunity to beg mercy of God.'[2] After the battle against the Amalekites, Saul claimed to have listened to the voice of the people in sparing the best of the spoil (1 Sa. 15:21, 24), contrary to the command of the prophet (1 Sa. 15:3), and McCarter comments, 'Democracy is no more acceptable a replacement for prophetic theocracy than is monarchy!'[3] But at least in the Western world the voice of the people speaks very loudly and persistently; Saul could therefore appear to have been treated somewhat unsympathetically, but the fact remains that he did not exercise real leadership.

At Endor Saul displays the same basic character as in the earlier episodes. On the one hand he wanted the best: he had cleared the land of those who practised necromancy and

---

[1] If Saul had been fasting as a dutiful act of piety before battle, as he did in 1 Sa. 14, by accepting the proffered meal he would be deliberately breaking his fast and the commitment it implied: 'he signals for the last time a willingness to sit loose from the constrictions of the sacral world', Gunn 1980, p. 109.

[2] Gunn 1980, p. 66.

[3] McCarter 1980, p. 270.

sought to make contact with the dead, because for Israel God had decreed to speak through his prophets. If his fast (v. 20) was part of prescribed battle ritual, Saul was still endeavouring to fulfil the externals of religion as he had done in offering the sacrifice (1 Sa. 13:12). Moreover, Saul was still dependent for his security on Samuel: 'There is pathos in the fact that Saul should even at this stage seek out the advice of his long-standing antagonist. Above all we are given to understand the grip that Samuel has upon Saul . . . [Saul] needs certainty and is paralyzed without it.'[1] Indeed Saul had asked for guidance from the Lord. What he had not fully taken in was the fact that he had already received the guidance that was appropriate in his circumstances. No amount of further requesting could change the information he had already been given.

The whole sequence of events demonstrates powerfully that for Saul everything hung on that matter of willingness to sink his own will in that of the Lord his God. He had wanted to savour the authority and power associated with the kingship, and therefore had asserted himself rather than accept the total domination of the prophet. He did not realize that there is in all valid human leadership the need to be subject to a higher authority, ultimately that of God himself, and that this is a relief rather than a humiliation.

If Saul could but have realized the fact, he became humiliated as a result of his attempts to take control of events. Samuel's confrontation with Saul, witnessed by his troops, both at Gibeah and at Gilgal, was profoundly humiliating for the king. Now at Endor, when judgment is about to fall upon him and his family through the defeat by the Philistines, Saul is a nervous wreck, in no fit state to lead the army. The pride of Saul, combined with jealousy of David, had together cost him his throne and his dynasty.

As for the wider implications of the Endor incident, the reader learns how pervasive and entrenched were Canaanite practices, even among the Israelites. Though violation of the law carried the death penalty, and necromancers were officially banished from the land, they were still to be found, ready to operate if given an assurance of protection. People evidently wanted their services and were ready to pay for

---

[1] Gunn 1980, p. 108.

the privilege. Whether they were deceived, or whether they
genuinely saw and heard the ghosts of the dead, the biblical
writers do not say. They lay stress on prophecy, God's way
of speaking to his people, as opposed to necromancy. Even
after his death, the prophet Samuel speaks. 'Neither cavern
nor tomb, neither space nor time, limits the effective power of
God's word . . .',[1] but Saul receives the very message he had
already heard. In the end, he had to do what he would in any
case have done – face the enemy. The additional information,
that within twenty-four hours he and his sons would be dead,
was no help at all to his morale. Indeed he would have been
better without it. He did himself no good by doing what he
had decreed to be unlawful. God's word stood and could not
be altered. He should have believed it instead of thinking that
by further consultation he could reverse its judgment. The
Lord did not answer him, because there was no more to be
said.

iii. David's providential rejection from the Philistine army (29:1–11).
In the meantime, for Saul's visit to Endor
belongs a little later though it is recorded first, David and his
men had been preparing to fight their own Israelite kith and
kin because there appeared to be no way of avoiding involvement with Achish in the fateful battle.

1. *Now the Philistines gathered all their forces*: these words pick
up the subject from 1 Samuel 28:1, where Achish was presumably in Gath. Here the Philistines are some thirty miles (48
km.) further north at Aphek, well on their way to the Valley
of Jezreel, but still about forty miles (64 km.) short of Shunem
(1 Sa. 28:4). At that time the Israelite forces were in Jezreel,
a meeting-place of routes, before being deployed on Mount
Gilboa (1 Sa. 28:4) for the battle. The *Fountain*, the source of
the river Harod, at the foot of Mount Gilboa, is now part of
a public park.

2–5. The Philistine army was on the march in orderly array,
each section under the eye of the ruler of the city from which
it was mustered. Achish brought up the rear, with David and
his men in attendance. The army generals felt uneasy at the
presence of David the Israelite and his men, here referred to
as *these Hebrews* (*cf.* the commentary on 1 Sa. 4:5–9). Achish

---

[1] Beuken, 'Hammer of Witches', p. 14.

must have been under David's spell not to foresee objections from the forces which, after all, were going to war against the king of Israel. Though Achish reckoned that he had evidence of David's loyalty, the battles of the *days and years* (evidently some considerable period) had been in the far south, not against the king in his traditional northern territory. Above all they suspected David, in the light of public opinion expressed after he killed Goliath (v. 5), of having aspirations for the throne. David, they argued, could become acceptable to Saul and Israel only by putting Philistines to death, so they demanded that he should be sent back to his *place*, namely Ziklag.

6–8. *As the Lord lives* is unexpected in a Philistine oath; can it be that Achish has committed himself to David's Lord, or is he being courteous to David in not swearing by Philistine gods? The latter is perhaps more likely.

I have found nothing wrong (Heb. *rāʿā*, 'evil') *in you*: already he has said *to me it seems right* (Heb. *ṭôb*, 'good'), so the 'good' and 'evil' theme continues, but with a twist, for Achish fails to appreciate that David is playing a double game. It is providential for Achish as well as for David that the Philistine 'lords' are discerning and insist that David be far removed from military operations. As Achish saw the situation, however, it was embarrassing to have to dismiss the man he had appointed as his bodyguard, and he was at pains not to offend him.

Go peaceably implies that David had the right to protest against this sudden reversal, and protest he did, as though he were suffering an injustice, whereas he was inwardly relieved to be out of the battle. Or was David so double-faced that when he objected *that I may not go and fight against the enemies of my lord the king*, he had in mind the enemies of King Saul, and was 'truly reluctant to quit the march and lose a chance to be "an adversary in [the Philistine] camp" '?[1] This may well have been David's veiled meaning; he could turn any situation, however daunting, to his advantage.

9–10. *You are as blameless* (Heb. *ṭôb*, 'good') *in my sight as an angel* (or messenger) *of God* is fulsome praise, unless it happened that David was literally the bearer of God's message to Achish, in which case David's insincerity was the more

[1] McCarter 1980, p. 427.

reprehensible. Whatever lies behind these words, there is no ambiguity about David's instructions: he and his men are to be away at first light.

In one of the LXX manuscripts (Vaticanus) verse 10 is longer than the Hebrew text, adding after *came with you*, 'and go to the place I assigned you. Let there be no rancour in your heart, for to me you are blameless' (JB). The translators of the NEB included the additional clauses, having judged that they had been omitted unintentionally from the MT and therefore from the standard English versions. In the GNB and NIV, however, the shorter text has been retained.

11. David and his men *return to the land of the Philistines*, having been honourably dismissed; while the Philistine troops went to Jezreel to fight against King Saul, David's army would be the only fighting men remaining in the land.

iv. David and the Amalekites (30:1–31). Though David had seen God's providential purpose in sparing him from fighting against Saul, he faced a desperate situation on his return to Ziklag, and might have concluded that the Lord had deserted him. It was the culmination of bitter attacks from enemies throughout his period of preparation for the throne.

1–6. *On the third day* indicates that David and his men covered about twenty-five miles a day on the march south from Aphek to Ziklag, where they would arrive tired, hungry and expecting all the comforts of a welcome home. The sight of a burnt-out, totally deserted town was more than the troops could bear. The Amalekites, whom Saul had failed to exterminate (1 Sa. 15:17–33), had taken advantage of the departure of the fighting men to wreak havoc, but at least their wives and families had not been killed. Instead the Amalekites had taken them all captive, regarding them as part of the spoil to be enjoyed or sold (v. 16), but there was at least some hope of recovering them from the enemy. David had suffered in exactly the same way as everyone else, losing his two wives, but he was held responsible for the disaster, all the pent-up anger and indignation being laid at his door, *for the people spoke of stoning him*. Never since his flight from Gibeah and Saul had David stood so alone, though he had often been in danger of death, *but David strengthened himself in the Lord his God*. Far from blaming God for allowing the destruction of the city, David took the reprisal of the Amalekites as one of life's hazards, in which he could draw on the resources of a faithful covenant Lord. As the psalms attributed to David assert over and over again, David poured out his feelings freely in prayer: 'I am lonely and afflicted. Relieve the troubles of my heart, and bring me out of my distresses' (Ps. 25:16–17) could have been composed in a situation such as this.

7–10. When he needed specific guidance, David could call on Abiathar the priest (*cf.* 1 Sa. 22:20–23) to bring the ephod, which would give a positive or negative answer to the question, *Shall I pursue after this band?* (Heb. *gᵉdûd*, 'a raiding party'; *cf.* 2 Sa. 4:2). Given a positive and encouraging response, David set out immediately with all his soldiers; despite their weariness, action was the needed antidote to their feelings of frustration and aggression. Nevertheless, the extra travelling proved too much for a third of David's soldiers, who went only as far as *the brook Besor*, probably the Wadi Ghazzeh, on which Beersheba and Arad are situated; they would have travelled some twelve miles or so south-west of Ziklag, on top of the march already that day.

11–15. Travel in the unpopulated desert of the south had special hazards; in particular there was rarely anyone to ask for directions, and there was no way of knowing where the Amalekite raiders were to be found, until David's men happened upon a half-dead Egyptian, whom they coaxed back to life. As it turned out, he had accompanied his Amalekite master on a series of raids until he had to be left by the roadside because of illness.

The Negeb of the Cherethites: Cherethites are always mentioned together with the Pelethites or Philistines (*cf.* v. 16; Ezk. 25:16; Zp. 2:5), and both groups came from Crete. Understandably, they settled in adjoining areas on the coast of Canaan. Cherethites showed special loyalty to David and later formed part of his bodyguard (2 Sa. 8:18). The districts of Beersheba, which belonged to *Judah*, and Hebron, associated with *Caleb*, had suffered, in addition to *Ziklag*. David was likely to endear himself to several communities, therefore, if he could defeat and punish the raiders and recover the spoil they had taken.

The fears of the Egyptian slave give some indication of the way he could easily have been treated, but in exchange for the help he can give he negotiates for his life and freedom.

16–20. Thanks to their guide, David and his men found the camp of the Amalekites, and observed from some vantage-point the unrestrained merrymaking spread out as far as the eye could see.

And David smote them from twilight: the Hebrew *nešep̱*, translated 'dawn' in Job 7:4 and Psalm 119:147, has this sense here, so JB, NEB, GNB. Having noted the situation, David and his men took some rest and attacked at first light, when the Amalekites would be suffering from the soporific effects of the feast, and least able to defend themselves. Operations lasted till *the evening* (Heb. *'ereḇ*) of the following day, that is the period of the day we call 'afternoon', when the sun is declining.

David completely overwhelms the Amalekites, killing all except the four hundred who escape on camels, and recovering all the spoil, but more importantly the human captives. The honour belongs to David now, just as earlier he had been obliged to take the blame. The verbs reiterate his prowess: *David smote them . . . David recovered all . . . David rescued . . . David brought back all. David also captured all the flocks and herds.* Whereas the odds had been stacked against him, now that he has won the day everyone understands that *This is David's spoil*. The contrast between David's battle against the Amalekites and the punitive mission on which Saul was sent (1 Sa. 15:2–3), needs to be noted. Saul had had a specific task to fulfil, which he well understood, but which deprived him of any share in the spoil. David, however, was under no such instructions, and was free to keep what he recovered in the battle.

21–25. The question of the spoil dominates the remainder of the chapter, however. When those who had been left at the brook Besor (v. 9) went out to welcome the returning victors, they met with a grudging attitude on the part of some. Each was permitted the return of his wife and children, but the *wicked and base fellows*, who may even have been a majority, wanted to exclude them from any share in the spoil. David exercised his prerogative, laying down the principle which became standard practice, and establishing a legal precedent. First he expounds the reasoning behind his decision. The outcome of the battle has been the Lord's doing, therefore the spoils come from the Lord. This theological interpretation of events, *the Lord has given . . . he has preserved us*, is well understood and widely accepted: *Who would listen to you in this matter?* It provides a good illustration of the way the faith of ordinary Israelites undergirded Israelite law, and made it workable.

Those who remained at the base camp with the baggage had equal shares with those who fought in the battle. David's sense of justice was instructed by his experience of the mercy and generosity of his Lord, and for that reason surpassed ordinary human standards of what is just and right.

26–31. Though the spoil technically belonged to David, his men had reserved the right to express an opinion as to the way in which it should be used, and David had no intention merely of enriching himself with it. For one thing, it was right that those who had been raided should receive some compensation; for another, David no doubt had an eye to the future, and intended to make the spoil work on his behalf. *His friends, the elders of Judah*, were heads of the communities of the region south of Hebron, whom David had got to know during his enforced exile. Many of them had endured raids, and now they would receive some reparation from *the enemies of the Lord*: loyalty to the Lord created the strongest of bonds.

Many of the places named are still recognizable in the modern place names. *Bethel* cannot be the well-known city to the north of Jerusalem; either there was another Bethel in the south, or the name should read Beth-zur (as in the LXX Vaticanus MS; *cf.* Jos. 15:58). There is a village called Beit Ṣûr to the north of Hebron. *Ramoth of the Negeb* is not known, but *Jattir* (Heb. *yattir*) is Khirbet Attir, about thirteen miles (21 km.) south of Hebron and close to *Eshtemoa*; both these places were Levitical cities (Jos. 21:14). *Aroer*, called Adadah in Joshua 15:22, is the modern 'Arʿarah, ten miles (16 km.) southeast of Beersheba. *Racal* is 'Carmel' in the LXX, the place where Nabal had his farm (1 Sa. 25:2), and for *Borashan* the LXX has Beersheba. The remaining place names are unidentified.

On their return from Aphek, David and his men had faced their ruined and abandoned homes; everything seemed lost, and David was in danger of being stoned to death. His status as the future king, 'the Lord's anointed', was no passport to an easy life, and he had to face the ambiguities of human experience every bit as much as Saul did. David's genius was his spiritual resilience. He expected to find the resources he needed in the Lord his God, and he was not disappointed, whereas Saul had made a habit of 'doing his own thing', and deliberately refusing to carry out the instructions he was given by Samuel. David refused to interpret obstacles as signs of

God's opposition to him; rather they provided opportunities to see what he would do in answer to the prayer of his servant. To find the energy and resolve to rally for another campaign men who were already needing food and rest was in itself a great achievement (contrast Saul's tendency to wait for something to happen); the inner resources of David resulted in action which would not have been possible without his faith in God. The 'chance' encounter with the slave of an Amalekite was part of the provision that enabled David's troops to get the better of the Amalekites. That they were in no fit state to defend themselves was the result of their own misjudgment. The hand of the Lord is to be seen in all these diverse but interwoven aspects of the episode, in which David is able to achieve something positive out of a bitter calamity.

v. Saul's last battle (31:1-13). The event to which the last chapters have been leading, the death of Saul, comes swiftly now. The account is brief and factual, and the more moving for that.

1. *Now the Philistines fought against Israel*, as they had done at the beginning of Saul's reign (1 Sa. 13:5), and even earlier (1 Sa. 4:1-11). Saul's divine commission had been to save Israel from their hand (1 Sa. 9:16), but ironically he dies at their hand, such is the measure of his failure. The narrator, omitting all detail, records Israel's retreat and the slaughter on Mount Gilboa.

2-7. The sons of Saul are the first named casualties (*cf.* Samuel's words in 1 Sa. 28:19), but Saul is also much sought, and is wounded by the archers, though not killed outright. David, who had once been Saul's armour-bearer, would have approved of the one who refused to run his sword through the king, out of awe for the person of the Lord's anointed. Saul heroically fell upon his own sword rather than have the uncircumcised Philistines *make sport* of him, as they had done with Samson (Jdg. 16:25); there was no telling what indignity they might inflict on him, so death was preferable to capture. The armour-bearer chose to die with his master *and all his men*, the chosen troops with whom he surrounded himself.

Troop movements could be seen from *the other side of the valley*, from the Hill of Moreh and the hills on the north side of the Valley of Jezreel, as well as from vantage-points east of Jordan. The bad news caused a mass evacuation from Israelite towns in the region, so leaving them open to Philistine occupation.

8–10. Though Saul did not live to witness the scene, the Philistines did enjoy themselves at his expense; in particular, they made capital out of their victory by congratulating their gods, and by dedicating Saul's armour to become a trophy in *the temple of Ashtaroth*, in much the same way as Goliath's sword had been treasured in Israel's sanctuary (1 Sa. 21:9). The foreign deity had triumphed, and the decapitated body of Israel's anointed king was hung, exposed, on the city wall of Bethshan, the easternmost of the line of old Canaanite fortress cities across the country from the Mediterranean to the Jordan, which the Israelites had not conquered (Jos. 17:11). Excavation has established that from the fifteenth to the thirteenth century BC the city was under Egyptian control, and in the twelfth-century remains, anthropoid clay coffins, characteristic of the Philistines, indicate that Philistine garrisons were stationed there by the Egyptians. 'In level V (*c.* 11th century) two temples were uncovered, one (the S) dedicated to the god Resheph and the other to the goddess Antit, and Rowe has suggested that these are the temples of Dagon and Ashteroth in which Saul's head and armour were displayed by the Philistines . . .'[1] It remained in Philistine hands in the time of Saul, and we are reminded what a formidable enemy he had in these deeply entrenched and well-armed troops.

11–13. *The inhabitants of Jabesh-gilead*, remembering their debt to Saul, who had rallied the men of Israel and come to their aid when they were intimidated by Nahash the Ammonite (1 Sa. 11:5–11), took the opportunity to demonstrate their continuing loyalty to him. They removed the impaled bodies of Saul and his sons, risking their lives in so doing, took them back to Jabesh, and *burnt them there*. Burning the dead, apart from penal and sacrificial cases, is mentioned elsewhere only in Amos 6:10. There the reason is the contagion of a plague; similarly, in this situation there could have been a risk of infection from the quickly decomposing bodies.[2] The

[1] T. C. Mitchell, art. 'Bethshean, Bethshan', *IBD* 1, p. 190. A. Rowe was one of the excavators of the ancient site, 1925–1928.

[2] The change of wording suggested by Driver, on the grounds that the verb *sāraþ*, 'burn', had another meaning, 'to anoint with spices', though preferred by Hertzberg (p. 233), has not been widely adopted. It appears in the NEB, 'and anointed them there with spices' (v. 12).

intention, however, was to give these great ones of Israel a decent burial *under the tamarisk tree*, the place of importance, and a sacred site. Eventually the remains of Saul and his sons were removed to the family tomb (2 Sa. 21:12–14).

There was some consolation for Israel, therefore, in the circumstances of Saul's death. Though the Philistines became the victors, they were deprived of the satisfaction of torturing and deriding Israel's king. He died an honourable death, and his burial recalled his heroic leadership against Philistine aggression in his early days as king, when he had rescued the oppressed, and had won the allegiance of all the people. But there is no denying that between the initial victory at Jabesh-gilead and his burial there, Saul had been a tragic hero, whose career has been the subject of much artistic and literary work, as well as of theological debate. He had had so much going for him: his height gave him a commanding presence; he had been chosen by sacred lot and designated by a prophet of the Lord, and had won popular acclaim by his valour in avenging wrong. Israel recognized moral worth and appreciated those leaders who cared about the oppressed, as Saul had so manifestly done. The majority stood by him through thick and thin, continuing to fight alongside Saul but aware of David's valiant defensive action.

In assessing the tragedy of King Saul, Christian writers have usually thought of him as a foil to David. Whereas Saul's life was a failure in terms of his calling to kingship, David succeeded in defeating Israel's enemies, in organizing the kingdom and in setting up a dynasty; in short, he became a model for future generations, who were taught to look for an ideal society led by another David. Saul, by contrast, is a study in failure. But was this altogether his fault? Several writers have contended that Saul was dogged by a fate beyond his control, a viewpoint explored by David M. Gunn: 'Does Saul fail as king because of his own inner inadequacy as a human being, or because he is brought low essentially by external forces or circumstances?'[1] Gunn concedes that Saul contributes to his own downfall, most obviously by his jealousy, and by his refusal to accept the rejection of himself and

---

[1] Gunn 1980, p. 115. The very title of Gunn's book, *The Fate of King Saul*, is significant; *cf.* Fokkelman's subtitle to his second volume on the books of Samuel, *The Crossing Fates*.

his dynasty, but Gunn shows that the announcement of Saul's rejection had a bearing on his attitude to David: he was not going to hand over to anyone without a struggle. Thus the divine oracle given through Samuel increased the wariness and suspicion of Saul, making him increasingly hostile, not only to David, but also to his own son Jonathan, who supported David. In view of the explanatory note, 'Now the Spirit of the Lord departed from Saul, and an evil spirit from the Lord tormented him' (1 Sa. 16:14), the theological and moral implications should not lightly be dismissed.

Gunn is of the opinion that Saul saw what he calls 'the dark side of God', in much the same way as did Job:

> The story makes it absolutely clear that Saul's moodiness, his rancour, jealousy, and violence, are all provoked deliberately by Yahweh through the medium of an 'evil spirit' . . . If the story is to be assessed in moral or theological terms then it is beside the point to dispose of the evil spirit by explaining it as a primitive way of speaking of mental illness (cf., for example, Mauchline, 130.). The evil spirit points unambiguously to Yahweh's manipulation of Saul.[1]

This plain speaking demands careful consideration and assessment. Moreover Gunn continues, 'God can pour out his favour upon Israel, upon David, and even upon Saul; but he can also be unpredictably terrible, jealous of his own status, quick to anger and impatient of the complexities of human action and motivation.'[2]

It would probably not be far wrong to say that this is the impression of God that many people in our churches associate with the Old Testament. Does not the second commandment endorse the point: 'I the Lord your God am a jealous God . . .' (Ex. 20:5)? This aspect of God's character is not altogether missing even from the New Testament, where Ananias and Sapphira met with sudden and inescapable death for deceit (Acts 5:1–11), and sin received its immediate judgment in an alarming way. The condemnation of Elymas the sorcerer, who was struck with blindness (Acts 13:8–11), and the death of Herod Agrippa I, who had killed James and imprisoned Peter, was a divine judgment: 'an angel of the Lord smote him' (Acts 12:23). The possibility of rejection features in the teaching of

---

[1] Gunn 1980, p. 129.   [2] *Ibid.*, p. 131.

Jesus (Mt. 7:19, 23); the foolish man who built his house upon the sand of disobedience (Mt. 7:24–27) could even have been suggested by the example of Saul. There is danger in eliminating this theme of inescapable judgment from the Bible's total message. There is also the added mystery that we do not know why some people receive what seems to us humans to be peremptory treatment, while others have an easier life.

Despite all the evidence he has found to the contrary, Gunn concludes on this more reassuring note:

> Perhaps in the final analysis, even in this story, the 'light side' may be seen as dominating the picture – Yahweh is early portrayed as the God who, in long-suffering loyalty, stands by his people and delivers them from their enemies; who is a shepherd, a bulwark and a refuge for his servant David; whose hall-mark is good, *not* evil.[1]

The dark side has to feature in God's dealings with both David and Saul, as with all mankind. The astonishing sequel was that the darkness in all its depth was borne by Jesus on the cross, and did not overcome him. Saul did not have that knowledge to enable him to accept his 'fate', and keep faith with the prophet Samuel. Had he been able to take a rebuke, repent, and exercise his kingship alongside the young man who would eventually become king his place, Saul could have overcome the Philistines, and established the Israelite kingdom, as he was intended to do by the Lord who called him.

The evidence suggests that Saul had a brooding temperament, and was given to melancholy; it was easy for him to retreat from the limelight and become intensely jealous of a rival. But was his inherited temperament part of his 'fate'? It was a potent factor in Saul's life; but the text indicates that Saul was responsible for his deliberate, stubborn refusal to admit when he had done wrong, and humble himself in repentance. This stubborn streak in Saul brought about a rift in relationship with Samuel, which left the king without the spiritual support he needed, and this increased his isolation, depression, and fits of mania. Saul calls forth our sympathy because his human frailty reminds us of our own, but his failure was not inevitable: he was responsible for his rejection

[1] *Ibid.*, p. 131.

of instructions from the one who had appointed him king, and he paid the penalty.

Another aspect of Saul's experience is 'the deterioration of charismatic gifts into madness', in which 'we plumb to the depths of a human psyche'.[1] We know that 'the spirit of God came mightily upon him, and he prophesied' (1 Sa. 10:10), so fulfilling the prophecy of Samuel that he would 'be turned into another man' (1 Sa. 10:6). This sign of divine equipment for his future task of ruling over the Lord's heritage stood for the strength on which he was to depend when he was in office, a strength far exceeding his own. But later, after the rift with David, when the Spirit of God came upon Saul he was thereby prevented from harming David. The gifts of the Spirit were not permitted to be used to oppose the work of God. It may be that here lies the key to the disintegration of Saul's powers that so characterized his last years. Though in the eyes of many modern writers Saul appears to have been painted blacker than he really was,[2] there can scarcely be a more dangerous plight than to be found in opposition to God. This was where Saul's disobedience landed him. He may have been more upright than David, in terms of human standards of social behaviour, but the biblical writers judge first and foremost in terms of the first commandment: as a man is in the presence of his God, so is he. By that test Saul stood condemned.

Meanwhile, the Lord, who does not judge by outward appearance but looks on the heart, had been putting David through his paces.

[1] A point made, but not developed, by W. Lee Humphreys, 'The Tragedy of King Saul: A Study of the Structure of 1 Samuel 9 – 31', *JSOT* 6 (1978), p. 25.

[2] We have already made reference to Gunn, who considers that Saul was 'essentially an innocent victim of God' (Gunn 1980, p. 123). *Cf.* also J. A. Soggin, *Introduction to the Old Testament* (London: SCM Press, 1976), 'To the modern reader Saul might hardly seem to be a "sinner", and we might doubt whether his "sin" made much impression on the reader or hearer of that time' (p. 195).

III. THE REIGN OF DAVID (2 SAMUEL 1:1 – 20:26)

a. David's rise to power in Judah (1:1 – 4:12)

i. David receives news of Saul's death (1:1–16). David's fortunes, at a low ebb since he had been forced to take refuge with the Philistines years earlier (1 Sa. 29:3), had been only slightly improved by the successful sortie against the Amalekites. He and his men were still recovering from the battle, and still needed to restore their charred homes, when, on their third day back, they received news of the battle against the Philistines.

1–3. The messenger announced beforehand, by his dishevelled appearance, that he was the bearer of bad news, for torn garments and hair caked with soil were signs of mourning. By falling to the ground before David, he implies that he recognizes the new king, and he expects a reward for his service in running to Ziklag with the latest news from Israel's camp.

4–5. A general retreat, the death of many, including Saul and Jonathan, summarized the situation, but David wanted some verification concerning the death of the king and his son.

6–10. At this request the messenger, elaborating the story to ingratiate himself with David, as he thinks, misjudges the reaction of the one he wants to impress. The reader knows that his story does not tally with the events already recorded: Saul had not needed assistance in dying by his own spear. It was ironic that David had only just returned from fighting the Amalekites, and here was an Amalekite daring to admit that he had slain the king. In proof he produced the distinctive regalia of the king, his *crown*, which identified him even in battle, and his *armlet*, a royal bracelet, worn on the upper arm.

11–12. Far from rejoicing, David and his army plunged into mourning at the news they had received, expressing communally their grief at the disaster that had befallen the people of the Lord. Though forced out of Israel, David and his men still regarded themselves as part of *the house of Israel*, and there was no longer any need to make a pretence of having deserted to the Philistines.

13–16. The messenger repeated that he was an Amalekite, but resident in Israel; his father may have joined the household of a citizen of Israel, working for him on the farm. It is not clear whether he fought for Israel. Expecting now to receive a handsome reward for having served David's interests, the messenger was instead called to account for having presumed to kill *the Lord's anointed*. As a resident, he could hardly plead ignorance of the awe that surrounded the person of the king in Israel, and David regarded him as deserving death. Surely he would have known that David had studiously avoided putting Saul to death, on the grounds that he was the Lord's anointed and therefore sacrosanct. The death of the Amalekite would be accepted as just by Israelites generally; even if he had fabricated his killing of Saul, the man was condemned by his own mouth, and David would be cleared of possible suspicion of having rejoiced in the death of Saul.[1] Such a magnanimous attitude on the part of one who had suffered so much at Saul's hand is incomprehensible apart from a deep commitment to the Lord, whose covenant made costly demands, but who undertook to save those who trusted him. David had already learnt to live by faith in this God before ever he was anointed by Samuel (1 Sa. 17:36, 46–47), and he was not going back on it now.

Your blood be upon your head means 'the blood you have shed is the cause of your own death'. The themes of verse 1 recur in inverse order in verse 16, and David's slaughter of the Amalekites was completed by the judicial death of this one Amalekite.[2] Whereas Saul had incurred his rejection through Amalek, David has now triumphed over this persistent enemy, and vindicated the right by punishing sacrilege, for to kill the anointed of the Lord was to turn against the Lord himself. This was David's deep conviction, and should not be regarded as a cloak for political intentions. All the same, David's action was observed, remembered and recorded, and it had a bearing on his reputation, as it did on his acceptance as Israel's king, but that was incidental. David's motive in sparing Saul had been reverence for the one whom the Lord had chosen and anointed; neither he nor any other human being had the right

[1] A different view is taken, *e.g.*, by Mauchline, who thinks that the Amalekite's narrative rings true, and regards David as blameworthy for disregarding the man's 'honourable motives and humanitarian considerations' (p. 197). Hertzberg, on the contrary, believes that 'he [the Amalekite] receives the due reward of the plunderer of the battlefield' (p. 237). Different interpretations call for discernment on the part of the reader.

[2] So Fokkelman 1986, p. 645, '. . . who is not so much an individual but stands as an example for the detested tribe'.

to end the life of the anointed of the Lord, and so force the Lord's hand.

ii. David's lament (1:17–27). With this poetic outpouring of his distress, David's Philistine period is brought to a conclusion, and the way prepared for a new departure (2 Sa. 2:1), and a new phase in David's life. There are two verses of introduction before the poem begins.

17–18. *And David lamented*: whereas in verses 11 and 12 all the crowd lamented together, now David uses all his creative ability to express the overwhelming agony of bereavement.

Saul and Jonathan his son: why does the writer repeat this apparently redundant phrase (*cf.* vv. 4, 12)? Is it to draw attention to Jonathan's self-effacement to the end? He had shown great potential in fighting the Philistines (1 Sa. 13:3; 14:1–15); he had recognized a kindred spirit in David, and had submitted willingly to his hero, giving him all the support of which he was capable; yet he remained faithful to his father right to the last battle. He was a son of whom Saul should have been proud.

It should be taught to the people of Judah (*cf.* the NIV, 'and ordered that the men of Judah be taught this lament of the bow'): the contrast draws attention to the Hebrew text, which reads literally, 'And he said to teach the sons of Judah the bow' (Heb. *qāšet*), which makes good sense if 'the bow' is used as a title (*cf.* Jesus' use of 'the bush' to refer to Ex. 3 in Lk. 20:37). The RSV adopts the LXX reading and omits the noun. David already has in view his authority over Judah, and provides a text which will ensure that all his people learn and remember the significance of the history that has been enacted on Mount Gilboa. Though the Hebrew has 'sons of Judah', the lament is addressed also to the 'daughters of Israel' (v. 24), and the RSV is surely right to translate 'people of Judah'.

The Book of Jashar, meaning 'the upright', is mentioned also in Joshua 10:13; it evidently contained a collection of early poetry, commemorating outstanding events and providing a source-book for later writers of our Bible books. It was evidently known to the writer's contemporaries.

All poetry is best appreciated in its original language, and the subtleties of Hebrew make this especially true of Old Testament poems, which rely for much of their effect on assonance, brevity and word play: this lament is no exception. Since none of these can be reproduced in another language, some technical explanation is unavoidable if the force of the Hebrew is to be appreciated.

19. *Thy glory, O Israel* represents the first two words of a total of eight which form the introduction to the lament in Hebrew. No names are mentioned and 'the glory' (Heb. *haṣṣᵉbî*) has the second meaning 'gazelle' (used in 2 Sa. 2:18). The ambiguity here, and the tension created by such words as *slain* and *high places*, which would normally be the last to be conquered, makes the unconventional opening to a highly original lament: 'The gazelle, O Israel – on your heights it lies slain'.[1] By contrast, *How are the mighty fallen!* is simple, understandable, and the kind of phraseology that is expected, but the eight words taken together avoid the obvious and evoke the horrors of defeat in battle. Verse 19b, repeated in different combinations in verses 25 and 27, is a catch line which expresses the recurring grief that cannot adequately be expressed. At the technical level, it provides an indication of the structure of the poem.

20–21. Though he had been living among the Philistines, all David's sympathies were with Israel, and he could not bear to dwell on the thought that the news being conveyed to Philistine cities would be met with excited rejoicing. *Tell it not in Gath* is alliterative and therefore memorable in Hebrew (*cf.* Mi. 1:10, which suggests that the saying had become proverbial). The longer name, *Ashkelon*, lends itself to more expanded but parallel ideas. The two cities stand for the whole of Philistia.

David could picture the welcome home, with the women singing and dancing in praise of the victors in the same way that the Israelite women had welcomed David after the defeat of Goliath (1 Sa. 18:7). That the *uncircumcised* should *exult* over Israel's king was too painful to contemplate, and David calls for a double calamity to befall *Gilboa*, so that its landscape mourns in sympathy by becoming dry and unproductive.

Nor upsurging of the deep is a rather vain attempt to make sense of an enigmatic expression, which means literally 'nor fields of offerings' (AV; *cf.* the NIV's 'nor fields that yield

---

[1] The translation is that of Fokkelman 1986, p. 653. I am greatly indebted to his detailed study of David's lament.

offerings of grain') 'for Dagon' being implied. A possible translation, which keeps the sense parallel with the previous line,
is adopted by the NEB, 'no showers on the uplands', but it
means adding the words 'no showers'.[1] Judges 5:18 has a
similar expression, 'on the heights of the field'.

Having called for drought on the Gilboa hills, David comes
at last to the name of the king who has lost his life there, but
so painful is the subject that he approaches it obliquely, via
the shield of the mighty . . . the shield of Saul. What he could not
have brought himself to say about the king, he can say of the
shield: it *was defiled* with the blood and dirt of war, and it was
not anointed with oil. It would be somewhat prosaic for David
to refer to the practice of oiling the shield (both to keep it
bright and to cause missiles to glance off it), were it not for
the reference to 'anointed' (Heb. *māšîah*), which applies most
specifically to Saul, and by its sound even suggests his name.
'There the shield of mighty heroes was defiled – yes even the
shield of Saul, whose consecrated person shared the common
fate as though he had never been set apart as the Anointed
of Jehovah'.[2] Thus, by the use of metonymy, David has come
to the heart of his lament.

22–23. Memories of Jonathan and Saul at the height of
their powers come flooding back. They had been courageous
in battle: Jonathan, characteristically, with his *bow* (which
suggested, perhaps, the title of the lament), and Saul with his
sword, so that they *returned not empty* from battle, but brought
with them rich spoils. They were accustomed to victory.

Indeed David has almost changed his poem into a victory
song, so enthused is he as he contemplates how deeply beloved
and how lovable these two great men had been. But as he
uses the word *life,* the stab of pain that demands the word
death forces him to face reality. He finds cause for praise in
the togetherness of father and son, which the enemy has not
been able to destroy, and so introduces a small climax in the
middle of the lament. The two comparisons, *swifter than eagles,
stronger than lions,* evoke the wide open spaces, powerful movement and formidable strength. Saul and Jonathan had been
in a class apart.

24–25a. Thinking now specifically of Saul, David can only

[1] For a history of this interpretation of the Hebrew, see Fokkelman 1986,
p. 740.

[2] Kirkpatrick 1881, p. 55.

mourn, and he calls on the *daughters of Israel*, unlike the Philistine women (v. 20), to *weep* for Saul, who has *clothed* them all like king's daughters. *How are the mighty fallen*, repeating as it does verse 19b, takes us back to the beginning and shows how the poet has made that line into a refrain, and at the same time has filled out its meaning: 'the mighty' (Heb. *gibbôrîm*), though plural, relates to King Saul. Thus the women are to take their share in the lament for the one who fell *in the midst of the battle*, in costly self-giving.

25b–27. Now, at the beginning of this last section the identity of 'Thy glory' in verse 19 is subtly revealed. The 'gazelle', or as we might say the 'jewel' of Israel, was Jonathan, whose name is inserted in this repetition of the first line of the lament. David speaks directly to Jonathan now, the one he has wanted to honour from the beginning, and for the first time the first person verb is used, *I am distressed for you*. 'The poet finally expresses his own feelings and thus explicitly puts "me" face to face with "you" ', and repeats the words of verse 19a. 'The death of Jonathan has become the first and the last subject of the entire poem – an arrangement that speaks for itself.'[1] While David had called on others to weep for Saul, David was consumed with grief for *my brother Jonathan*, whom he addresses as though he were still living, a common illusion in bereavement. *Very pleasant* does not express sufficiently strongly what the poet is saying here; 'very dear' (NIV) captures the emotion with which David remembers Jonathan. Indeed, David had never experienced such love as Jonathan had shown him. He did not need to spell it out, for everyone knew that Jonathan, the heir to the throne, had not clung to his rights, but had voluntarily renounced them in favour of David, whom he had protected and encouraged through the years. And this renunciation had been no impulsive act, but an ongoing generous attitude of heart and mind: Jonathan had allowed his own interests to be disregarded, in order that David's could prosper. True, that kind of love David had found in the women of his life – his mother and his wives – but even their love was not to be compared with the love which had motivated Jonathan. While Saul had distributed gifts which tended to win him support (v. 24), Jonathan's selfless, transparent goodness had not even looked for reward,

[1] Fokkelman 1986, pp. 670–671.

hence David's superlative praise: *your love to me was wonderful, passing the love [even] of women.*

David has spoken to Jonathan, but now he must face reality: Jonathan is among *the mighty fallen.* The battle is over, *and the weapons of war perished.* For all David knows, these two great men are still lying untended on the war-torn slopes of Gilboa, their weapons useless beside them, impotent despite their destructive power. The scene is an eloquent and moving statement about human greatness, and brings to a fitting end David's poignant lament.

This, then, is the poem which David wanted all Judah to know by heart, and which was written in the nation's anthology of great events. Indeed, all the great families had a place in this lament, having supplied their own 'mighty men' to fight alongside Saul and Jonathan, and so it became their lament also. As the mourning women wept for their own sons and husbands, so they would weep for the king and his son. Such is the power of poetry, that the mountains of Gilboa are well known by name even in the twentieth-century materialistic West, yet the name occurs only in connection with Saul's last battle.[1] We, too, find ourselves caught up in a world of destruction and death, in which David's lament still plays its part in verbalizing the grief which can never find adequate expression.

Interestingly, David had assumed the role of interpreter of events to his people. His gifts were such that he could not suppress the urge to write, and no doubt he knew within himself that he would mould the thinking of Israel through his poetry as well as by his political skill as king. Above all, it is his spiritual perception which will give authority to his leadership, yet in the lament this is nowhere expressed. He does not even mention the name of God, nor does he suggest that God's providence has had any part in the events he commemorates. That would in the circumstances be inappropriate, but his silences are as eloquent as his words, and a suitable time will one day enable him to express with full conviction his assurance of God's faithfulness in guiding him throughout his life (*e.g.* 2 Sa. 22:31–32; 23:5).

The lament brings to an end the account of Saul's reign,

[1] Fokkelman 1986, p. 740, expresses surprise that the name occurs only in this connection in Scripture (1 Sa. 28:4; 31:1, 8; 2 Sa. 1:6, 21; 21:12; 1 Ch. 10:1, 8).

but at the same time marks the beginning of the reign of David.

iii. David king in Hebron (2:1–4a). The death of Saul was the signal for David's departure from Ziklag and Philistine vassaldom, but the best way to proceed was far from obvious. Saul had left sons and men of power over his army who were capable of asserting their authority, and who had the backing of those who had supported Saul. In particular, they could count on the loyalty of Saul's tribe, Benjamin. The Philistines had their outposts as far north and east as Beth-shean, and had established their military hold over Israel, driving a wedge between the northernmost tribes and the central area of Ephraim and Benjamin. Israel's territory east of Jordan was more or less intact, but the general picture was one of fragmentation and uncertainty in the absence of one commanding figure to establish a lead and unite the country.

1–3. *David inquired of the Lord*: without doubt he had a possible course of action in mind, but unlike Saul he was not relying on his own judgment alone. There were good reasons for him to move into the territory of *Judah*: it was geographically close at hand, it was the tribe to which he belonged, and he had had recent contact with 'his friends, the elders of Judah' (1 Sa. 30:26), who might be expected to welcome his approaches. When he consulted the priest Abiathar, who had the ephod (1 Sa. 23:9), the Lord's answer through the sacred lot confirmed that David should proceed to Judah, and, when the cities of Judah were named, it was Hebron that received the affirmative answer. Accordingly, Ziklag was abandoned. The wives and families of David and his men are mentioned to reinforce the fact that this is a final removal from Philistine territory, in favour of *the towns of Hebron*, settlements in the neighbourhood of the larger walled city.

4a. Hebron, with its importance in the Abraham narratives and its associations as the burial-place of the patriarchs, was the most distinguished of Judah's cities. David's arrival was the signal for the men of Judah to anoint him *king over the house of Judah*. Years before, Samuel had anointed David without disclosing the significance of his action; now, in a public ceremony, the divine intention was beginning to be fulfilled, but the event is referred to almost in passing. Much still has to be accomplished.

183

iv. David's embassy to Jabesh-gilead (2:4b-7). David, concerned to know whether Saul and his sons had been given a decent burial, received the information that the people of Jabesh-gilead had rescued their bodies and had given them honourable burial. David took it upon himself to express appreciation of their loyalty, and to assure them that it would not go unrewarded, either by the Lord or by himself. *I will do good to you* implies that he will soon be in control, and virtually invites this city, strategically placed on the east side of the Jordan, some eighty miles (129 km.) to the north of Hebron, to give him its allegiance as the people of Hebron have done. Though no reply is recorded, his diplomatic approach will have been appreciated and remembered.

v. The rival kingdom (2:8 – 3:1). The reason why the city of Jabesh-gilead was in no position to give active support to David now becomes apparent. It already had a king.

8–9. *Abner*, cousin of Saul and captain of his army (1 Sa. 14:50), took the initiative in establishing as successor to Saul his son *Ishbosheth*, a survivor of the battle in which his three older brothers had lost their lives. The account clearly conveys Abner as the power behind the king; nowhere is any reference made to the reaction of the people to this imposed ruler. His name, usually interpreted as meaning 'man of shame', is given in 1 Chronicles 8:33; 9:39 as 'Eshbaal', which has always been considered to be his original name. The word *ba'al*, meaning 'master', 'lord', was also the name of the Canaanite male deity, and so was avoided by the writer of our text. Eshbaal will have meant 'the Lord's man'. Ishbosheth may, however, mean 'man of strength'.[1]

Mahanaim, associated with Jacob (Gn. 32:1), was east of Jordan, probably near the Jabbok. In view of the Philistine occupation of the Gilboa range, and the Israelite withdrawal to the east of Jordan, the enthronement of Ishbosheth had to be at a safe distance from enemy lines. The territory over which he was regarded as king included, in addition to Gilead, northerly Ashur (probably Asher), and *Jezreel*, *Ephraim* and *Benjamin*, at the heart of Israel's territory, much of which was in Philistine hands; indeed *all Israel*, still had to be reclaimed.

---

[1] M. Tsevat, 'Ishbosheth and Congeners: The Names and Their Study', *HUCA* 46 (1975), pp. 71–87.

The declaration was an ideal rather than a reality.

10–11. Ishbosheth, who was younger than Jonathan, was *forty years old* when he began to reign, whereas David was thirty (2 Sa. 5:4). Since David and Jonathan appear to have been about the same age, this difference is surprising, and Saul's reign, which began when he was quite a young man, is not usually thought to have been a long one. Moreover, the length of the reign of Ishbosheth, *two years*, is hard to reconcile with the seven and a half years that David reigned in Hebron. It may be that there has been a mistake in the transmission of the text, as in 1 Samuel 13:1. The names Israel and Judah are used to refer to the kingdoms as they were known after the division of the kingdom (1 Ki. 12:16–17).

12–13. Stalemate between the opposing claimants to the throne was broken by Abner, who *went out* (on a military exploit) to the ancient city of *Gibeon*, close to Geba, from which Saul came. It had featured prominently in Joshua's conquest of Canaan, and was described in the account as 'a great city, like one of the royal cities' (Jos. 10:2). It is known today as el-Jib, 5½ miles (9 km.) north of Jerusalem, and therefore close to the border of Judah's traditional territory,[1] hence the active involvement of David's men, under the leadership of *Joab*. *The pool of Gibeon* was so famous that no explanation was needed. Even today there are two water systems to be seen which from the iron age onwards provided access to spring-water during time of siege. One of these, a cylindrical hole in the rock, about 37 ft. (over 11 m.) in diameter and over twice as deep, led by means of a staircase cut round the side of the pit and down into the rock below to a spring, which evidently at times filled the cavernous hole almost to the top. This, or the spring below, may have been the pool referred to.

14–17. What started as a competitive skirmish ended as a battle to the death. *Let the young men . . . play before us* is not easy to interpret. 'Young men' (Heb. *nᵉʿârîm*) refers in military contexts to professional soldiers (1 Sa. 21:2–5; 25:5; 26:22; 2 Sa. 16:2).[2] The verb *śāḥaq*, from which the name Isaac is

---

[1] The discovery during excavations of el-Jib between 1956 and 1959 of thirty-one jar handles bearing the name *gbʿn* established that this was the site of ancient Gibeon. *Cf.* J. B. Pritchard in M. Avi-Yonah (ed.), *Encyclopaedia of Archaeological Excavations in the Holy Land* (London: Oxford University Press, 1975), II, art. 'Gibeon', pp. 446–450.

[2] De Vaux, *Bible and ANE*, p. 130; Yadin, *Art of Warfare*, p. 267.

derived, means 'sport' and, in this context, 'take part in a tournament or duel' (*cf.* the NIV's 'fight hand to hand in front of us', though the verb nowhere else has this meaning). With twelve men on each side, some kind of contest was agreed upon, but swords were drawn and fatal wounds inflicted. It was not the kind of fight of which David would have approved, but it was remembered by the name given to the spot in Gibeon, Field of *Haṣṣurîm* or 'rocks', referring perhaps to the rock-like obstinacy of the individuals who fought there, as well as to the terrain. In Psalm 89:43, however, the same word is used to mean 'sword edge', hence the marginal reading, 'the field of sword-edges'; the other two suggestions arise from the LXX. The death of the young warriors caused the tournament to escalate into a full-scale battle, which ended in favour of David's men.

18–23. The three sons of David's sister, Zeruiah, made it their aim to follow up the victory by eliminating *Abner*, and so enabling David to become king of the whole of Saul's territory. *Asahel*, the youngest, was noted for his speed as a runner, *swift ... as a wild gazelle* (*cf.* the commentary on 2 Sa. 1:19, where the word 'glory' means 'gazelle'). Abner, the experienced warrior, knew his opponents well, and had no wish to kill Joab's brother, but was forced to do so in self-defence by the younger man's persistence. Abner suddenly stopped and pointed his spear behind him; Asahel could not prevent himself from running on to the spear, which pierced him through. He died instantly. His valiant exploit on David's behalf was so much appreciated that travellers coming to the spot *stood still* as a mark of respect.

24–28. In the heat of the battle, however, *Joab* and *Abishai* continued the pursuit after Abner, whose eastward route required a valley to take him towards the Jordan. The *hill of Ammah* and *Giah* are unidentified; *the wilderness of Gibeon* should probably read 'of Geba', for Geba, further east, is close to a ravine that leads down to the Jordan valley (*cf.* 1 Sa. 14:5). On a hill in that inhospitable country, Abner was able to rally his men behind him and confront his pursuers. His aim was to achieve some respite, hence his appeal to Joab to call off the chase. Joab's reply, *The men would have given up the pursuit ... in the morning*, needs the insertion of the word 'only' to give the sense; *i.e.* the men would not have stopped pursuing Abner until the morning (*cf.* NIV, GNB). Joab makes out that his men

186

could still have plenty of strength in reserve, but reluctantly, in response to a special request, Joab *blew the trumpet*, so signalling the end of the episode, for the time being.

29–3:1. Abner's men took the remainder of the night and half the next day to reach *Mahanaim*; they had the longer trek. The aftermath of the battle is recorded by David's supporters, who set their loss of twenty men in all against a much larger number in Abner's ranks. *Three hundred and sixty* dead implies an army of several hundreds, much larger than the account had led us to expect. Picking up Asahel's body on the return journey, they buried it in his family tomb at *Bethlehem*, in accordance with custom. The account is well authenticated by this and other local traditions and names, and by the memory that *the day broke upon them at Hebron*. Indeed the vivid detail suggests that it is the work of an eye-witness, who sees the significance for the future of the superiority of David's troops. It was a trend that continued (3:1), and a sign to those who believed of the unseen working of God's hand in history.

vi. David's sons and heirs (3:2–5). Already during David's reign at Hebron the state archives contained records of those who might qualify as heirs to his throne. Sons born later in Jerusalem are listed in 2 Samuel 5:13–16 (*cf.* 1 Ch. 3:1–9). Michal does not feature, because she bore no children. David's firstborn son is *Amnon*, whose death is recorded (2 Sa. 13:28–29) at the hand of the third in line of succession, *Absalom*, who was born to the daughter of a northern king. Between them came *Chileab*, who in 1 Chronicles 3:1 is called Daniel; nothing more is said about him, and he disappears from the scene. *Adonijah* was to make a bid for the throne when his father was dying (1 Ki. 1:5–53); simply on the grounds of seniority, he had a claim. David was ensuring that, even at this early stage, he would have a son to succeed him as king, and his household of six wives was a sign of prestige. It is not clear why the last-named, *Eglah*, is singled out as *David's wife*, as though the other five were not wives; probably nothing more than the avoidance of repeating the word 'wife' lies behind this.

vii. Abner defects to David (3:6–21). Estrangement between Abner and Ishbosheth was one element in the decline of Saul's successors, and it resulted in advantage to David.

6-7. Ishbosheth was aware that Abner was growing powerful at his expense, and he found occasion to challenge him when Abner helped himself to *Rizpah*, the concubine of Saul, whose sons were Mephibosheth and Armoni (2 Sa. 21:8). To take the wife or concubine of the late monarch was to appropriate his property and to make a bid for the throne, to judge from the conduct of Absalom (2 Sa. 16:22) and of Adonijah (1 Ki. 2:22). Abner repudiates the suggestion that he has designs on the throne, but though he makes light of the affair, he can hardly have been surprised that this construction was put on his action.

8-11. The anger of Abner at the accusation indicates his powerful position. *A dog's head of Judah* means a contemptible running dog of Judah; the NEB has 'Am I a baboon in the pay of Judah?', following Symmachus, a Greek translator of the third century BC, who sought to be idiomatic, but the Hebrew *keleb* means 'dog'. After all he has done for Ishbosheth, Abner takes offence that his conduct should be questioned; he implies that Ishbosheth owes everything to Abner's loyalty (Heb. *ḥesed*, 'faithfulness to a covenant', 'kindness'), as indeed he probably did. By way of retaliation, Abner will transfer his allegiance from the house of Saul to that of David, so accomplishing *what the Lord has sworn to him*. The word of Samuel to David, though spoken in the private family gathering (1 Sa. 16:5), and unrecorded except as Samuel's instruction from the Lord, had become widely known. Now even Abner, who had willingly flouted what he knew to be God's revealed purpose, finds himself helping to fulfil it. He knows that in the near future David will unite the kingdoms of Israel and Judah *from Dan to Beersheba*, the northern and southern extremities of the 'promised land'. Without the support of Abner, Ishbosheth becomes merely a puppet, powerless to oppose his general.

12-16. David was not caught off guard by the messengers Abner sent to him. He was being invited to enter into a covenant with a man who was betraying his master, and who claimed to have the power *to bring over all Israel* to David. Such a ruthless leader threatened to be a rival to David in future. For this reason David had his condition ready: *bring first Michal, Saul's daughter*. He had fought for her (1 Sa. 18:27), she had been given to him in marriage, and, though she had been given to another man, he had the right to demand her return.

It was a shrewd political move, because the presence of Saul's daughter as his wife would give to David a strong claim to the throne of Saul, while a son would unite the two houses, but it was also a bold move to approach the reigning king direct with such a request. David had read the situation aright: he was not rebuffed. Ishbosheth, flattered perhaps to have been given his royal status instead of having the usual intervention of Abner, complied and arranged for Michal to be escorted to David. *Paltiel*, called Palti in 1 Samuel 25:44, her husband, accompanied her as far as *Bahurim*, a village on the north-east side of Jerusalem (*cf.* 2 Sa. 16:5; 19:16), where Abner ordered him home. No sympathy was permitted for Michal nor for her stricken husband; affairs of state had to take precedence over personal feelings.

17–19. Abner fulfilled David's condition, by seeing to it that Michal went on to join David, but Abner himself convened a conference of elders representing the northern tribes. Benjamin, sandwiched between north and south, he consulted separately, on his way south to Hebron (v. 19), for Saul's own tribe needed specially sensitive handling. Abner's assertion that there had been a general demand of David's kingship may simply have been an example of his strategy in public relations. His suggestion made compliance the obvious next step, while his quotation of the Lord's promise, made originally concerning Saul (1 Sa. 9:16), gave religious authority to Abner's proposal. This divine pronouncement concerning David is not recorded apart from Abner's use of it. Having obtained a unanimous agreement, Abner was ready to return to David.

20–21. David received the delegation under Abner's leadership with royal hospitality, and was all prepared to become king of the northern tribes when Abner returned with their representatives to Hebron. Mutual trust and respect between David and Abner was growing so that *he went in peace* and safety (with 'safe conduct', NEB).

viii. The death of Abner (3:22–39). 22–25. The arrival of *the servants of David* with Joab when Abner's visit was still the latest news introduced a protest group that had to be reckoned with. Courtiers who were uneasy at David's new alliance knew they would find a champion in Joab. There were two good reasons: Abner had killed Joab's brother,

Asahel, albeit unwillingly and in self-defence (2 Sa. 2:22–23), and in addition Joab would have recognized in Abner a rival for high office in David's court. Full of indignation, he rushed into the king's presence and criticized the policy David had adopted, accusing him of naïvety in trusting the motives of an erstwhile enemy. The fact that no response is recorded may indicate that David was having second thoughts which caused him to be influenced by Joab's strong assertions, but Joab was exceeding his office in taking it upon himself to counter the decisions of the king and frustrate his intentions. To do so was virtually to assume royal power, and a lesser man than David would have dealt accordingly with Joab.[1] Perhaps afterwards he wished he had punished Joab (*cf.* 1 Ki. 2:5, 32).

26–30. The text specifically says that *David did not know about* Joab's messengers, sent to fetch Abner back from *the cistern of Sirah*, which is probably the modern Ain Sarah, a mile and a half (2.5 km.) north-west of Hebron. Joab acted with all speed. He met Abner at the gate of Hebron and treacherously killed him in cold blood *for the blood of Asahel his brother*. Joab would probably have justified his action on the grounds of the ancient system of family obligations (Heb. *gō'ēl*; *cf.* Nu. 35:16–21). The 'avenger of blood' had to see that the murderer was himself put to death, and Abner was aware of the possible implications of his deed (2 Sa. 2:22), but Asahel had been put to death in the aftermath of war, and it is questionable whether in such a case the avenger of blood had any such obligation. David indeed implies that Joab and Abishai his brother, who is later implicated (v. 30), were both guilty of shedding the blood of Abner without cause, while David declared himself *guiltless before the Lord*, an expression that David would not use lightly. The curse for which he calls to be on the house of Joab as well as on Joab himself is frightening: *one who has a discharge* would be perpetually unclean and therefore debarred from worship (Lv. 15:2), as would the *leprous* person. One *who holds a spindle* implies a

---

[1] Hertzberg raises the question 'whether Joab did not from the beginning have a secret understanding with David or at least whether Abner did not "die very opportunely" for David' (p. 261). Undoubtedly David came under suspicion, and he was sensitive about the possible charge of complicity, but the account implies that David's understanding with Abner was made in good faith. It was Joab's arrival that brought about its reversal, so Joab takes the blame.

disability that required a sedentary occupation (*cf.* 'or who leans on a crutch', NIV). These five afflictions would be signs of the Lord's righteous judgment on Joab's action, and future generations would note how the curse was fulfilled.

31–39. David put Joab in his place by ordering him to take part in the official mourning for Abner. Since he was the cause of the death, it was out of keeping that he should wear *sackcloth* as though he grieved for the loss of this man. The anomaly would not be missed by the crowds, who would see that David had not condoned the action of his general. David's desire to honour the memory of Abner was displayed by his place as first mourner in the funeral procession, by the fact that he led the expressions of grief, and by the poem he composed for the occasion.

In this lament David displays once more his originality as a poet. In the brief compass of four lines, he captures the pathos of this untimely death by likening it to the execution of a criminal. There is a correspondence of form and content between lines 1 and 4, 2 and 3, making an aesthetically satisfying pattern of thought (a, b, b, a) which conveys all that needs to be said. *Should Abner die as a fool dies?* The great man with so much potential had died like a 'fool' in the sense that the Bible uses the word: like a rebel against God and his law, hence 'the lawless' (NIV). He had been put to death like a criminal, yet he was nothing of the sort. Addressing him directly, David declared Abner's freedom from handcuffs and chains: a free man, he fell *as one falls before the wicked*, a direct reference to Joab, yet refraining from calling him a murderer. Joab had sufficient justification in the social laws to clear him of that accusation, while Abner should have been astute enough to be on his guard in the light of the death of Asahel. David said just enough to convey his own regret at what had happened and to express the public grief, without incriminating anyone else in a capital crime.

David was careful to match his words by his deeds. Not for him the funeral feast when he was in mourning, and the king's abstinence *pleased all the people*, who appreciated this sign of genuine feeling in their leader. Indeed, *all Israel* got the message that the death of Abner *had not been the king's will*. If there had been any hint that Joab had acted with David's connivance, even David would not have escaped the condemnation of a discerning populace. All the same, David left

191

nothing to chance, and the words of the king to his servants were no doubt meant for mass consumption and quotation: *Do you not know that a prince* (Heb. *śar*) *and a great man has fallen this day in Israel?* Moreover, David found himself *weak*, in the sense that he could not accomplish what he wanted to do because his plans were thwarted by Joab and his brother. The task of keeping within bounds these headstrong soldiers was one of David's recurring difficulties, and his complaint, *the sons of Zeruiah are too hard for me*, becomes almost a refrain (*cf.* 2 Sa. 16:10; 19:22). These relatives of his took too much upon themselves, acting without the king's authorization and against his wishes. As he had done in respect of Saul, David looked to the Lord to work out his justice in the matter. He felt sufficiently secure in his throne not to take punitive action on his own account.

ix. The downfall of Saul's house (4:1–12). Once Abner was dead, the end of resistance to David's rule came swiftly, and to that extent Joab's initiative had benefited David. Ishbosheth had depended, albeit unwillingly, on Abner's ability, and without him found he could not maintain his position as king.

1–3. The death of Abner was the turning-point, not only for Ishbosheth, but also for Israel as a whole. There was nothing to stop ruthless men taking advantage of the power vacuum, and asserting their own self-assigned authority. In this connection we are introduced to two soldiers in the employ of the Israelite king: *Baanah* and *Rechab*, experienced leaders of guerrilla bands, and, as Benjamites, trusted supporters. The details concerning *Rimmon*, their father, from the town of *Beeroth* on the northern border of Benjamin/Ephraim, have every appearance of being a contemporary note, prompted by the need to explain that the original Canaanite inhabitants fled from Beeroth to *Gittaim* (site unknown, but in view of the fact that Gittaim is the plural of Gath, it may have been in Philistia), to avoid harassment. In the time of Joshua, Beeroth had been allied to Gibeon, and therefore Joshua permitted the Canaanite inhabitants to remain unharmed (Jos. 9:16–21). It would not have been surprising if the non-Israelite inhabitants had murdered Ishbosheth, but the writer includes a reminder that this was not the case. The tribe of Benjamin had taken over the place, and at the time of this event it was a couple of Benjamites who had risen against their own leader.

4. A note of Saul's grandson is slipped in here. Though it interrupts the narrative, it is not entirely out of place in a chapter that is concerned with Saul's successors, and it introduces Jonathan's son *Mephibosheth*, whom David would honour (2 Sa. 9:1–13). The fact that he was handicapped and physically incapable of going to war made him an unlikely contender for the throne.

5–8. Ishbosheth appears to have had no suspicion that he might have traitors among his troops. The easy access these two men had to the person of the king is astonishing; even an ordinary household could be expected to be more security-conscious, especially during the afternoon rest hour. There are textual differences concerning the details. In verse 6 the RSV follows the LXX, whereas the AV, RV and NIV, following the Hebrew, make no mention of the sleeping doorkeeper: 'They went into the inner part of the house as if to get some wheat, and they stabbed him . . .' (NIV). The NIV makes good sense of the following verse by making it explanatory: 'They had gone into the house . . . After they stabbed and killed him, they cut off his head.' Even so, the text does appear repetitive, though Hebrew style favours such expansive additions. The motive for the murder is obscure, unless it was to curry favour with David, who was clearly going to be king of all Israel. The two men hastened to carry their trophy, dead Ishbosheth's head, to David at Hebron, travelling by way of the *Arabah*, the dry rift valley of the Jordan and Dead Sea, to avoid meeting other travellers. Their claim, *The Lord has avenged my lord the king*, was presuming on God's approval of their deed, as though they had acted on the Lord's express orders.

9–12. They had completely misread the policy of David, who immediately disowned them. His opening words, *As the Lord lives*, assert not only his commitment to the Lord but also his faith in the Lord's direct involvement in the outcome of daily events. David implicitly rejects the hypocrisy of Rechab and Baanah in claiming to be the Lord's executioners; he testifies that the Lord *has redeemed* [*his*] *life out of every adversity*, for David had not taken the initiative to rid himself of Saul, and he had not permitted others to do so. If these two were after a reward, they should know that David rewarded with

193

death the one who carried the news that Saul was dead, and their cold-blooded murder deserved at least the same sentence. Ishbosheth he describes as *a righteous man,* for though he was Saul's son he was not personally involved in his father's guilt, and had done nothing to deserve death. The two men are punished by death, mutilation, and public exposure as a warning to others. The head of Ishbosheth is given a suitable burial in the grave of his general, Abner.

The murder of Ishbosheth is a further example of the interference of opportunists, who prevented David from pursuing to the end the policy on which he had set his heart. Yet the outcome was to make possible the extension of David's kingdom to all Israel. Evidently David was cleared of any suspicion in connection with the death of Ishbosheth and, in the absence of any suitable survivor of the house of Saul, David was the obvious choice for king.

b. David king over all Israel (5:1 – 9:13)

i. David's covenant with Israel (5:1–5). Abner had already prepared the way for the elders of the northern tribes, including Benjamin, to make David their king (2 Sa. 3:17–19). Though Abner did not live to see the ceremony, the representatives of the tribes of Israel appear to have lost no time in assembling at Hebron to swear allegiance to David (v. 3). They explain their decision on three counts: i. the ties of kinship are strong (*cf.* Dt. 17:15); ii. David has already proved himself as a military leader under Saul (1 Sa. 18:30), and on his own account when Saul was after his blood; iii. most impressive of all, he had divine approval. Now he had won the confidence of the people, and the providential sequence of events which led up to this occasion confirmed the prophetic oracle which, though not previously recorded in the book, seems to have been widely known (*cf.* 2 Sa. 3:9–10).

You shall be shepherd of (lit. 'you will shepherd') *my people*: the symbol of the shepherd to represent the duties of a ruler was widely used in the ancient Near East.[1] In the Old Testa-

[1] 'In the ancient East, shepherd at an early date became a title of honour applied to divinities and rulers alike. This usage is found in a stereotyped form in the Sumerian king-lists, in Babylonian courtly style and in the pyramid texts (the books of the dead). The custom was followed throughout antiquity,' E. Beyreuther, 'Shepherd', *NIDNTT* 3, p. 564.

ment the word 'shepherd' (Heb *rō'eh*) describes the Lord's care of his people in the early poetry of Genesis 49:24 (*cf.* Gn. 48:15), as well as in the Psalms. The consciousness that the Lord was the shepherd of Israel (Pss. 23; 74:1; 77:20; 78:52; 80:1; 95:7) meant that Israel's human shepherds had before them the highest possible model of faithfulness, justice and loving kindness. By their exercise of these qualities they were judged.

King David made a covenant with them . . . before the Lord; the covenant agreement was made on the basis of the 'shepherd' model, which guarded against the oppression commonly associated with kingship (1 Sa. 8:10–18), but on the part of the people ensured their loyal support. The exact wording of such a covenant has not survived.

They anointed David king over Israel: the event is soon over and even more quickly recounted, but it marked the end of a long patient wait for God's time, and the start of a life-work to which David had been anointed in private many years earlier (1 Sa. 16:6–13). Now the public anointing sets him apart as 'the Lord's anointed', chosen and equipped by the calling and gifts of the Lord God himself to be king over the whole people of Israel.

A chronological note gives an overview of the outworking of David's reign. *Thirty years old* was regarded as an ideal age at which to take on responsibility (*cf.* Nu. 4:3; Lk. 3:23), and a *forty*-year reign does seem to have been considered a norm (Jdg. 3:11; 5:31; 8:28; 1 Sa. 4:18; 1 Ki. 11:42), but the figure could still be an exact one for David's reign. The breakdown of the two parts of his reign shows that the writer intended the figure to be taken literally. He has not previously mentioned Jerusalem, but takes this opportunity of recording another far-reaching move on David's part, the capture of this strategic city, which thus far had remained independent.

ii. David makes Jerusalem his city (5:6–16). This event may have followed the defeat of the Philistines, described in verses 17–25; once David had been proclaimed king over all Israel, the Philistines ceased to tolerate his exploits and saw him as a serious threat to their power. It made good sense that they should attack without delay (v. 17), and therefore David is unlikely to have had opportunity first to take the

Jebusite citadel.[1] Nevertheless, the capture of Jerusalem was so important and far-reaching an event that in the mind of the writer it was given pride of place, not least because the reversal of past failures (Jos. 15:63; Jdg. 1:8, 21) set the seal of divine favour on David.

The description of David's highly original method of taking the city is cryptic, and difficult to interpret, though excavation of the site of the Jebusite city has helped a little (see the Additional Note: 'Excavation of ancient Jerusalem', pp. 199–202).

6. *The king and his men* suggests that David took the relatively small army which had supported him in his fugitive days; loyal and resourceful, they could be depended upon to vie with each other in achieving the impossible.

The *Jebusites* were one of the minority peoples of Canaan, frequently mentioned in connection with Jerusalem, which was also known as Jebus (Jdg. 19:10). *The inhabitants of the land* would be better translated 'of the area' (*cf.* 'the Jebusites, who lived there', NIV; the Hebrew *hā'āreṣ*, 'the land', can mean anything between 'the locality' and 'the earth', depending on the context). The Jebusite defenders of the city considered themselves impregnable, *You will not come in here.* The wedge-shaped site consisted of a ridge, rising towards the north, with a slope on the west towards the Tyropoeon valley, and an even steeper and longer slope down on the eastern side to the Kidron. A city wall of heavy stones protected the citadel, and from the top stones could easily be rained down on attackers, even by *the blind and the lame.* As we might say, it was child's play.

7. *David took the stronghold of Zion* against all the odds, and in view of the fact that he had masterminded the operation it was appropriate that Jerusalem should have become his property, *the city of David.* The name is in use today in connection with the archaeological excavations on the south-eastern hill of Jerusalem, south of the Temple Mount. This was the area previously known as the stronghold of *Zion* (meaning uncertain, perhaps 'eminence'), not to be confused with modern Mount Zion, which is further west. The Jebusite city was a fortified area encircling a citadel, whose water supply

[1] Bright, p. 194, records the Philistine battles before David's capture of Jerusalem. Y. Aharoni, *The Land of the Bible* (London: Burns and Oates, 1967), p. 260, on the other hand, retains the order of events in 2 Sa. 5.

was the spring of Gihon, near the base of the eastern slope.[1]

8. Having established the most important fact that David made the city his own, the writer allows himself a brief account of the method by which the stronghold was captured. Unfortunately there are uncertainties as to the exact meaning of the text here. The RSV interprets the challenge as *get up the water shaft* (Heb. *ṣinnôr*), an ancient and attractive translation, which makes good sense because there were natural channels in the limestone rock through which it could have been feasible to enter the city, but the word is rare and occurs elsewhere in Scripture only in Psalm 42:7, where it is translated 'cataracts'. The NEB's 'let him use his grappling-iron' (*cf.* NIV mg., 'use scaling hooks') is based on the LXX 'dagger'. A recent scholar has claimed that 'The *ṣinnor* . . . should be understood as the fortress'.[2] The traditional understanding, 'water channel', remains possible, and is perhaps the most likely translation. The verb translated 'get up' (Heb. *nāgaʿḇ*) usually means 'to touch'; this interpretation requires therefore what S. R. Driver called 'a questionable paraphrase'.[3] Nevertheless the verb has the meaning 'assault' in 2 Samuel 14:10. The situation called for an unusual activity, so we should not be surprised at an unusual use of words, but the fact is that this verb does not at present enable scholars to arrive at certainty as to what the activity was.

Having entered the city by some surreptitious means, David's men were to deal with his enemies, who are described in the terms used by the Jebusites of the defenders of their city; *who are hated by David's soul* needs to be understood in context, and is better translated 'to reach those "lame and blind" who are David's enemies' (NIV). The remainder of the verse is an additional note, which could well be in brackets, explaining the origin of a commonly accepted saying. *The house*

---

[1] The settled area of the hill was 'about 60 dunams in extent', Y. Shiloh, *Excavations at the City of David 1978–1982*, Qedem Monograph (Jerusalem: Hebrew University, 1984), 1, p. 3, but since in peacetime habitations grew up outside city walls, the citadel itself is likely to have been smaller than this, not more than a couple of acres.

[2] For this information I depend entirely on an abstract in *OTA* 9.1, Feb. 1986, of V. Scippa, 'Davide Conquista Gerusalemme', *BeO* 27 (1985), pp. 65–76. He evidently supports this from Aram. *ṭinnār*, 'fortress', and the *Tg. Ps–J. kĕrakkā*': 'Whoever will strike the Jebusite and touch (*i.e.* assault) the fortress . . .'.

[3] Driver 1913, p. 199.

could be either the Temple or the palace, neither of which was in existence at the time, but association of ideas connected the saying with this incident. What happened to the original inhabitants of the citadel is not mentioned.

9–10. At last David was in a position to take up permanent residence in a city which he had conquered, and which had no established connections with any one tribe. As *the city of David*, it transcended tribal rivalries and therefore made possible a new concept of unity by providing as a focal point a capital, which has continued to this day to capture the imagination of Abraham's descendants. But first the foundations needed to be secured. *The Millo* is a transliteration of the Hebrew word, the meaning of which is probably 'supporting terraces' (NIV). The Jebusite city walls were built on the slopes of the hill, which was particularly steep on the west side, hence the need to have secure buttresses resting on terraces, which would not slide (even imperceptibly) downwards towards the valley. Even within the city there was more levelling in order to make building possible. David evidently turned his attention to this substructure early in his occupation of Jerusalem.

Ultimately David's continuing progress was to be attributed, not to his undoubted gifts, but to his spiritual resources: *the Lord, the God of hosts, was with him*. The divine name, *Yahweh, 'elōhê ṣ'bā'ôt*, is a variation of *Yahweh ṣ'bā'ôt* (*cf.* the commentary on 1 Ša. 1:3–8). David, borne along by the presence of the God of all authority and power, could not but grow in importance, as did his city: 'God is in the midst of her, she shall not be moved . . . The Lord of hosts is with us . . .' (Ps. 46:5, 7, 11). Though Israel did at times misapply this truth and presume upon it, so that the prophets had to threaten destruction (*e.g.* Je. 7:1–4, 13–15), truth it remained. 'God with us', Immanuel, was no empty triumphalism (Is. 7:14; Mt. 1:23; 28:20).

Two pointers are included to ways in which David would consolidate his hold on his new capital. One concerned foreign relations and the other sons and heirs.

11–12. *Hiram king of Tyre*: Tyre, an important port which already at the time of David had for centuries been trading in the eastern Mediterranean, made friendly overtures to David, who was beginning to win respect beyond Israel's borders. The hinterland of Tyre was noted for its cedars, and the port boasted skilled workers in wood and stone, some of whom were loaned to David. They took a gift of cedar wood and constructed the palace in Jerusalem.

Foreign recognition was indeed a new development; David was conscious of the encouragement this offered, but the writer notes that David put it down to the Lord's doing *for the sake of his people Israel*, not for the sake of David personally. This awareness of the Lord's concern for all his people kept David from exaggerating his own importance (Dt. 17:20) and from extravagant policies involving oppressive taxation.

13–16. If David knew Deuteronomy 17:17, he interpreted it in a way that permitted him to keep a harem, in the manner of oriental monarchs.

More concubines and wives . . . more sons and daughters: in the parallel passage (1 Ch. 14:3), no mention is made of concubines because their sons would not have been reckoned in the succession to the throne, and that may be the reason why concubines are mentioned before wives in our text, which includes the former for the sake of completeness, but dismisses them because the subject in question is the order of inheritance. The first six in that order were listed in 2 Samuel 3:2–5; of the eleven mentioned here, only two reappear. Surprisingly, the tenth son, Solomon, succeeded as king, while his brother, Nathan, is named in the genealogy of Joseph (Lk. 3:31). Both were sons of Bathsheba (1 Ch. 3:5).

Additional Note: Excavation of early Jerusalem

The spring Gihon, in the Kidron Valley, is the clue to the identification of the earliest city, which was built on the ridge above its water supply. It was in an effort to trace the tunnels and shafts connected with this spring that excavations early in the twentieth century were conducted by M. Parker (1909, 1911) and R. Weil (1913–1914), and in 1923–1925 the Palestine Exploration Fund sponsored extensive excavations under the direction first of R. A. S. Macalister and J. G. Duncan, and then of J. W. Crowfoot. Though small areas were opened up on the summit of the hill and on its western slope in an attempt to locate the ancient walls, the results were at that time inconclusive. All these excavations were outside the walls of the present city, on the spur of the hill which runs approximately southwards from the eastern end of the south wall, to the east of Dung Gate; this area was rightly surmised as being

ADDITIONAL NOTE

the site of the citadel conquered by David.

The water supply

The earliest water supply was identified during the Parker expedition by L. H. Vincent. A vertical shaft through the rock, already discovered in 1867 by Captain Charles Warren, gave access to water in a tunnel from the spring, and the shaft was reached from above by means of steps. In normal times women would no doubt walk out of the city to fetch water, but whenever danger threatened it would have been reassuring to have supplies accessible, especially in the case of siege, without any risk to life. Other cities, such as Megiddo, Hazor, Gibeon and Gezer, had similar systems. In the nature of the case dating is difficult, but they are generally thought to have been cut first during the Late Bronze Age.[1]

At Jerusalem two shafts began at the same opening into the hill, but one of them came to a sudden end, stopped by a stratum of very hard rock. The other became:

> a stair-case down to a platform, which led into a horizontal semi-circular tunnel at a level about half-way down to the spring. At the end of the tunnel is another shaft going further down into the mountain. The bottom of this shaft ends in what was then a water-filled channel which leads to the spring Gihon . . . by lowering a bucket down the last shaft, the Jebusites could reach the water.[2]

If this work was accomplished by the Jebusites, as Shanks suggests, there must have been some military threat to the city for such elaborate engineering feats to be attempted, and

[1] At Hazor Y. Yadin excavated 100 metres of tunnels which formed a network under the lower city. These dated from the Middle Bronze period. Evidently tunnelling technology had been developed long before the Iron Age (Y. Yadin, *Hazor* [Oxford: Oxford University Press, 1972], p. 43). In the upper city a large underground reservoir with inlets that drained water from the surface belonged to LB I or MB II (p. 127), but this was not connected to a spring, as was the system at Jerusalem. The elaborate tunnel and shaft water system at Megiddo 'must have been cut in the first half of the ninth century . . . most probably by Ahab' (p. 164). The fully developed water system at Hazor dates from the first half of the ninth century BC (p. 178), when it was necessary to prepare to withstand a long siege. Y. Shiloh, however, dates the first water system in Jerusalem, as at other royal centres, to the reign of David (Shiloh, *Excavations at the City of David*, pp. 24, 27).

[2] H. Shanks, *The City of David, A Guide to Biblical Jerusalem* (Tel Aviv: Bazak, 1973), p. 29.

it could be that the entrance of the Israelites into Canaan posed such a threat. By achieving their aim to have a water supply during attack and siege, the Jebusites felt secure against David's onslaughts, some two hundred years later. It would be another two hundred years before the Assyrian threat drove King Hezekiah to excavate another tunnel to take water from Gihon to Siloam, where it could be collected and stored.

From the Spring Gihon the first sixty-five feet (20 m.) of tunnel, reused by Hezekiah, are the work of the Jebusites, and can still be visited. At this point Hezekiah's tunnel goes off to the left, whereas the Jebusite tunnel goes straight ahead to a point where the Jebusite shaft comes down, though it is now blocked off. This shaft, about forty-nine feet (15 m.) deep, is the rock-climb that David's men would have had to scale to enter the city by the tunnel and steps above. Though extremely difficult, it was the kind of exploit that would appeal to David's mighty men, and, like commando troops today, they needed to have opportunity to achieve the 'impossible'. Kathleen Kenyon's considered opinion was:

> There is every reason to suppose that this is the method by which the Jebusites had access to the spring in time of war, and that it was the means whereby the capture of the town by David was achieved. The position of the head of the shaft would be inside the town, while the spring would be outside the walls.[1]

Once one man had pioneered a way the rest of the troops would follow until a sufficient number could make their surprise attack inside the city.

The city walls

During early excavations in this area of Jerusalem, a city wall had been located on the crest of the ridge. This raised a problem in relation to the water channels and shaft, because the tunnel entrance was nearly thirty yards (27 m.) outside this wall. It was this anomaly, among others, that Kathleen Kenyon had in mind when she undertook her excavations there in 1961, which culminated in 1967. At a point over fifty-

[1] K. Kenyon, *Royal Cities of the Old Testament* (London: Barrie & Jenkins, 1971), p. 26.

two yards (48 m.) further east and lower down the slope she located this older wall. 'The dating evidence was clear. It was originally built c. 1800 BC. It was still in use in the 8th century BC, and must therefore have been the wall of the Jebusite town that was captured by David, and that was thereafter repaired by him as the wall of his own city.'[1] She surmised that a gate leading to the spring was likely to have been situated in approximately the point at which she was excavating, close to the present path down to the spring from the summit, but she was not able to verify this possibility.

Excavation in the City of David began again in 1978, under the direction of Yigal Shiloh, of the Institute of Archaeology of the Hebrew University in Jerusalem. Some twelve areas have been opened up, including one which continued the excavation of the Jebusite city wall:

> The wall has been exposed by the present expedition for a length of 90m., and some 20m. more were revealed by Kenyon ... This location was suitable mainly from the topographical aspect of the bedrock, which forms a scarp here, at the middle of the slope – and the wall was built atop it.[2]

No further evidence of a gate into the city appears to have come to light as yet.

As excavations continue, clarification of some of the controversial issues may be expected. Meanwhile, what is not in doubt is the site of the Jebusite city, its water supply at the spring, and its fortified wall, half way up the hillside. The fact that the spring gushed forth its waters in a cave made its protection from the enemy in time of war reasonably simple; once the water could be obtained from inside the city, the cave mouth could even be blocked up. Once David had conquered the city it remained the capital of the Judean kings until the armies of the Babylonians proved too powerful for it in 587 BC.

iii. David twice defeats the Philistines (5:17–25). So long as David was king only of Judah, the Philistines were content to tolerate his rule, but when he was proclaimed king of all Israel he became too powerful to be trusted, hence these

---

[1] *Ibid.*, pp. 26–27. [2] Shiloh, *Excavations at the City of David*, p. 28.

two concerted efforts to divide his territory, and so weaken his effectiveness. *The valley of Rephaim* is within sight of Jerusalem, among the precipitous hills to the south-west of the city (see map on p. 222). Whether or not the capture of the Jebusite city had already taken place, the Philistines were attacking at the point where David's kingdom was arguably at its weakest, for this was an area which the Israelites had not been able to hold, and David had not yet had time to build up his defences. Furthermore, this northern border of Judah was adjacent to Benjamin, the tribe from which Saul came, and from the enemy point of view it made good sense to exploit any uncooperative elements in David's newly extended kingdom.

The importance of these two battles was obvious, not only to those who lived through them, but also to future generations in Israel. Had the Philistines been successful in defeating David at the beginning of his reign over the united tribes, it is doubtful whether he would have been able to command the allegiance which brought him to eminence among the peoples of the region. Isaiah was able to make passing reference to the event and expect it to be immediately meaningful, more than two centuries later (Is. 28:21). For Israel it must have had all the emotional overtones that Trafalgar has for the British, together with the awesome sense of God's overruling associated with the evacuation from Dunkirk, the Battle of Britain and with the D-day landings during the Second World War. This was one of Israel's remarkable deliverances.

17–18. *All the Philistines* united against David, as they appear to have done against Saul, but this time there is emphasis on their total mobilization. David was an even tougher enemy than Saul had been. *Went up in search of David* sounds as though they were still thinking of David as a lone fighter, with a small bodyguard, whom they could locate and kill. Indeed, David's retreat to *the stronghold* suggests that his tactics were to resort to the kind of guerrilla warfare to which he had been accustomed. It is not possible to know which of the many strongholds (Heb. *mᵉṣādôt*) mentioned in 1 Samuel 23:14 is intended here (*cf.* 1 Sa. 24:22).[1]

19–20. *David inquired of the Lord*: he lived by his faith, and expected guidance in matters concerning the kingdom which

[1] The word for 'stronghold' is well known today as the name of the mountain near the Dead Sea, made famous by Herod and by the massacre that took place at Masada in AD 73.

he believed the Lord had given him. To both of his questions the oracle gave an affirmative answer. He could be assured of victory. The name of the place, *Baal-perazim*, 'Lord of the breakthrough', commemorates the fact that David was able to break through the enemy lines, so decisively that it seemed to him as if the Lord had burst through ahead of him, *like a bursting flood*. The power of his God had been demonstrated, decisively controlling events and directing history, just as Isaiah foresaw happening in the Assyrian attack on Jerusalem (Is. 28:21).

21. *The Philistines left their idols there*: far from having power, these deities could not save themselves. David and his men took them as trophies of war, which were later burnt (1 Ch. 14:12). Thus they proved to be 'no gods', as opposed to Israel's God, whose covenant symbol survived capture and was returned (1 Sa. 7:1).

22–25. In a second attempt to gain the upper hand over David, the Philistines attacked once more in the same valley. David did not take for granted that his God-given strategy on the previous occasion would succeed a second time, nor did he trust his own expertise but asked afresh for guidance. This time he was not to go to meet the enemy head on. Instead, he was to make a surprise attack from the rear, which would have the advantage of cutting off the Philistine retreat route.

Opposite the balsam trees: the Hebrew word *bākā'* comes only here (*cf.* 1 Ch. 14:14, the parallel account) besides Psalm 84:6, 'the valley of Baca' (or 'weeping', RV). The 'balsam', or 'mulberry' (AV), or 'aspen' (NEB), are uncertain translations, though 'balsam' is the traditional Jewish interpretation of the word *bākā'*. The name resembles the Hebrew word for 'weep', a reference, perhaps, to the sap which exudes from balsam when it is torn or cut. More important than the identification of the species is the sign that the Lord will give, *the sound of marching in the tops of the balsam trees*. The wind which would cause a sound like a rushing of feet was in this case the wind of the Spirit of God, *for then the Lord has gone out before you to smite the army of the Philistines*. Once the sign is given, there is to be no delay: *bestir yourself* or 'move quickly' (NIV). David must move with the Spirit of God if he is to fulfil God's purpose to defeat the enemy. There was a place for waiting, but a place also for action. David accomplished what Saul had failed to achieve, because *David did as the Lord commanded him*, and triumphed once again. The secret of success, obedience, had been an option open to Saul, but he had not chosen it. David was, indeed, one of a rare company of people, rare even in the Bible, of whom it could be said that they did as the Lord commanded them.

He *smote the Philistines from Geba to Gezer*, or 'from Gibeon to Gezer' (LXX and 1 Ch. 14:16; *cf.* Is. 28:21). Gibeon is more likely to be correct, and geographically Gibeon is right. The defeated Philistines, knowing that their direct line of retreat westwards was blocked by David's army, had to make a detour northwards to Gibeon before they could turn downhill towards Gezer, on the edge of the lowland plain. Gezer remained a Canaanite city until the time of Solomon, who received it from the hand of his father-in-law, probably Pharaoh Siamūn,[1] as part of the dowry of the Egyptian princess who became his wife (1 Ki. 9:16). The Philistines made no further attempt to thwart the rise of David. So decisive was this battle, that from this time on the Philistines ceased to be a serious menace to Israel, though they continued to cause trouble during the period of the monarchy.

iv. David makes Jerusalem the city of God (6:1–23).
One of the themes of the books of Samuel is the history of the ark of the covenant, taken captive by the Philistines, but returned to Israelite territory when it proved to be embarrassingly powerful to humiliate both them and their god (1 Sa. 5). Not that the decorated gold box was of itself powerful, but everyone knew that it was the symbol of the presence of the Lord God of all the earth, who had made himself known in a special way to Israel, so that they became his people and he pledged himself to be their God. It was unthinkable that the ark should remain in obscurity in a private house on the border of the land, and once Jerusalem had become the city of David the king purposed that Jerusalem should be the city where the Lord was honoured and worshipped. By enshrining the ark, the symbol of God's presence, there, David transformed the old Jebusite stronghold into the place where the One God was pleased to make himself known, the centre of the earth, the site of his throne, the connecting link between

---

[1] K. A. Kitchen, *Third Intermediate Period in Egypt* (Warminster: Aris and Phillips, 1972), pp. 273ff., 280ff.

earth and heaven. David's intention was good, but problems arose in carrying it out. The account is realistic, portraying eager enthusiasm alongside perilous disregard for God's holiness.

1–2. *Thirty thousand* chosen men is often thought to be too high a number.[1] The problem is to know how the word *'elep* is being used in this context, which is no longer strictly military, though soldiers may fulfil a ceremonial role in worship and a strategic victory had just been won. *All the people who were with him* suggests David's civil and religious leaders, mentioned separately from the military commanders. The parallel account explicitly refers to commanders and leaders, and includes in the company who went to bring the ark 'priests and Levites', who must surely have been present (1 Ch. 13:1–2). Even if 'all the assembly of Israel' (1 Ch. 13:2) means only representatives of all the tribes, the occasion still involved large numbers and considerable pageantry, which, together with orchestral and choral music, united the huge crowd taking part in the historic event.

The ark had been last mentioned in connection with the family of Abinadab, whose son Eleazar had charge of it at Kiriath-jearim, but since then twenty years had passed (1 Sa. 7:1–2). It is surprising, therefore, to find the name *Baale-judah* used instead, except that the names are alternatives in Joshua 15:9, where it is called Baalah (*cf.* Jos. 15:60, where the name is Kiriath-baal). The names compounded with Baal suggest that it may have been a Canaanite high place; Kiriath-jearim means 'city of forests', a name which would again be appropriate today in the light of the reafforestation that is transforming the landscape to the west of Jerusalem. It is now known as Kuriet el-'Enab, or Abu Ghosh, about nine miles (14 km.) from Jerusalem, on the Jaffa road.

The ark of God, which is called by the name, avoids the notion that God is somehow to be located in the ark, and yet retains the distinctive function which the Lord had designed that it should fulfil as the place where he would meet with his people and speak with them (Ex. 25:22). The specific name (the word comes twice in the Heb.) connected with the ark, *the name of the Lord of hosts who sits enthroned on the cherubim*, envisages the

[1] See the commentary on 1 Sa. 4:2, explaining that the Hebrew *'elep*, the usual word for 'thousand', may have had other meanings, such as 'captain'.

golden cherubim as the footstool of an invisible throne 'high and lifted up' (Is. 6:1), and the God of the armies of Israel (1 Sa. 17:45) as supremely worthy of worship. But it is in connection with worship at Shiloh that the name first occurs in the Bible (1 Sa. 1:3, 11; 4:4), so the 'hosts' were supremely the angels who surrounded the throne rather than Israel's armies. The fact that these angels did God's bidding meant that they accomplished his will, hence the more meaningful translation 'the name of the Lord Almighty' (NIV) instead of 'Lord of hosts'.

3–4. *And they carried the ark of God upon a new cart*, no doubt with every good intention, but without due concern for the holiness of the ark, which was fitted with rings and poles to indicate that it was to be carried by the poles (Ex. 25:12–14). So transported, it would not have needed to be steadied or touched. The RSV has abbreviated the Hebrew text, relegating to the margin the omitted portions, which appear to have been repeated by mistake. Eleazar, to whose care the ark had been committed (1 Sa. 7:1), is not mentioned here. Instead, his brothers *Uzzah and Ahio* have responsibility for the oxen and the cart, with its special load.

5. The slow pace of the cart permitted the procession to engage in dancing and singing *before the Lord with all their might*. The participle *making merry* (Heb. *mᵉśaḥᵃqîm*, from the verb with which 'Isaac' is connected, and which means 'to laugh') has the force of unrestrained celebration in worship.

With songs (Heb. *bᵉšîrîm*) is a correction of the Hebrew (from 1 Ch. 13:8) which reads *bᵉrôšîm*, 'fir trees'. The names of musical instruments are understandably difficult to translate; the first two are stringed instruments, of which the second is first mentioned in 1 Samuel 10:5 in the Bible. It may therefore have been of Phoenician origin. All the others are percussion instruments. It is interesting to observe that the last, *cymbals*, always occurs in a religious context.[1] For Israel, all life's great occasions were God-centred and connected with worship, and the same was true of Israel's music.

6–7. Suddenly the joyous celebration came to a tragic end at *the threshing floor of Nacon* (*cf.* the NEB's 'a certain threshing-floor', which implicitly draws attention to the fact that the name 'Nacon' is problematic, for it occurs nowhere else; in 1 Ch. 13:9 'Chidon' is the name). Two verbs with which *nacon*

---

[1] For further detail, *cf. IBD* 2, art. 'Music', pp. 1031ff.

could be connected are *kûn*, 'to be fixed or prepared', or *nākāh*, 'to smite'; indeed the latter occurs in verse 7, *God smote him*. The name may have been coined to encapsulate memories of the disaster, witnessed by the great company of worshippers. Uzzah, by handling the ark, albeit in a spontaneous action to prevent it falling to the ground, committed sacrilege and was killed by the contact with God's holiness. In so far as David had decreed how the ark was to be transported, he was responsible for Uzzah's death, but some blame must have attached to Uzzah and Ahio, whose family had for years been in charge of the ark. From David's point of view, the death of Uzzah under these circumstances was not only a tragedy for the family of Abinadab, but also a colossal loss of face for the king.

8–11. David, for whom everything had been going so well, reacted with hot indignation: he *was angry* at the Lord's intervention, recalled in the new name for the threshing floor, *Perez-uzzah* '[the Lord's] break out on Uzzah'. David in his humiliation blamed God for the incident and opted out of the task of taking the ark on to Jerusalem, partly because he was also *afraid of the Lord*. He who had experienced wonderful protection over the years from the Lord his God, and had known unusual intimacy with him, had to come to terms with the fact that he had overstepped the mark, and presumed upon the relationship, by failing to observe the regulations laid down to safeguard respect for God's holiness. Though Jesus taught us to call God our Father, he also taught us to pray 'hallowed be thy name', implying the need to pay careful attention lest privilege becomes presumption. As A. F. Kirkpatrick observes, 'If such reverence was due to the symbol, with how much greater reverence should the realities of the Christian Covenant be regarded?'[1]

Obed-edom the Gittite: Gittite means 'from Gath', but Obed-edom is unlikely to have been a Philistine from the city of that name, and was probably a Levite, in view of his being entrusted with the ark. At least three Israelite towns had names compounded with Gath, from one of which this man originally came. Possibly he should be identified as the descendant of Korah, named in 1 Chronicles 26:4, 8. Over a period of three months, people observed that this man and

---

[1] Kirkpatrick 1881, p. 92.

his household received signs of God's favour: *the Lord blessed him*.

12–15. News that Obed-edom had experienced the Lord's blessing caused David to fulfil his intention to bring the ark into Jerusalem. *Those who bore the ark* implies that this time men carried the ark in the prescribed way, by its poles, but even so, after only six paces had been taken, David offered sacrifices. 1 Chronicles 15 adds considerable detail, explaining that this time 'Levites carried the ark of God upon their shoulders with the poles' (1 Ch. 15:5; *cf.* Ex. 25:14), and indicating that the Levites sacrificed seven bulls and seven rams because God helped them (1 Ch. 15:26). David's sacrifices also will have been part thanksgiving for a good start on the journey, and part prayer for its safe completion.

David danced before the Lord with all his might: the verb (Heb. *mᵉkarkēr*) is a participle, meaning 'whirling', and occurs only in this passage (vv. 14, 16). David apparently used an old ritual dance, which was unknown when the Chronicles account was written, the author substituting verbs in ordinary use. David expressed no less enthusiasm than on the former occasion (v. 5), but now he had learnt that sincerity and enthusiasm were not enough. He had also paid attention to the ritual requirements which God's law had laid down. He had even replaced his royal robes by *a linen ephod*, the priestly dress, which as king of a kingdom of priests he was entitled to wear, and which was particularly appropriate for the festal ceremony. Similarly, the *shouting* was part of the ritual (*cf.* 1 Sa. 4:5), and was associated with religious fervour as well as with battle cries. So was the *horn* (Heb. *šōp̄ār*), as Psalm 47:5 (a psalm which probably recalls this procession with the ark) illustrates, 'God has gone up with a shout, the Lord with the sound of a trumpet (*šōp̄ār*).'

16. At the moment of David's triumph, when the ark had successfully entered Jerusalem, his wife Michal took exception to all this religious excitement and display. Her idea seems to have been that the king should avoid mixing with the people, and be aloof and inaccessible. As it was, *she despised him* for the very qualities that made him great, namely devotion to the Lord and spontaneity in worship.

17–19. Once in the city, the procession made for the tent which David had carefully prepared to receive the ark; the tabernacle remained at Gibeon (1 Ch. 16:39). Only after

Solomon had built the Temple was the tent of meeting brought to Jerusalem (1 Ki. 8:4), but from this point onwards in David's reign the presence of the ark of the covenant in Jerusalem ensured that here was the place *par excellence* where worship should be offered, because this was where the Lord was pleased to make himself known. David responded with *burnt offerings and peace offerings*, which expressed total commitment and thanskgiving; the peace offerings, or 'fellowship offerings' (NIV), unlike the burnt offering, were not consumed on the altar, or used to provide food for the priests; instead most was returned to the offerer (Lv. 7:11–18), who used the meat for a communal feast as part of the rejoicing. David also *blessed the people in the name of the Lord of hosts*, claiming for them the blessings which the Lord had pronounced on his covenant people (*e.g.* Ex. 19:5–6; Dt. 7:6–11), before distributing food to all.

There are some unusual words in verse 19. *A cake of bread* (Heb. *ḥallaṯ leḥem*) is used elsewhere only in sacrificial contexts of the Pentateuch (*e.g.* Ex. 29:2; Lv. 2:4; Nu. 6:15); it means a flat loaf of bread. *A portion of meat* (Heb. *'ešpār*) occurs elsewhere only in 1 Chronicles 16:3, and the meaning of the word is totally unknown,[1] hence the variant translations, *e.g.* 'a portion of dates' (JB), 'a cake of dates' (NIV), based on the food usually carried by the Eastern traveller. *A cake of raisins*, mentioned in connection with Canaanite worship two centuries later (Ho. 3:1), was nevertheless staple food; 'flagon of wine' (AV) is no longer considered to be the meaning of this term.

20. David returned to his home, full of all the joy of achievement, and of shared excitement at the prospects for God's future blessing of his family and city, only to be greeted on the way by his disapproving wife. Her sarcasm, *how the king of Israel honoured himself today*, was a prelude to scathing condemnation. What had her hopes been when she first fell in love with David, who killed two hundred Philistines for the privilege of marrying her (1 Sa. 18:20–27)? She preferred the 'brave warrior' image to that of the humble, worshipping king, stripped of all his royal regalia, and, as she saw it, *uncovering himself*, or maybe 'showing off'.[2] Michal interprets the situ-

---

[1] The conclusion of Driver 1913, pp. 207–209.
[2] So Gunn 1982, p. 74, 'not necessarily "uncovering himself" literally'.

ation to justify her alienation from her husband; though she does not come across as an attractive person, she had nevertheless had a perplexing and tragic married life after David left the court (1 Sa. 19:11–17; 25:44; 2 Sa. 3:13–16), and the changes were not of her choosing. Now her angry outburst put an end to such reconciliation as might have been possible.

21–23. David in his reply did not mince his words. The derogatory reference to her father and family, though true, was sure to wound, with its insistence on the contrast between Saul and himself in relation to *the Lord, who chose me above your father . . . over Israel, the people of the Lord*. The election promise of 2 Samuel 5:2, precious to David and the people of Israel, and a source of conflict for Michal, is echoed here. She could not 'win' the argument, because she could not accept the divine purpose, which the *maids* (*i.e.* 'maidservants') joyously celebrated. Like her father before her, she found herself working against God. David in no way regrets what he has done; *I will be abased in your eyes*, while it makes good sense, is not what the Hebrew says. It has 'in my eyes', indicating that David is more concerned to honour the Lord than to foster his own reputation, for he does not need to boost his own ego, nor does he lack popular support.

In the context, Michal's childlessness implies that from this point on marital relations between her and David came to an end. The relationship between them had irrevocably broken down.[1] There is, however, a difference of opinion among commentators as to the meaning of this verse, *e.g.* John Mauchline says it should be interpreted 'as quoting her childless condition as the penalty of her contempt of David the anointed king, and as the deprivation of the house of Saul of continuance, and especially of providing the mother of the successor to the throne'.[2] The two views are not, of course, mutually exclusive.

The installation of the ark in Jerusalem was the first momentous achievement of David's reign after the capture of the city. It has been pointed out that no public ceremony took place there to proclaim David king or to enthrone him in Jerusalem; this great festival connected with the arrival of the ark was all the more impressive as the proclamation of the

---

[1] The reference to sons of Michal in 2 Sa. 21:8 (AV, RV) should probably read Merab (*cf.* 1 Sa. 18:19), following two Hebrew MSS and the LXX.

[2] Mauchline, p. 226.

Lord as King in Jerusalem, with David as his appointed prince (Heb. *nāgîd*, v. 21; *cf.* 2 Sa. 7:8). Jerusalem was now the city of the Lord of hosts, sanctified by his presence and protected by his power, though not unconditionally, as later generations were to discover.

Much has been made of the political astuteness shown by David in incorporating the ark and all it stood for in his capital. The fact is that devotion to God is not essentially opposed to prosperity in the wider world of national and international affairs, and the book of Proverbs insists many times over that the first and most important requirement, for kings as for everyone else, is the fear of the Lord. Saul failed at this point as surely as David put the Lord first. That his devotion brought him advantages should not occasion any surprise, nor is a cynical and self-regarding interpretation of David's action appropriate.

v. A house for the Lord (7:1–29). The building of David's palace has been dismissed in one verse (2 Sa. 5:11), so incidental is it to the writer of the books of Samuel, and an interval of time is implied between 2 Samuel 6 and 7, in particular by the note that his battles against aggressive neighbours had already been fought (*cf.* 2 Sa. 8:1–14). The importance of the contents of this chapter is such that it has priority over the formal accounts of David's wars. It also follows up the themes of the previous chapter, in that the Temple would have enshrined the ark, and the question of an heir, touched on by implication in connection with Michal, became the subject of God's special purpose.

The context of this chapter is wider than the career of David, however, and goes back to Israel's commitment as the covenant people of Yahweh, adopted by him as his people. The book of Deuteronomy enshrined the fundamentals of that commitment, including instructions regarding kingship in Israel (Dt. 17:14–20), though surprisingly they are not directly referred to here. It had also given directions for a dramatic act of worship once Israel had rest in the land (Dt. 12:10–11). But the covenant had not originated with Deuteronomy. Israel's occupation of the land of Canaan was proof that the covenant with Abraham still stood (Gn. 15:18), and in the divine word through Nathan there are verbal reminiscences (*e.g.* 'rest' and 'a great name') which recall that early covenant. Even though that word 'covenant' does not occur in Nathan's pronouncement, it is used in later references to David's dynasty (2 Sa. 23:5; Pss. 89:3, 28, 34; 132:12), and confirms that it was regarded as an enduring, unconditional promise, sworn on divine oath. As such, it brought David into prominence within the historic covenant, so adding a dimension to the original Abrahamic covenant.

Two distinct but related themes in the subsequent literature of the Bible have their source in this chapter. First, the Davidic line is given the right to rule *for ever*, and the Lord gives his word that he will not withdraw his *steadfast love* (Heb. *ḥesed*, the covenant term) from David's son as he did from Saul (v. 15). Thus the Lord is to build David's house; that is, David will found a dynasty:

> 2 Samuel 7 is rightly regarded as an 'ideological summit', not only in the 'Deuteronomistic History' but also in the Old Testament as a whole. The Nathan oracle constitutes the title-deed of the Davidic house to the rule of Israel and Judah, which rule it did indeed exercise over Judah for fully four centuries.[1]

The fact that its rule came to an end, and had been seen by the prophets to be failing, gave rise to the second theme which developed as a reinterpretation of the promises to David: his booth would be repaired (Am. 9:11); a Davidic child would establish his throne with justice and with righteousness (Is. 9:6–7); a branch from the stump of Jesse would yet create an ideal kingdom (Is. 11:1–9, *cf.* Je. 23:5; Zc. 3:8).[2] In other words, this chapter was to become the source of the messianic hope as it developed in the message of prophets and psalmists.

1–3. *The Lord had given him rest from all his enemies round about* (*cf.* v. 11), is taken word for word from Deuteronomy 12:10, where the promise is made that the land will belong to the twelve tribes, who will overcome their enemies and be shown one place where worship is to be made. Having seen the promise at least partially fulfilled, David wanted to give greater glory to God by housing the ark more in accordance with the style and permanence of his own dwelling. This would have been considered by the Canaanites to be the duty

[1] Gordon 1986, p. 235.
[2] *Cf.* J. G. Baldwin, '*ṢEMAḤ* as a technical term in the Prophets', *VT* 14/1 (1964), pp. 93–98.

of the king; anything less would be a snub to the God who had given him his victories.[1]

Nathan the prophet, first mentioned in this connection, is the king's adviser and confidant; his immediate reaction is to encourage the king to go ahead and build. There was no obvious reason against the plan, and the king's intention was good, though there was the subtle inference that David was asserting himself by changing the long-established tradition of a tent shrine.

4–7. The Lord now takes the initiative by giving his word to Nathan for David. First he raises the question whether *a house to dwell in* is either necessary or appropriate for the Lord who had been guiding his people and so manifesting his presence in Egypt, and in every part of their journeying. A movable tent had therefore been a more meaningful symbol of his dwelling among them than a permanent building could ever have been. Moreover, no divine command had ever been issued that *a house of cedar* should be built. All the materials for 'a desirable residence' were, after all, part of the Lord's creation, and there is gentle irony in both the questions contained in these verses.

Did I speak a word with any of the judges?: where the RSV reads 'judges' (Heb. *šopṭê*), having taken the word from 1 Chronicles 17:6, the Hebrew has *šibṭê*, 'tribes'. Keil and Delitzsch argue that if 'judges' had been the original expression used in the text, it would be impossible to explain the origin and general acceptance of the word 'tribes'. The leaders were identified with the tribes to which they belonged.[2]

8–9a. *My servant David* (*cf.* v. 5) is an honoured title, but at the same time a reminder to David that, though he is king, and surrounded by those who serve him, he too has his servant role in relation to his God. It is worth pondering that it was by 'servant' imagery that the role of Jesus was most profoundly foreshadowed in the Old Testament: 'Behold my servant . . . in whom my soul delights' (Is. 42:1) or 'with whom my soul is well pleased' (LXX; see Mt. 12:18; *cf.* Mt. 3:17). If David had his eyes on greatness, it would begin with submission and

---

[1] F. M. Cross, *Canaanite Myth and the Hebrew Bible* (Cambridge, Mass. and London: Harvard University Press, 1973), p. 243. The fact that David did not build a temple testified to David's acceptance of a limited kingship, unlike Canaanite concepts of kingship.

[2] Keil and Delitzsch, p. 342.

service to the Lord God.

Secondly, the Lord directs David to keep in mind that day when he had been *following the sheep* and *I took you*. The agency of Samuel is not mentioned, important though he had been at the time; the Lord directly intervened in David's life so that he should be *prince over . . . Israel*. This was the very phrase used of Saul (1 Sa. 9:16; 10:1). The Lord spoke of *my people Israel*, all the tribes descended from Jacob/Israel, over whom he was king (Dt. 17:19; Jdg. 8:23); the human rulers were called 'prince' (Heb. *nāgîd*) to make the point that they were subservient to Israel's real king.

I have been with you . . . and have cut off all your enemies: David had been 'the brilliant general' in the eyes of his contemporaries, but he owed his success to the one who had accompanied him unseen through all his life.

9b–11. For this reason, David also has a future. *A great name* is a promise that looks far ahead of his own lifetime, when a greater than David would nevertheless crown with new significance all that David had stood for as king, and cause the name 'David' to be known world-wide. *A place for my people Israel* had already been put on the map, but there is a long forward look in this promise also, which would provide hope and solace in troubled times (*e.g.* Je. 32:37), and a vision of security (*rest*; *cf.* v. 1) still future (Ps. 89:22–24). Finally, in a play on the word 'house', the tables are turned and the Lord undertakes to build for David *a house* in the sense of 'dynasty'.

12. The question of a successor for David is now faced, for though his death was by no means imminent it was nonetheless inevitable that he would *lie down with* [*his*] *fathers*, an expression which suggests fellowship beyond the grave.

I will raise up your offspring (Heb. *zar'ăkā*, 'your seed'): the original implies not only one generation but many. In God's perspective, history is seen whole, its purpose clear and certain to be achieved. Nevertheless, the immediate reference is to David's heir and successor, whose kingdom the Lord will establish, as he had established David's.

13. *He shall build a house for my name* returns to the original question of the building of the Temple. The idea of the Lord making his name dwell in the place which he will choose comes several times in Deuteronomy (Dt. 12:11–12, 21; 14:23–24; 16:2, 6, 11; 26:2). One interpretation of the meaning of this phrase is that 'Deuteronomy is replacing the old crude idea of Jahweh's presence and dwelling at the shrine by a theologically sublimated idea.'[1] The 'name' replaced Yahweh's actual presence. Over against that view is evidence from ancient texts and inscriptions that 'the phrase is an affirmation of ownership, the equivalent of taking possession'.[2] The widespread occurrence of the idea of 'the name' points to an idiom which was well established and understood in the ancient Near East; even Deuteronomy 'regards God as present in heaven and in his sanctuary'.[3] Though the exact meaning of 'the name' is elusive, the context of 2 Samuel 7 demands that Yahweh, who alone could show his servant future generations (v. 19) and therefore directed the course of history, should also be accessible to his servants on earth. The Temple, like the Tabernacle, would provide the means of access to the great God who had condescended to name for himself this one spot on earth. A dedication stone may have borne the name Yahweh, thus pointing to a literal meaning, the written name indicating ownership (*cf.* Is. 43:1). But a theology of transcendence could hold its place alongside that of God's immanence (1 Ki. 8:27). The tension between the two apparently irreconcilable concepts was, and still is, a necessary element in worship of the living God who delivers his servants from the paw of the lion and the paw of the bear, and so proves he is with his servants (1 Sa. 17:36; 20:13), and yet remains the Sovereign Lord (2 Sa. 7:18–22, NIV).

14–16. *I will be his father, and he shall be my son* discloses a relationship of privilege which had not been true in the case of Saul, but it is a relationship which implies discipline: *I will chasten him with the rod of men*, that is, like a human father; the generation that endured the destruction of Jerusalem saw it as divine discipline, 'under the rod of his wrath' (La. 3:1). But this promise enabled even the direst disaster to be accepted, because it implied a loving purpose, *I will not take my steadfast love from him*, or as the poem in Lamentations goes on, in an echo of the Davidic covenant, 'The steadfast love of the Lord never ceases' (La. 3:22). The oracle to David through Nathan

---

[1] Von Rad, *Studies in Deuteronomy*, p. 39.

[2] R. de Vaux, *Revue Biblique* 73 (1966), p. 449, quoted by G. J. Wenham in 'Deuteronomy and the Central Sanctuary', *TynB* 22 (1971), p. 113, together with other evidence.

[3] Wenham, *ibid.*, based on work by de Vaux. See *e.g.* Dt. 26:2–3, where 'a dwelling for his name' permits a worshipper to address 'the Lord your God'.

ends with an emphatic restatement of the main thrust of the covenant promise: *your house and your kingdom . . . sure for ever; your throne . . . for ever*, and all this because David expressed a desire to honour the Lord. He received far, far more than he could ever have hoped to give, and any disappointment at having to allow someone else the privilege of building the Temple was far outweighed by the assurance of blessing that extended into eternity.

17. The task of the prophet, to convey the message of the Lord faithfully and accurately, is carried out by Nathan, though it involved contradicting what he had already said to David by way of personal opinion. He had not spoken on that occasion in the name of the Lord.

In the light of all this marvellous revelation of his part in God's purposes, David cannot but respond in worship. His prayer is, in a nutshell, that all that the Lord has spoken may be fulfilled and that through it all the greatness of the Lord may become obvious to all.

18. *King David went in and sat before the Lord*, no doubt in the tent which he had set up to house the ark, and to symbolize the divine presence. Though as Christians we no longer need an ark, because the Lord is accessible in every place, prayer is nevertheless appropriate and therefore made easier in a place where worship is regularly offered by God's people. Nothing could be more humbling than to hear the word of the Lord, spoken directly to one's situation, hence David's question, *Who am I, O Lord God, and what is my house . . . ?* 'House' in both its senses is the recurring theme of the prayer, and David begins by using the word in reference to his family background, which was undistinguished.

19–21. Yet not only had he become established as king, but he had also been promised an ongoing dynasty extending far into the future. The last clause of verse 19 has been emended in the RSV, but the Hebrew has been kept in the NIV: 'Is this your usual way of dealing with man, O Sovereign Lord?', a somewhat free translation. It nevertheless fits the context, because David goes on to deduce from all that he has learnt through Nathan's prophecy that the revelation is *according to thy own heart*, in keeping with God's character, and therefore typical of his dealings with mankind. God not only makes great plans for his servants, but he also graciously makes his plans known.

217

22–24. *Therefore thou art great*, and the measure of God's greatness here is his capacity to refer to the future as easily as to the past, so demonstrating that he is master of mankind and of human history. He is incomparable, in a totally different category from all other so-called gods. Already this had been apparent in the events of the exodus, when God *went to redeem* [*Israel*] *to be his people, making himself a name*. Egypt in particular, and the nations in general, had seen demonstrated before their eyes the greatness of Israel's God when he over-threw the peoples of Canaan and their gods to give Israel the land. No other nation had ever experienced anything compar-able, especially the covenant setting in which all this had come to pass. By virtue of the covenant, David and all the family of Israel were *his people*, so that David could pray, *thou didst establish for thyself thy people Israel to be thy people for ever; and thou, O Lord, didst become their God*. By recalling the exodus events and the establishment of Israel's tribes in the land of Canaan, David is declaring his faith in the God of his fathers, and identifying his role in God's developing purpose as the sequel to all that had gone before. The living God unified history, giving meaning to both past and present.

25–29. *And now* indicates a new departure, as David makes specific requests (*cf.* 28–29). Up to this point he has been entering into all that the Lord has done in the past; only after that does his mind turn to the interests of his own kingdom, seen in relation to God's kingdom, and therefore in true perspective, but still important in its own right. It is easy to read with knowledge of the fulfilment of the promises in mind, and forget that for David the establishment of his dynasty was still hidden in the unknown future, and to be accepted by faith, every bit as much as the 'eternal' element in the promise. So David reasons with himself (v. 28), i. *thou art God*, ii. *thy words are true*, iii. *thou hast promised*, to all of which the logical conclusion is that God's word must be fulfilled. But, like us, David needed to trace the steps in the argument in order to be certain that his feet were on sure ground, and by turning the promise into prayer he both endorsed his acceptance of God's word and also, by repetition, underscored it for future generations. He ends his prayer, not with petition, but with an assertion that his house will be *blessed for ever*.

Thus it came about that David gave up his intention of building the Temple. Though he was king of Israel, he accepted that he had to defer to a higher authority, that of the God of Israel, to whom he owed his calling through the prophet Samuel, his preservation in mortal danger at the hand of Saul, and his accession to the throne by common consent of the people. Recognition on the part of the king that he owed the throne of his kingdom to the sovereign Lord God involved humble acceptance of the role of servant, *thy servant*, as David calls himself ten times over in this prayer. David was far from perfect, as the subsequent narrative is to demonstrate, but he had grasped this all-important truth about himself, and it was because he valued so highly his call to serve the Lord God that he was sensitive to rebuke and repented when he stepped out of line. For this reason, he knew forgiveness and restoration of fellowship, both of which had eluded Saul because he could never bring himself to take his hands off the reins of government, or readily admit to being in the wrong. Saul, by clinging tenaciously to what he regarded as his kingly prerogative, lost the kingdom; David, more concerned about honouring the Lord than guarding his own reputation, had his kingdom made sure for ever. It was this promise that gripped future generations, especially in troubled times, and caused the Davidic line to be recorded with more than usual care by different branches of the family, so that when the Gospels came to be written, the evangelists Matthew and Luke each used a genealogy of Jesus that included David but differed in intention and details (Mt. 1:5–6, 20; Lk. 3:31).

vi. The establishment of David's empire (8:1–14).

One aspect of David's success as a ruler was in the diplomatic and military spheres, for when he came to power his kingdom was threatened by the surrounding peoples, who had been accustomed to take advantage of any weakness and invade at will. Though Saul had defeated the Philistines and the Ammonites early in his reign, his frenetic hunt for David deflected the army from defence of the kingdom, and his death at the hand of the Philistines at Mount Gilboa, far to the north and east of their territory, indicates their supremacy at that time. David's decisive victory over this persistent enemy has already been recorded (2 Sa. 5:17–25), and 2 Samuel 8 takes up the story where 2 Samuel 5 left off.

1. *After this* may be used here as a general connecting link rather than as a strictly chronological reference (*cf.* 2 Sa. 10:1;

15:1), but in the author's original source it could have had the latter function. No such place as *Methegh-ammah* is known; the word 'methegh', meaning 'bridle', could indicate that David gained control (*cf.* 'David took the bridle of the mother city', RV, taking the phrase as a reference to Gath, as in 1 Ch. 18:1); it could be a place name (*cf.* 'hill of Ammah', 2 Sa. 2:24), but the context requires a place of importance. The LXX translates 'tribute', but this appears to be a guess, in line with verse 2.

2. The Moabites had been entrusted with David's parents, who resided in Moab under the protection of the king during the period of danger from Saul (1 Sa. 22:3–4), and David was related to Moab through Ruth the Moabitess (Ru. 4:17). Here, however, David deals ruthlessly with his defeated enemy, putting to death two thirds of those lined up in rows on the ground, so severely reducing the power of the Moabite army, and subjugating Moab as a vassal state. The regular payment of *tribute* indicated ongoing subservience. What caused David to treat Moab with such severity is not known.

3. Mention of *Zobah* takes David's campaigns far to the north of the territory which had thus far belonged to Israel. Saul had had cause to fight against Zobah (1 Sa. 14:47); David went on the offensive to attack this mountainous kingdom to the north of Damascus. He chose a moment when the king, *Hadadezer*, was campaigning to recapture territory that had belonged to him to the north, including part of the Euphrates river, so opening up a second front.

4–5. David's strategy was effective, enabling him to take captive a sizeable number of men and horses. The decision of David to cripple the chariot horses by cutting the tendons in their legs, so rendering them useless for warfare, may have been a realistic decision on a campaign. There would be limits to the number of horses he could keep fed and cared for, and in the mountainous terrain chariots were of limited value. Chariots had not greatly helped their enemies thus far (*cf.* Ex. 15:19; Jos. 11:6–9; Jdg. 4:15–16), hence David's wariness of the advanced military vehicle, though he retained a hundred of them. When the Syrians of Damascus went to the aid of Hadadezer, David could have been trapped between the two armies, but such was his ability as a commander that his army overcame their enemy and put large numbers to death.

6–8. *David put garrisons in Aram of Damascus*: the conquest of territory so far away from Jerusalem raised problems as to effective means of keeping the population in subjection. The garrisons would have provided his local governors with armed backing, so upholding David's authority, even if, as seems probable, Hadadezer remained on his throne as a vassal.

And the Lord gave victory to David wherever he went: the expansion of Israel's influence impressed David's contemporaries as nothing short of miraculous, even taking into account his great gifts as a leader and strategist. The spoil from these wars was also impressive: *shields of gold*, which had belonged to the Syrian officers, provided the nucleus of a collection which was to be greatly expanded by Solomon (1 Ki. 10:17), and depleted by Shishak king of Egypt in Rehoboam's reign (1 Ki. 14:26; but *cf.* 2 Ki. 11:10).[1] In the time of David, however, such a collection would be a new source of pride and prestige, and David characteristically dedicated his booty to the house of the Lord (2 Ki. 11:10). Of the two places from which *very much bronze* was taken to add to the treasure, only *Berothai* is identified sufficiently to be marked on the map. It is thought to be the modern Bereitan, about seven miles (11 km.) south of Baalbek.[2] (1 Ch. 18:8 has Cun, perhaps a later name for the same place.)

9–12. As a result of his victory over Zobah, David's prestige rose to such an extent that the *king of Hamath* on the Orontes river, over a hundred miles north of Damascus, took the precaution of forestalling any attack on his territory by sending his son as an ambassador to David. King *Toi*, or Tou (1 Ch. 18:9), which is generally preferred, by volunteering tribute, was pledging his support for the newly victorious

[1] Yadin, *The Art of Warfare*, p. 360, has the picture of a basalt orthostat from NW Mesopotamia depicting a cavalryman with a round, bossed shield slung over his shoulder. It belongs to the tenth century BC, approximately the time of David, and came from the geographical region where David was fighting. It seems likely that the shield was made of wood or leather, stiffened with metal, in this case with a metal boss. 'Shields of gold' may have been similar to the one depicted, the gold of the boss making them particularly desirable. The Heb. *šeleṭ*, translated 'shields' in the RSV (AV, RV also) is in the NEB 'quivers'; BDB suggests 'arms', 'equipment', but 'shields' makes good sense in the contexts where this word occurs (2 Ki. 11:10; Song 4:4; Ezk. 27:11).

[2] *IDB* 1, p. 386.

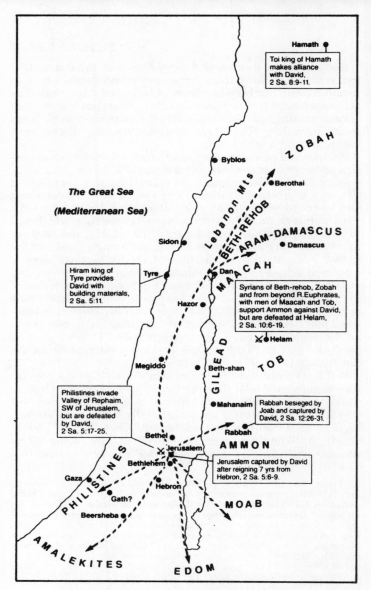

Hamath •

Toi king of Hamath makes alliance with David, 2 Sa. 8:9-11.

ZOBAH

Byblos •

The Great Sea
(Mediterranean Sea)

Berothai •

BETH-REHOB

Lebanon Mts

ARAM-DAMASCUS

Sidon •

Damascus •

Hiram king of Tyre provides David with building materials, 2 Sa. 5:11.

Tyre •

Dan •

MAACAH

Hazor •

Syrians of Beth-rehob, Zobah and from beyond R. Euphrates, with men of Maacah and Tob, support Ammon against David, but are defeated at Helam, 2 Sa. 10:6-19.

Helam •

GILEAD

TOB

Megiddo •

Beth-shan •

Philistines invade Valley of Rephaim, SW of Jerusalem, but are defeated by David, 2 Sa. 5:17-25.

Mahanaim •

Rabbah besieged by Joab and captured by David, 2 Sa. 12:26-31.

Bethel •

Rabbah •

Jerusalem

AMMON

Bethlehem •

Jerusalem captured by David after reigning 7 yrs from Hebron, 2 Sa. 5:6-9.

PHILISTINES

Gaza •

Gath? •

Hebron •

Beersheba •

MOAB

AMALEKITES

EDOM

WARS DURING THE REIGN OF DAVID

222

Israelite king. In this way further riches were added to the treasury, and while on the subject the writer refers to the enemies nearer home whom David had forced to pay tribute. For the moment they are merely listed; the reference back to Hadadezer (*cf.* v. 3) acts as a literary bracket round these verses, indicating that they belong together and were once part of an independent account.

13–14. As the marginal reading indicates, most Hebrew texts have 'Syrians' where the RSV text, following the LXX, Syriac and some Hebrew MSS, has *Edomites* (*cf.* 1 Ch. 18:12). The *Valley of Salt*, to the south of the Dead Sea, certainly implies Edom rather than Syria (Heb. Aram and Edom were easily mistaken). The large number of Edomites put to death implies an attempt to invade Israel from the south, and so preserve their monopoly on trade routes through the desert to the Red Sea port of Ezion Geber.[1] On this occasion they were crippled by heavy losses, and forced to submit. David *put garrisons . . . throughout all Edom, and all the Edomites became David's servants*, so establishing his trade monopoly there and opening the way to communications with Arabia and Africa, which were to develop significantly during Solomon's reign (*cf.* 1 Ki. 9:26–28).

And the Lord gave victory to David wherever he went: the repetition of verse 6c concludes a section which in a modern history of a reign would have had far greater space, for it is usual to reckon a leader's victories in battle as his major achievements. These military operations must also have been time-consuming, occupying much of David's best years, and displaying his brilliance as a general; but the scriptural writer, far from cultivating a hero-cult, attributes David's success to the Lord who called him and enabled him to succeed, and gives emphasis to other aspects of David's character in the chapters that follow.

vii. David's delegation of duties (8:15–18).
Expansion of David's empire demanded adequate organization and efficient

---

[1] I. Finkelstein, 'The Iron Age Sites in the Negev Highlands – Military Fortresses or Nomads Settling Down?', *BAR* 12/4 (1986), p. 53, points out, 'There was no need for the kings of Israel to vanquish the desert dwellers militarily. The disruption of Negev trade, which was their chief economic support, brought about the collapse of the special infra-structure that made their sedentarization possible.'

personnel at the heart of the domain in Jerusalem, and therefore this extract, probably from an official archive, is in place at this point.

15. *David reigned over all Israel*: in the light of all that has just been recorded, we feel the need to add 'and beyond', but this discrepancy is one of the indications that these verses constitute a quotation. Not only was David king, but he also kept in his own hands the judiciary. He was the final court of appeal, so that he made sure that *justice* (Heb. *mišpāṭ*) and *equity* (Heb. *ṣᵉdāqâ*) were available *to all his people* without prejudice or discrimination. The pattern for the judge was the goodness and reliability of God himself (*cf.* Dt. 32:4; Ps. 37:27–29), and presupposed godliness in the one administering justice. Leadership in the land up to and including the time of Samuel had been in the hands of 'judges' (Heb. *šōpᵉṭîm*, a word cognate with *mišpāṭ*), and therefore it was to be expected that David would take over the office of supreme judge, such as Samuel himself had held, with its overtones of deliverer and 'saviour' (*cf.* Jdg. 2:16). It was to be the sphere in which his son Absalom was to question his effectiveness (2 Sa. 15:1–6)' and set up as a rival.

16–18. *Joab the son of Zeruiah*, David's nephew (1 Ch. 2:16), having put to death Abner (2 Sa. 3:27), who might have been in competition for the post, became the army general, though the *Cherethites and the Pelethites*, mercenary soldiers with special responsibility for guarding the king, were under the separate command of *Benaiah the son of Jehoiada*, a valiant soldier (2 Sa. 23:20–23). By employing foreign guards to ensure the safety of the king David would minimize the possibility of becoming the victim of inter-tribal rivalries; these men from Crete could give whole-hearted allegiance to him (*cf.* 2 Sa. 15:18; 20:7).[1]

The *recorder* (Heb. *mazkîr*), whose title derived from the Hebrew 'to remember', had a most important role at court, with responsibility for keeping the king informed, advising him, and communicating the king's commands.[2] Interestingly,

---

[1] The likely derivation of the names Cherethites and Pelethites may conveniently be found in *IBD* 1, art. 'Cherethites', 'the distinction between them was that though they both came from Crete, the Cherethites were native Cretans, whereas the Pelethites had only passed through the island in their travels from some other original homeland' (pp. 263–264).

[2] Bright, p. 201, refers to the *mazkîr* as the royal herald.

the Lord is also depicted, like the human king, as having 'recorders', though the word is translated 'remembrancers' (RV, AV mg.); their responsibility was to keep reminding him of his stated intentions until they were completed (Is. 62:6). This is an aspect of prayer which is easily overlooked, though it is implicit in the Lord's prayer: 'thy kingdom come, thy will be done . . .'

Two chief priests were appointed to work side by side (*cf.* Zc. 4:14); *Ahimelech*, whose father was Abiathar, and is later himself called Abiathar, had been with David since escaping death at the hand of Saul (1 Sa. 22:20), so his appointment was no surprise, but *Zadok the son of Ahitub*, who had responsibility for the ark (2 Sa. 15:24–29), appears here for the first time. His genealogy in 1 Chronicles 6:50–53 is traced back to Aaron through Eleazar, and includes the name of his father Ahitub, as in our text. But Ahimelech's grandfather was also called Ahitub (1 Sa. 22:20), and ever since 1871, when J. Wellhausen called into question the genealogy of Zadok given in this verse, various other ways of accounting for his origin have been proposed.[1] Great importance attaches to the genealogy of Zadok because, after Abiathar supported Adonijah and was banished to Anathoth (1 Ki. 2:26–27), Zadok became the chief priest of Solomon, and the first of a line which controlled temple worship to the exile and beyond.

The royal *secretary*, whose office was obviously of great importance, is named, and finally David's sons are described as *priests* (Heb. *kōhᵃnîm*), a designation which the Chronicler does not use; instead they are called 'chief officials in the service of the king' (1 Ch. 18:17). There have been suggestions that *kōhēn* may have had a wider meaning than 'priest' in certain contexts. The NIV, for example, has 'David's sons were royal advisers', and the JB, while keeping the word 'priests' in the text, explains in the margin that the probable meaning

---

[1] There is, of course, no reason why there should not have been two men by the name of Ahitub, and F. M. Cross, *Canaanite Myth and Hebrew Epic*, pp. 195–215, has put forward arguments which affirm that Zadok was indeed an Aaronide. He sums up: 'David's unusual choice of two chief priests, like many of his decisions relating to Israel's new central sanctuary in Jerusalem, was based on sure diplomatic grounds; he chose a priest from each of the great, rival priestly families: Abiathar of the Shilonite house of Eli which claimed descent from Moses, Zadok from the Hebronite clan which traced its line to Aaron' (p. 215). For a summary of the various hypotheses, see *IDBS*, p. 976.

was that 'David's sons assisted or deputised for him in those priestly functions for which the king was qualified; cf. 6:13–20.' In support, one recalls that Moses had performed priestly functions (*e.g.* Ex. 19:22, 24), as had Samuel (1 Sa. 10:8); Saul had been reprimanded for going beyond the express instruction of Samuel (1 Sa. 13:8–14), his fault usually being interpreted as intrusion into the priestly role. David and Solomon, however, certainly had a cultic dimension in their concept of kingship, and were not rebuked for exercising a lead in sacrifices and worship. John Mauchline comments that 'such service by laymen was common at this period although, in some cases at least, the service of a regular priest was regarded as preferable'.[1] He may well be right. The division of roles as it would work out in practice was still being settled, even though guidelines had already been laid down.

viii. David honours a possible rival (9:1–13). After all he had suffered at the hands of Saul, it would have been understandable if David had conveniently forgotten his promise to Jonathan (1 Sa. 20:14–15, 16, 42), especially in view of the fact that Jonathan had initiated the covenant agreement. But it was one of David's strengths that he did not forget what he had undertaken, even though many years had passed since that covenant had been made. The chapter provides an indication of the passing of time: Mephibosheth, who now has a young son (v. 12), was five years old at the death of his father (2 Sa. 4:4). David had seen his enemies defeated, his throne secured, and his empire established. He was therefore in a position to fulfil the obligation he had undertaken to show loyalty to Jonathan's descendants.

1. *Is there still any one left of the house of Saul?* David throws the net wider than his promises required, extending his generosity to any of Saul's surviving sons or grandsons, though his motive is clear: he is neither soft nor weak, but intends to show *kindness* (Heb. *ḥesed*) *for Jonathan's sake*, for he remembered how much he had owed to Jonathan. Members of the previous king's household had made themselves scarce, hence David's need of information.

2–5. One who can give the needed information is a man who has served in Saul's palace, by name *Ziba*, and who now

[1] Mauchline, p. 238. He refers to Jdg. 17:5, 13; 1 Sa. 10:8; 13:8–15.

calls himself David's *servant*. He was a man of some standing, with twenty servants of his own (v. 10). The only person he mentions as a descendant of Saul, to whom David might show *the kindness of God* (*cf*. Eph. 4:32), happens to be Jonathan's son, crippled in a fall (2 Sa. 4:4), though it transpires that there were others who might have had some claim (2 Sa. 21:8). *Mephibosheth*, who is called Merib-baal in 1 Chronicles 8:34 and 9:40 (the word 'baal' being avoided in Samuel because of its idolatrous associations), had been living in relative obscurity in *Lo-debar*, usually identified with Debir in Gad's territory (Jos. 13:26), east of Jordan, but close to the southern end of the Sea of Chinnereth (Jos. 13:27). Amos made a disparaging reference to it (Am. 6:13). *Machir the son of Ammiel*, who had provided a home for the prince of the deposed house of Saul, was to appear again in a hospitable role when David was in need (2 Sa. 17:27).

6–8. Despite the close relationship between his father and David, Mephibosheth would never before have been to the court of the king, and it would hardly be surprising if he felt both fear and resentment at the summons he had received, hence David's reassurance to him, *Do not fear; for . . . I will restore to you all the land of Saul*. The property of the previous regime would have come into David's possession, and to restore that property to a member of his predecessor's family was to run the risk of encouraging thoughts of usurping the throne. What was intended as a generous gesture without any ulterior motive could in this way backfire (*cf*. 2 Sa. 16:3).[1]

Mephibosheth, who had apparently been dependent up to this point on the hospitality of a generous individual, suddenly became a rich man, the owner of wealth-producing property (*cf*. 1 Ch. 27:25–31, where David's estates are listed; Saul's may have been less extensive but were no doubt ample). *You shall eat at my table always* ensured not only a place of honour at court but also access to those who were directing the affairs of state. He could now be 'in the know'. His reference to himself as *a dead dog* is unnecessarily disparaging, and reflects what would now be regarded as a morbid self-image, induced

[1] The suggestion that David acted out of 'calculated prudence' and aimed to bring people who could be a potential threat to him under watchful supervision (Mauchline, p. 241) seems to me unjustified. In my judgment it would have been more prudent to have left the situation alone, but David was not afraid to take risks, and went out of his way to be unusually generous.

perhaps by his disability.

9–10. It was all very well to bestow property on Mephibosheth, but it required management, hence the involvement of Ziba as chief steward, a man of substance who would realize what was required. *That your master's son may have bread to eat* is an understatement: he will have independent means. Ziba's *fifteen sons and twenty servants* ensure that there will be people with the necessary training and skill to manage the estates efficiently.

11–13. Ziba took over this responsibility as requested, and Mephibosheth lived at court like one of the royal princes, for whom the arrangement could have proved irksome. By sheer repetition, the account lays stress on Mephibosheth's lameness, his place at the king's table, and on the servants he needed. David's kindness involved a cost, to others as well as to himself. There was one other relevant factor, he had *a young son, whose name was Mica*. As it happens, he is not heard of again, but at the time he could have appeared as a possible threat to the throne of David, especially if Mephibosheth developed ideas about asserting the rights of the house of Saul, as Ziba reported (2 Sa. 16:3). The kindness of God (v. 3), on which David modelled his kindness, was not limited, but freely given to the undeserving as an act of free grace. Jonathan had given gracious help to David when he was driven from the king's table, and now David has been able to show kindness in return by giving to Jonathan's son security and honour. 'Thus the love between David and Jonathan attains a new stature'.[1]

c. David's personal crisis (10:1 – 12:31)

i. War with Ammon (10:1–19). David's well-intentioned embassage to the new king of Ammon initiated a whole train of events which were to his disadvantage, and must have raised the question whether it is prudent to 'show kindness'. This theme provides an obvious link with the events of 2 Samuel 9, including use of the characteristic quality of kindness (Heb. *ḥeseḏ*).

The Ammonites had come into the story at the beginning

---

[1] Fokkelman 1981, p. 30. These words conclude an analysis of the chapter, and its parallels with 1 Sa. 20, of which 'David, once a fugitive, now a king, mirrors as well as inverts this situation.'

of Saul's reign, when they had made cruel threats to the city of Jabesh-gilead (1 Sa. 11), but David had succeeded in establishing good relations with its king, Nahash, and intended to do all he could to maintain the alliance. The capital city of Ammon, Rabbah of the Ammonites (2 Sa. 12:26), is the present-day Amman, capital of Jordan.

The fact has already been noted that 2 Samuel contains no detail about David's brilliant conquests, nor is his skill as a military tactician explored. The question therefore arises why so much should be made of this particular exploit, which belongs to the period of David's success, when he could enjoy his achievements, and relax a little after the long uphill struggle.

1–2. A change of sovereign is still the occasion for diplomatic visits, and David was not acting in an unusual way in sending his ambassadors to offer his condolences and affirm his continuing good will. The expression *deal loyally* is the same in Hebrew as the 'show kindness' (Heb. *ḥesed*) of 2 Samuel 9:1, 3; in each case faithfulness to a covenant lies behind the words, though English requires a different turn of phrase for the political agreement. From Jerusalem to Amman was a journey of about fifty miles (80 km.).

3–5. In response to the suspicions expressed by his advisors, Hanun reversed the policy of his father and, by insulting David's ambassadors, asserted his independence of the kingdom of Israel. The accusation of spying was an already ancient ploy (Gn. 42:9), but it made a good excuse to humiliate David's ministers by sending them away with half a beard and half-naked. The outrage was virtually a declaration of war, its provocation demanding a suitable rebuff.

6–8. The Ammonites, expecting reprisals, prepared for battle and hired mercenaries from the *Syrians*, that is, the very people whom David is recounted as having defeated in 2 Samuel 8:3–12. Probably that summary of his achievements takes account of several exploits and their final outcome, in which case the events of this chapter would belong to an earlier stage of relationships between Israel and Syria/Aram, while contributing to the final victory of David. *Zobah* was an important kingdom of southern Syria, ruled by the house of Rehob (2 Sa. 8:3), which presumably stemmed from the place, *Beth-rehob*, called simply *Rehob* in verse 8. *Maacah* and *Tob* were nearer neighbours of Ammon in Transjordan.[1] The combined forces from these lands presented a formidable army, to attack on the flank, while the Ammonites ahead defended their city, presumably Rabbah.

9–12. Joab is seen here to advantage in his role as general of Israel's army. He did not panic in the face of the formidable odds, but strategically deployed his forces so as to allow for flexibility as the battle progressed. Moreover, he took on the most difficult task himself, commanding the small special force against the Arameans, while permitting his brother *Abishai* to fight the Ammonites, on the understanding that each would reinforce the other's army in case of need. Finally, Joab revealed himself to be a man of faith, fighting *for the cities of our God*, and praying, not expressly for victory, but for the Lord's outworking of his will. 'Joab will apply his forces and strategic genius to the full but, as a believer, he remains aware at the same time that the decision rests in God's hands, and he resolves himself to this.'[2] It comes as something of a surprise to find the tough Joab exhibiting faith in this way; now we know him a little better, and see him as a worthy general of David's army.

13–14. Joab succeeded in routing the Arameans, and the Ammonites similarly gave up the struggle. For the time being the battle was at an end.

15–19. The federation of Aramean states was too powerful to take the defeat as decisive and, reinforced by allies *beyond the Euphrates* (lit. 'beyond the river', but the Euphrates is meant), Hadadezer's army commander, *Shobach*, marched his forces to *Helam*, probably the modern 'Alma, some thirty-five miles (56 km.) east of the Sea of Galilee.[3] So significant was the outcome of this battle that David commanded the army in person, and won a resounding victory against their chariots and cavalry, even mortally wounding their commander. Not

[1] Damascus and its surrounding kingdom of Syria (known before *c.* 1000 BC as Aram), which lay between Zobah and Maacah, 'was one of the Aramean districts in the confederation under the leadership of Aram-zobah, whereas the kingdom of Maacah and the land of Tob . . . were not Aramean as yet' (B. Mazar, 'The Aramean Empire and its relations with Israel', in D. N. Freedman and E. F. Campbell, Jr., *The Biblical Archaeologist Reader* 2 [Garden City, NY: Doubleday, 1964], p. 131).

[2] Fokkelman 1981, p. 48.

[3] The name 'Helam' possibly occurs on an Egyptian inscription of *c.* 1800 BC, depicted in *IBD* 2, p. 633, but it is not otherwise known.

only the Arameans but also all their allies became subjects of David. This meant that the consolidated Israelite tribes had subjugated the powerful Aramean states to the east and north, and secured control over the main trade routes that connected Egypt and Arabia with Syria and further afield. As a result, Israel gained political dominance and economic advantage, while at the same time depriving Ammon of military allies. The Ammonites, who had been observing developments from the sidelines, had had opportunity to recover their strength.

ii. David's adultery (11:1–27). 1. During the inclement weather of the winter months, hostilities normally ceased, only to be resumed *in the spring of the year*, when travelling became bearable. It may have been just a year before that David had sent his envoys to offer his condolences to Hanun.[1] Joab led the total Israelite forces against Rabbah, having defeated the Ammonites in the field. *But David remained at Jerusalem* is the all-important circumstance, anticipating all that follows, including the final outcome of the battle (2 Sa. 12:26–31). While others spent themselves and risked their lives, he was 'killing time', acting like one of the kings of the nations round about, and exercising a kind of *droit de seigneur*.

This incident is closely interwoven with the account of the Ammonite war. In the past it has been usual to assert that the author skilfully inserted the Bathsheba affair into the accounts of the Ammonite war, but more recently a literary approach to the text has encouraged a reassessment of presuppositions regarding the history of the text. True, the Bathsheba incident is omitted totally from the parallel account in Chronicles, but an omission there does not prove an intrusion here. Indeed, far from being an intrusion, it could even be the reason why these particular battles are included in such detail. The biblical writer is more concerned about the character of the man God chose to head up the dynasty in Jerusalem, and the way God dealt with him, than with his splendid military achievements or wealth.

[1] Fokkelman 1981, pp. 50–51, points out that, by removing one *'ālep* from the MT, the word 'kings' has generally been read here, whereas by keeping the consonantal text and reading 'messengers' it makes better sense: 'And it happened with the coming (literally "return") of the new year, at the (same) time as the envoys (i.e., diplomats, consolers) had marched out, that David sent out Joab, etc.' (p. 50).

2–4. The account of what happened is brief and objective.
The king has an afternoon siesta, followed by a stroll on the
roof, which of necessity involves going backwards and
forwards, getting nowhere, a sense conveyed by the Hebrew
verb form.[1] From his vantage-point high above the homes of
his citizens (note the double mention of the roof), the king is
master of all he surveys. On this occasion he catches sight of
a woman, and she is *very beautiful*; the Hebrew idiom adds 'to
look at'. The glance becomes the gaze. Enquiries identify her
family and her husband. Ignoring the fact that she is the wife
of one of his serving troops, and aware only of his own desire
(which he does not yet identify as lust), he overrides her
personal feelings in the matter by sending messengers to take
her. The bald facts are stated, including the detail that she
was not pregnant when she came to David. Indeed, *she was
purifying herself* when he took her: 'Opposite the man who is
the prey of blind passion stands Bathsheba, and by contrast
her purity receives an emblematic aspect'.[2]

5. *And the woman conceived*: in keeping with the viewpoint of
the narrator, who has David in mind throughout, Bathsheba
is not named. To David she had been merely 'the woman'
rather than a person; moreover, no mention is made of the
agony of uncertainty she had suffered, all the more so because
a child of the king was involved. Now it was David's turn to
be dismayed.

6–8. A cover-up appears to David to be the obvious way
forward, so he sends to the battle lines for *Uriah the Hittite*; the
reader notes that he is not a member of Israel's covenant
community. What sort of person will he prove to be? He is
received at court, asked about the welfare (Heb. *šālôm*) of
Joab, the army and the battle, but, as Fokkelman notes, 'The
answer Uriah gives is not included in the narrative – a significant gap which symbolizes that David just lets him talk, not
paying any particular attention to his account.'[3] By contrast,
direct speech is used for what really matters to David (v. 8).
A royal gift is meant to encourage Uriah to consider himself

[1] The *hithpaʿēl*, one meaning of which is to express action upon or for oneself;
in one's own special interest (E. Kautzsch, *Gesenius' Hebrew Grammar* [Oxford
University Press, ET, ²1910], section 54, 3c, p. 150).
[2] Fokkelman 1981, pp. 52–53. This narrative is full of subtle nuances which
Fokkelman's approach highlights, and on which I draw in this section.
[3] Fokkelman 1981, p. 53.

specially favoured, and therefore to relax and enjoy his opportunity to go home and be with his wife.

9–11. *But Uriah slept at the door of the king's house . . . and did not go down to his house*, choosing instead to remain *with all the servants of his lord.* Three times the point is made that Uriah did not go home, for, despite what the king had said, Uriah knew where his duty lay; he was not on leave. David had expected and hoped that Uriah would prove to be like himself; instead he proved to be a man of integrity, whose first loyalty was to the king's interests rather than to his own pleasure. At the risk of arousing Uriah's suspicions, David asked why he had not gone home, and he answered, *The ark and Israel and Judah dwell in booths . . .* Astonishingly, this Hittite mentions the covenant symbol before everything else that has influenced his behaviour. He is aware also of his solidarity with the fighting men at the front, over whom he will not steal an advantage. Both of these considerations applied even more forcibly to the king, who had final responsibility for the war, and had laid much stress on covenant loyalty himself, but now a foreigner is showing him to be despicably lax.

12–13. David remains too occupied with his problem to concern himself with the moral issues. He has one more stratagem in mind: he will entertain Uriah, and there is just the chance that when Uriah has feasted and drunk at the king's table his resolve will weaken and he will go home to make love. But no; once again he spends the night *with the servants of his lord*, faithful still to his sovereign ('ādôn) and to his own high resolve. The cost of such loyalty will prove to be high: he insists on what is right and loses his life.

14–17. *David wrote a letter* to Joab, and made Uriah carry his own death warrant. It was all part of David's attempt to screen himself from exposure, yet ironically the incident has become one of the best known in Scripture. Only the essential information of the letter is quoted: David hands over to Joab the murder of an innocent man. This puts Joab in the unenviable position of conflict between loyalty to the king and loyalty to his own conscience. Even his professional competence as general is put at risk by the necessity to comply against his better judgment with what the king commands. In the event there was considerable loss of life, including *some of the servants of David*, and Uriah.

18–21. *The messenger* sent back to the king goes with an oral report on the battle, and his fulfilment of his errand is recorded in verses 22–24, but 'Joab's worries about the report (vv. 19–21) are given much more, even central attention.'[1] Central to his argument is something that the messenger did not need to say, but which was of great moment in the thinking of Joab: 'Who struck Abimelech son of Jerubbaal?' The reference is to Judges 9:50–57, where in the siege of Thebez Abimelech went so close to the wall that a woman was able to kill him by hurling an upper millstone on top of him. Joab, the military commander, knew better than to go close to the wall, but he had had to do so in response to the king's command; now the king must take the blame. The fact that a woman was involved is subtly hinted at by Joab, who has formed his own interpretation of David's activities in Jerusalem. He is not mistaken.

All the news about the fighting, which should be of paramount importance to David, is to be rounded off with the one name that really interests him: Uriah the Hittite.

22–24. The messenger reported *all that Joab had sent him to tell*, which had not been included in verses 19–21. Here was the information which had loomed large in the mind of Joab as he had got to grips with all that had been demanded of him: the near defeat, and then the advance towards the gate, which entailed new danger from soldiers on the wall, who caused the casualties. So worried has Joab been over all this avoidable bloodshed that the death of Uriah genuinely takes second place in his thinking, though because it had been forced upon him by the king Joab, in reporting the death to the king, virtually blames him for the heavy death toll. Joab is unhappy about the whole incident.

25. In his reply David fails to register any of the anger expected of him by Joab. Instead he takes the losses in his stride as part of the cost of the war, refusing to take notice of the inference that he had initiated the situation by his orders concerning Uriah. 'David poses as Joab's mild and understanding superior. However, in [14, 15] we have already been informed about the man behind this mask, and therefore v. 25 sounds all the more cynical and merciless.'[2] By saying to Joab, *Do not let this matter trouble you* ('displease thee', AV), David is

[1] Fokkelman 1981, p. 61, where a diagrammatic presentation of vv. 14–25 shows the skilful use of a chiastic structure, a concentric pattern.
[2] Fokkelman 1981, p. 63.

at the same time speaking to himself and placating his own conscience.

Strengthen your attack upon the city: David fully expects victory over Rabbah, and condescendingly tells the messenger to *encourage* (lit. 'strengthen') Joab.

26–27. *The wife of Uriah*: she is referred to not by her name but by her status in this passage. In this way the writer detaches himself from the new liaison and pays his respects to *Uriah her husband*, who *was dead*. At no point is the reader permitted to gather that Uriah's death was regarded as a matter of indifference. Once the mourning period was over David sent as he had done once before (2 Sa. 11:4) to bring her *to his house*, but this time *she became his wife*. Their son was born; time passed and, so far as appearances went, everything went on as before. Ministers close to the king knew what injustice had been committed, and yet it apparently went unpunished, though not for long, because *the thing that David had done displeased the Lord* (*cf.* David's very word to Joab in v. 25). The Lord in his infinite grace had allowed David's attempt at cover-up to fail, and was about to confront him. The writer is able confidently to make this statement because of the revelation he is about to record.

iii. The prophet confronts the king (12:1–15a).

Whereas in countries such as Egypt the king was regarded as divine, in Israel he had to submit to the Lord God who had chosen him, and observe all the commandments given to Israel (Dt. 17:15, 20). It was the task of the prophet of the Lord to encourage the king to fulfil these obligations, and to rebuke him in God's name if he failed to do so. The prophet Samuel had found King Saul stubbornly opposed to accepting a rebuke (1 Sa. 13:12; 15:13, 20); now Nathan was to discover how David would react to hearing the truth about his behaviour. Much would depend on the prophet's method of approach, which in this instance provides a model and reveals exceptional insight into human reactions to personal guilt and the failures of other people.

1. *The Lord sent Nathan*, who therefore went with full divine authority, however much he may have dreaded the delicate task of rebuking the king. *He came to him* is no redundant phrase, because it serves, together with verse 15, as a frame round the narrative. Nathan begins his audience with the king by sketching a case-study which could easily have come before one of the local courts. There is nothing to suggest that it is a parable, and David, the supreme judge, who could be expected to pronounce on hard cases, paid attention to the details, which the prophet outlined in sixty-one carefully chosen words.

The case concerns *two men*, one rich, the other poor. Even so little information arouses interest: life's inequalities are always with us.

2–3. The rich man's riches are in stark contrast with the poor man's *nothing*, his *flocks and herds* with the *one little ewe lamb*, the natural increase of stock with the need of the poor man to buy his one treasured possession. Now we are shown the poor man in such a way that we can come to know him. He hand-raises the lamb he has bought, treating it like a member of his family, spoiling it like a beloved daughter. They become inseparable.

4. A visitor comes to see the rich man, but rather than deplete his own stock in order to entertain the guest he takes possession of the poor man's pet lamb, which he proceeds to turn into the main course for his feast. Now we also know the rich man in all his meanness and heartlessness.

5–6. David has become involved with Nathan's two men; he can see exactly what they are like, and he reacts with righteous anger, and with a vehemence which may have surprised himself: *As the Lord lives the* [*rich*] *man . . . deserves to die*. The oath should not be necessary, but it is a sign of intense involvement. David passes the death sentence on the rich man. But why? He has not committed murder.

> David means to occupy himself with the reality outside of himself, the rich man and his misdeed, but, in actual fact, he is involved with himself and seeks to restore his feelings of well-being in this way . . . Nathan provides him with a projection screen for this very purpose, and, indeed, David projects vehemently. He means to pass verdict upon another but actually passes verdict entirely upon himself.[1]

David attempts to rid himself of his guilty conscience by passing judgment on someone else, while subconsciously passing judgment on himself. Only after that does he mention

[1] Fokkelman 1981, p. 77.

fourfold restitution to compensate the poor man for his loss, and explain the reasoning behind his verdict: the rich man *did this thing* and must therefore be held responsible, and his state of mind was also reprehensible, *he had no pity*. Here in David's reaction is proof, if any were needed, that humanity is endowed with a keen sense of justice which operates effectively, provided that the individual passing judgment is not personally part of the case. At the same time, the conscience of the individual who passes judgment betrays its guilt (or innocence) to the discerning onlooker.

7–12. Nathan has skilfully presented his case and gained an opening which enables him to deliver all he must say without waste of time or words: *You are the man*. David has condemned himself and suddenly has to come to terms with his own verdict, passed upon another but now unerringly applied to himself. There could be no more effective example of the power of the parable as a tool in counselling. All David's defences have been flattened at a stroke, and he stands naked before his judge.

Nathan has come to deliver the judgment of God, and therefore he dare not soften the impact of his words. Indeed he speaks in the first person the *ipsissima verba* of God himself. It is an awesome moment for both the prophet and the king. But the way has been prepared by the parable's appeal to his conscience, which has proved to be in working order, and has passed the death sentence on the king. David now has to allow the word of the Lord to probe deeply in order to bring to light the hidden, dark side of his personality, so that David acknowledges it as his own.

First, David must consider all that he has received from the hand of God: *I anointed you . . . I delivered you . . . I gave you*. He has been rich in that he has experienced the Lord's favour from his youth, when he was anointed by Samuel, when he was delivered from death at the hand of Saul, and when he inherited the kingdom and *your master's wives*. Evidently the custom was that the harem of the dead monarch was inherited by his successor, and by this rule David had already added to his household. In no respect could he claim that he had been deprived; he was the rich man. Moreover, if he had asked for more he could have had more, such is the extent of the Lord's generosity towards him.

Despite all this, David has done *what is evil in his sight*, thus despising the Lord's word and his authority. David knew what had happened to Saul when he rejected the word of the Lord (1 Sa. 15:23); now he was under sentence himself.

You have smitten Uriah the Hittite with the sword: though David had engineered this death from a distance, he was as guilty of murder as if he had thrust the man through with his own sword. How could he possibly escape the death penalty? Though by the law of the land he might be judged not guilty, he had no ground for appeal before the divine judge, who went on to uncover the adultery that motivated the murder.

The punishment which the Lord is going to mete out exactly reflects the crimes committed. *The sword shall never depart from your house* indicates that David's dynasty, unlike that of Saul, is to continue, but that good news is modified by the ongoing punishment of protracted war and bloodshed. In this the whole nation is involved, and generations to come will be reminded of David's sin as they fight continuing battles. Moreover, *I will raise up evil against you out of your own house*; so far as his wives are concerned, he will lose them to a neighbour. The Lord says, *I will take your wives*, as David took Bathsheba (2 Sa. 11:4); but whereas he acted in secret, *all Israel* will witness the Lord's retribution, as is necessary if justice is to be seen to be done, and the law of the Lord is to be upheld. 'From Nathan's perspective the issue is clear. It was Yahweh who gave the kingdom. Yahweh in turn will not then let his king's act of violent taking pass without consequences for his kingdom.'[1] The continuing narrative will show how those consequences worked out during the lifetime of David, bringing tragedy and loss to mark the later years of his reign, and not only to him. Nathan's reproof, spoken in the name of the Lord, gives the impression that the Lord himself will act directly to punish David; its outworking involves the interwoven schemes of different members of David's family, motivated by the very sins which had disgraced their father, and by the desire for prestige and power. The working of God's providence, affirmed throughout Scripture, is seen in all its mystery, because it is accomplished through the freely chosen actions of the human participants in the drama.

13–15a. The king makes his second response to the prophet

[1] Gunn 1982, p. 97.

with a verdict on himself which is closely connected with the
verdict he passed on the rich man (vv. 5–6), but this second
verdict is much harder to articulate than that had been. Now
David takes his courage in both hands and faces up to the
fact that he is without excuse and has incurred the death
penalty. Though he is king, he confesses his guilt before the
prophet who, despite being God's mouthpiece, is nevertheless
one of David's subjects. Such loss of face is incredibly hard to
bear, and could have been regarded as political suicide, but
the king, convinced of Nathan's integrity as a prophet,
humbled himself in confession. Immediately came the astonishing response: *The Lord also has put away your sin; you shall not
die.* This was the turning-point in the life of David, and the
clearest indication that he was different from Saul in the most
essential relationship of all, that of submission to the Lord
God. For that reason he found forgiveness, whereas Saul never
accepted his guilt or the rejection that followed from it. Psalm
32, traditionally accepted as expressing David's thoughts on
this occasion, is exuberant over the joy of knowing forgiveness
in place of guilt, restoration of fellowship after the pain of
conviction of sin. In place of death he has new life, so freely
does he enter into the grace of God.

This transforming experience does not mean, however, that
the judgments which the Lord has announced through the
prophet have been annulled. The consequences of David's
having *scorned the Lord* still have to be faced, and of that, one
further consequence will be a sign: *the child that is born to you
shall die.* With that the prophet has fulfilled his mission; he
departs, and the interview ends.

iv. The death of the child (12:15b–23). David is a
surprising person, so much so that those closest to him at
court did not understand the way his mind worked. He knew
from what Nathan had told him that the child born to
Bathsheba would die, and there would be justice obvious to
all in that event. In this way Israel and observers outside of
Israel would take note of the evidence that the Lord was
indeed a God of righteousness, by whom actions were weighed.
David, however, restored to fellowship with the Lord, was
overwhelmingly conscious of the Lord's loving-kindness in
granting him forgiveness and reinstating him, despite his
guilty past, as the covenant king of Israel. This permitted him

again to approach the Lord in prayer, and he meant to explore to the full the possibility that the Lord would grant him the life of the child in answer to his petition.

15b. This is one case in which Scripture associates illness with the sin of a parent (*cf.* Jn. 9:2), but, as in the case of the man born blind, the purpose was the glory of God. The biblical writer does not hesitate to attribute directly to the Lord the sickness of this child, in accordance with the prophet's word.

16–18. There is nothing merely perfunctory about the prayer of David on this occasion. His love for the child, who is not even named, is so great that he will fast for a week and go without sleep in order to give himself to prayer. This passionate man understood the meaning of the word 'love' in the light of the Lord's love to him, and longed for the baby to be spared. When the child dies, for his prayer receives a negative answer, no-one dares to tell him the news for fear of his reaction, but they had misinterpreted the king's mind.

19–20. Once he had established that the child was dead, David, instead of going into mourning, resumed his normal way of life, which his servants had tried unsuccessfully to induce him to do during the previous week. He even *went into the house of the Lord, and worshipped* in the tent where the ark of God had been installed (2 Sa. 6:17). This proves that David had accepted the Lord's judgment, despite his week of mourning, when he had given expression to his great grief in advance, as it were. Now that the death has occurred, he is able to break with convention, even to the extent of worshipping the God who has taken back the child. That done, he breaks his fast and asks for food.

21–23. The servants need an explanation of such topsy-turvy behaviour. David's answer to them has enabled every generation of readers to appreciate his reasoning. *Who knows whether the Lord will be gracious to me . . . ?* shows David's conviction that he was in touch with the God who deals with his children as individuals and responds to their faith. Thus, as he listens to the word of the Lord through Nathan (v. 14), he does not accept it fatalistically, but rather in the way a child hears the statement of a parent, who sometimes changes his mind about a punishment if the child behaves acceptably. David has understood an important element in prophecies of judgment, and one expressed by our Lord as he contemplated the coming judgment on Jerusalem: 'How often would I have gathered your children together . . . and you would not (*i.e.* were not willing)!' (Lk. 13:34). The Lord has blessings in mind for those who ask, and David is not going to miss them because he has not asked (Jas. 4:2).

Now that the child is dead, however, the answer is final: *I shall go to him, but he will not return to me.* David comes to terms with his own mortality, and even in that finds hope, because he looks forward to being reunited with his child. The Lord who had sent Nathan to David had had the last word and, though David was bereft, he was content.

v. The birth of Solomon (12:24–25). The birth of a second son to Bathsheba and David was certain to be a reminder of the illness and death of the first. Would this son live? The name given to him by his parents, *Solomon*, is derived from the Hebrew *šālôm*, 'peace', 'prosperity', so reflecting their hopes for this new life. Nathan came to bring a reassuring message, neatly expressed in a second name, *Jedidiah*, 'loved by the Lord'; this baby would not die.[1] Now David knew that he had indeed been restored to fellowship with the Lord, and of all his many children this one became especially precious.

Additional Note: The Bathsheba incident

Underlying the account of 2 Samuel 11 and 12, unseen but nevertheless foundational, is Israel's covenant law, the ten commandments of the Lord their God, which included the words, 'You shall not commit adultery' (Ex. 20:14). Indeed the nations around, as well as Israel, hedged marriage about with safeguards, such as monetary payments which had to be returned in the event of divorce, with the intention of securing the permanence of marriage. A man could have more than one wife, but he could not with impunity have a married woman, who belonged exclusively to her husband, with whom she had become one flesh. This was part of the social structure of Israel's society, and therefore could be taken for granted by the narrator. All Israel knew that adultery was wrong; the

[1] The name may be a title of royal legitimation, indicating divine protection and Yahweh's abiding love. N. Wyatt, ' "Jedidiah" and Cognate Forms as a Title of Royal Legitimation', *Biblica* 66 (1985), pp. 112–125.

241

question, then as now, was how to deal justly with the complex circumstances to which adultery gave rise.

In the case of David the king, the word of the Lord, spoken directly through the prophet, exposes the sordid reality in such a way as to strip off any suggestion of glamour. Nathan's parable brings out the cruelty of violating loving relationship, and the callousness of disregarding another man's feelings, not to mention appropriation of the object of his affections, which is mean and despicable. From all that the reader has seen of David thus far, he was not a callous man; but he was capable of falling to unsuspected depths of evil at a whim, so within one and the same person two people were struggling for supremacy. That evening when David caught sight of Bathsheba, the evil got the upper hand and all his understanding of the covenant commands went out of the window. David the king knew he was guilty, and so did the world of his day. That was why he had to devise a way of covering his guilt and became involved in murder.

The worrying feature is that David apparently benefits in the long run from his wrongdoing. True, he has a guilty conscience for a while, but he receives divine forgiveness, and with that is restored to fellowship with God and peace with himself. True, the child conceived in adultery dies, and his death goes some way towards indicating to the world the divine judgment on David's sin. Nevertheless, the fact remains that the woman he desired, but should not have had, became his wife, and many Christians today find that impermissible, especially for a believer, which David undoubtedly was. Did not the fact that the Lord granted to David restoration of fellowship encourage wrongdoing?

According to the letter of the law, David was free after the death of Uriah to marry Bathsheba. However, the Lord did not judge by the letter but by the spirit of the law, and by this standard David was guilty; indeed Nathan had explained the repercussions which would cause disturbances in his family for years to come. But one factor set David free from the guilt of his sin: he repented. He was genuinely grieved that he had taken matters into his own hand, despising the Lord he professed to serve in so doing. He could have known that, as king, all that he did would become known, and that his example would be imitated. In particular, his own children would tend to take their cue from their father. Primarily, however, his sin had been against the Lord, as he was to write:

> Have mercy on me, O God,
>   according to thy steadfast love;
> according to thy abundant mercy
>   blot out my transgressions . . .
> Against thee, thee only, have I sinned,
>   and done that which is evil in thy sight,
> so that thou art justified in thy sentence
>   and blameless in thy judgment.
>
> (Psalm 51:1, 4)

The fact is that David's prayer was acceptable to God because of his broken and contrite heart; and, as he goes on to express his experience in the psalm, it transpires that he found deliverance from bloodguiltiness, and – clean of heart and conscience – he knew once again the joy of God's salvation.

But society is not ready to forgive, and very often people who have committed grave sin are unable to forgive themselves, and so they cut themselves off from God and his church because they expect to meet with condemnation. And, indeed, that may be their experience if church leaders forget that the church consists of returned sinners whose task it is to reclaim other sinners in the name of Christ. If the church is faithful in that mission, it will be fulfilling the task committed to it by the risen Christ (Mt. 28:18–20; Mk. 16:15; Lk. 24:46–47; Acts 1:8; Jn. 21:15–19, which lays stress on the pastoral care of believers). Those who have been forgiven much love much, and are well placed to restore others who need forgiveness. Not that anyone fails to need forgiveness, but there is such a thing as shallow repentance, which is a matter of words rather than of conviction, and which breeds a pharisaic attitude. In this state of mind it is easy to condemn the scandals of other people's behaviour, because such criticism helps to bolster one's own ego, as David found when he reacted to Nathan's parable, and pronounced his judgment. Realization that he was the man in question, who stood condemned, cleared away all his hypocrisy and enabled him to make a clean breast of everything in the presence of his God. Without the depth of his conviction of sin and his certainty of forgiveness, cleansing and renewal, David would never have become everyman's psalmist. His writing is pertinent for every generation and for every human situation.

Every sensitive reader must also wonder what the whole episode looked like from the point of view of Bathsheba. She was the victim of David's lust, but the narrator deliberately omits her feelings from consideration, in order to concentrate on David. Nevertheless, she suffered much, losing her integrity, bearing an illegitimate child, losing her husband, marrying her lover and then losing her child. All the ingredients for a drama are here, and invite exploration, but the biblical narrator resisted any invitation to side-track. By treating Bathsheba with clinical objectivity, the writer cleverly conveys the self-centredness of David's lust. She is the wife of another, and yet he seizes her. Such an action cannot be described as 'love', and the Bible does not use that term, nor any other endearing word. Looked at from the divine standpoint, David's action has no redeeming features. Even so, this was not the end of all things; David did not need to consider suicide, for he came to repentance. Bathsheba, after all her agonies, bore David another son who was 'beloved of the Lord'. Though we find it difficult to understand why this son, of all David's children, should have been God's choice for David's successor, the fact that he was the chosen one endorses the message of this episode: there is a way back into fellowship with God even from the depths of evil. The word of the Lord has the power to touch the springs of conscience, deep within the human personality, and to bring to light the hidden things of darkness. Once this process has allowed full confession to express repentance, the Lord 'is faithful and just, and will forgive our sins and cleanse us from all unrighteousness' (1 Jn. 1:9). The choice of Solomon as king and, above all, the birth of Jesus into the line of David give practical expression to the reality of God's acceptance of sinners (Mt. 1:17; Lk. 3:23, 31). It is the outworking of this acceptance in real life that brings home the truth: God forgives repentant sinners.

vi. Conclusion of the Ammonite war (12:26–31). Almost certainly the siege of the Ammonite capital Rabbah was concluded during the season in which it began (2 Sa. 11:1), but the successful conquest of the city fits well at this point, supplementing the peace which David had obtained with his God with this victory which brings peace from war. 2 Samuel

10–12 are thus bracketed by the Ammonite hostilities and can be seen to be all of one piece. Another effect of dealing with the Bathsheba affair in one uninterrupted sequence is to give priority to the important outcome of David's crime in terms of punishment and forgiveness. 'There is no haste in settling accounts with the Ammonites, but there is considerable haste in settling accounts with David's crimes, for they may not remain undenied for even one moment.'[1]

26–28. Under the generalship of Joab, the city of Rabbah was about to capitulate. He reported to David, *I have taken the city of the waters*, and the use of direct speech vividly conjures up the excitement and expectation of victory. Rabbah of Ammon was situated near the source of the river Jabbok, which flowed to the south of the ancient city. It was usual for a city's water supply to be guarded by fortifications, and these Joab had already captured.[2] Excavation in the citadel area has revealed heavy fortification in an earlier period (*c.* 1750–1550 BC), and stratified remains of the Iron Age city (*c.* 1200–580 BC), including phases of the tenth to ninth-century defence wall, which may go back to David's reconstruction of Rabbah after its capture about 980 BC.[3] The citadel, which would be the last area to fall, would include the palace, and Joab in his loyalty wanted the honour of capturing the city and its king to go to David.

29–31. Strengthened by extra forces, David's army finished what Joab had almost accomplished; verse 29 repeats with David as the subject what verse 26 had attributed to Joab. It was an impressive conquest, assessed here in terms of the wealth which David acquired in spoil. The transfer of the crown from the head of the Ammonite king (whose name is not mentioned now, despite its repetition in 2 Sa. 10:1–5) to the head of David symbolized the transfer of power over Ammon to the Israelite king. The weight of the gold (the *talent* was about 30 kg., or 66 lb.) and the crown jewel were

[1] Fokkelman 1981, p. 95.
[2] Water works of the upper city were uncovered by the Italian archaeological expedition (1930–1941), but 'the results were published in a very fragmentary manner', M. Avi-Yonah – E. Stern (eds.), *Encyclopaedia of Archaeological Excavations in the Holy Land* (Oxford: Oxford University Press, 1978), 4, p. 987.
[3] G. M. Landes, *IDBS*, p. 724.

indicative of the splendour of Ammon's throne.[1] The population was subjected to forced labour, not to torture, as used to be thought (cf. 'put them under saws, and under harrows of iron . . .' AV, RV, but cf. RV mg.). A century ago the traditional interpretation was questioned.[2] It has now become the generally accepted view that forced labour, not torture, is implied by the text; the various tools and occupations suggest that David set up building projects throughout Ammonite territory. These would be needed in order to repair the fortifications damaged in the recent fighting, and probably also to house his own garrisons, whose task it would be to keep the conquered people subservient.

The return of the king and the people to Jerusalem marks the conclusion of the episode.

d. Like father like sons (13:1 – 19:40)

The rape of Tamar initiates a series of events which dominate the later part of David's reign and threaten to discredit him entirely, so that he almost loses his throne, together with any right to indicate which son should succeed him. The account is detailed and close-knit, with many signs of first-hand observations and of vivid reminiscences.

i. Amnon rapes his half-sister, Tamar (13:1–22).

The narrator introduces two of the grown-up sons of the king, who turn out to be 'chips off the old block'.[3] *Absalom* is mentioned first because it is his sister, *Tamar*, who is at the centre of the drama, but *Amnon* was the eldest in the family, and therefore the heir-apparent (2 Sa. 3:2–3). The king is already one step removed from all that is going on between the sons of his

[1] The words 'their king' (Heb. *malkām*) could be read as the name of the Ammonite deity (cf. Je. 49:1, 3; Zp. 1:5), but this has been generally rejected as a possibility because it is thought unlikely that David would have taken and worn the crown of an idol. Nevertheless, it is not so unlikely if the wearing of the crown showed the superiority of Yahweh over Milcom.

[2] G. Hoffmann, *ZAW* (1882), pp. 53–72, quoted in Driver 1913, pp. 227–229, argued i. for the meaning 'brick-mould', not 'brick kiln' (Heb. *malkēn*); ii. that the verb 'made them pass through' (AV) should be corrected to 'made them labour at' by the slight change of *r* to *d*. The preposition 'under' is not a usual rendering of the Hebrew *b*, for which 'at' is to be preferred. The NIV incorporates these points 'consigning them to labour with saws and with iron picks and axes, and he made them work at brickmaking'.

[3] The title of chapter 5 of Fokkelman 1981, dealing with 2 Sa. 13.

different wives, and behind the action itself there is another
preoccupation, that of the succession, for Chileab, David's
second son (2 Sa. 3:3), drops out of the story (we do not know
how or why) and Absalom is second in line to the throne.

1–2. *Absalom*, whose name is given prominence at the beginning of the chapter, is going to dominate the scenes to follow.
His *beautiful sister*, tragic in her beauty, is a royal princess.
Amnon, the crown prince, loves her, but, despite his privileged
status, he finds himself powerless to possess her. The reason
given, *she was a virgin*, might have meant in other circumstances that he was free to marry her (*cf.* v. 13), but she
was his half-sister and therefore he dismissed the possibility
(Lv. 18:9). Either that, or he was intending only a casual
liaison with her; in any case, Amnon had not considered
breaking the conventions which governed society in Israel in
these matters. Instead he *made himself ill*, to the extent that
other people noticed the change in his appearance.

3. *But Amnon had a friend*, an important and influential counsellor, no doubt, and a member of the royal family: his own
cousin, *Jonadab*. He is described as *a very crafty man* (Heb.
ḥākām, 'wise', 'shrewd'); the context dictates the exact nuance
of the word, and here its usual ethical content is conspicuously
lacking. He was 'wise' in the sense that he knew what he
wanted and how to get it.

4–6. Jonadab is sufficiently observant to notice that something is wrong with prince Amnon, and, on discovering that
he is love-sick, proposes a ruse which will not only bring
Tamar to him but will also make their father responsible for
her coming.

When your father comes to see you: evidently he was in the habit
of visiting any of his children who were ill, and was inclined
to be indulgent towards them. It was childish of a grown man
to make out that he would eat only what one particular
member of the family made specially for him; most mothers
would have had no patience with such a request, but there
appeared to be no harm in it, and Jonadab counted on David's
leniency towards his sons.

7–9. Tamar responded to her father's message and went to
Amnon's home (accompanied without doubt by at least one
lady-in-waiting) prepared to coax the invalid to eat the appet-
izing food she cooked for him. The scene is vivid; Amnon is
on his bed, in an adjoining room, but within sight of Tamar,

and we watch (as if through his eyes) the cook at work.

She took dough ... and made cakes ... and baked the cakes: the word for 'cakes' (Heb. *l*ᵉ*bibôt*) occurs only in this chapter and the word for 'baked' is more correctly 'boiled'. Some special invalid dish is implied, *but he refused to eat*. His original request (v. 6) had been for a couple of *l*ᵉ*bibôt*; the word is derived from the Hebrew *lēbāb*, 'heart', implying something like 'heart-shapes', a clue which David did not pick up. Now Amnon can't touch them, he is so ill. It is all part of the act. Ill as he is, he cannot bear all these people around, and in this way he contrives to be left alone with Tamar.

10–11. Amnon continues to play the invalid, who has no strength even to feed himself. His dutiful sister, apparently unsuspecting, approaches his bed, only to be grabbed: *he took hold of her* (Heb. *yah*ᵃ*zeq*) is a strong verb meaning 'over-powered' (*cf.* 1 Sa. 17:50, 'prevailed'). Even so, he speaks lovingly, calling Tamar *my sister*, a term which was used fig-uratively of the 'beloved' (Song 5:1), though with ambiguity here since Tamar was Amnon's half-sister.

12–14. Tamar, trapped, tries to reason with her brother. She refuses his suggestion on three counts: public opinion in Israel was opposed to rape, described as *hann*ᵉ*bālâ hazzô'ṯ* 'this folly' (*cf.* Gn. 34:7), she would have no future, and neither would he, because he would be regarded as *one of the wanton fools* (Heb. *hann*ᵉ*bālîm*; *cf.* the name 'Nabal' in 1 Sa. 25). Was this the sort of person Israel would want for a king, a man without principles, who took the law into his own hands and offended ordinary standards of morality in the land? Finally she makes her suggestion: Amnon should ask her father for her hand in the proper way, and marry her; the king would not refuse him. Though the law of Leviticus 18:9 forbad such a union, it was clearly to be preferred to rape; if Sarah was Abraham's half-sister, there could be a precedent, and Tamar was clutching at any escape from her plight. All argument proves useless against Amnon's intense passion, which was a travesty of love (v. 1), and he raped her.

15. The sudden reversal from love to hate, and the dismissal, *Arise, be gone*, are cruel, most of all to Tamar, but also in their revelation of Amnon's inadequacy as a person:

Amnon's act of violence reveals him as someone incapable of contact and as an uncouth egoist. The worst for him is that there is a witness present, and Tamar is this very witness. From then on he will no longer be able to see her, for such a meeting would be a repeated, extremely shameful unmasking and intolerable confrontation with his own shortcomings as a person.[1]

16–17. Once again Tamar attempts to persuade her brother to see reason: he is compounding his evil deeds in rejecting her after all his pretended love. Princess though she is, she is summarily bundled out of Amnon's presence, and referred to ignominiously as *this woman. Bolt the door after her* was Amnon's attempt to rid himself even of the memory of Tamar, whom he had so much wanted before. The relationship, if such it had ever been, was dead.

18. Tamar is dressed as an unmarried daughter of the king, distinctive in her *long robe with sleeves*. This is reminiscent of Joseph's 'coat of many colours' (Gn. 37:3, AV) or 'long robe with sleeves' (RSV); though the details are obscure, the dress was no doubt splendid, but all that it stood for was gone for ever. When Amnon's servant *bolted the door after her*, Tamar knew deep down that the door to marriage was bolted against her for good.

19. Tamar's sense of desolation was every bit as great as if she were in mourning, hence the expressions of grief that everyone she met could see and hear. At least there was for her no unhealthy repression of wounded feelings, though her future was bleak. Her face daubed with dirty marks (*cf.* 1 Sa. 4:12), her torn robe (*cf.* 2 Sa. 1:2) and her loud crying eloquently depicted grievous loss; *she laid her hand on her head* is a gesture mentioned in Jeremiah 2:37, but in reliefs and tomb paintings it appears to symbolize captivity.[2]

20–22. Absalom immediately jumped to the right conclusion on seeing Tamar, and he did his best to comfort her by making light of her experience. He made use of a diminutive form of Amnon's name (Heb. *'aminôn*), perhaps one used in the family,[3] and, by recalling that he was her brother, implied that she should not clamour for justice but leave the matter with him. She took shelter in Absalom's house, *a desolate*

---

[1] So Fokkelman 1981, pp. 107–108, in a section full of insight, explains the irrational behaviour of Amnon.

[2] *ANEP*, illustrations 634, 640.

[3] Hertzberg, p. 321, suggests that this is perhaps meant as an ironical diminutive.

woman (Heb. *šōmēmâ*), isolated from society, disqualified through no fault of her own from marriage. David reacted to the outrage with anger, 'but he would not hurt Amnon because he was his eldest son and he loved him' (the NEB adds these words from the LXX). Like Eli and Samuel, David failed effectively to control his sons, and his own bad example would inhibit any protest against Amnon. Absalom, however, showed his disapproval by refusing to have anything to do with Amnon, and, seething with anger, waited for an opportunity to avenge the wrong done to his sister.

ii. Absalom's revenge (13:23–39). 23. *After two full years*: with all the many demands on the king, David and others would have forgotten Tamar's plight, but not so Absalom, who now had his plans laid. Sheep-shearing had long been regarded as a time for festivities (Gn. 38:12–13; *cf.* 1 Sa. 25:2, 36); Absalom's sheep were being sheared at a little place *near Ephraim*, often identified with the better-known Ophrah, north-east of Bethel. The NEB has Ephron, another name for the same place (2 Ch. 13:19), but the NIV takes Ephraim as the tribe, 'near the border of Ephraim', which would indicate a place a little further south.

24–29. Though Absalom appears to be pressing the king to be present with his retainers at the feast, he must have expected that his invitation would not be accepted. If the king will not go, then Amnon, the crown prince, should stand in as his representative. David appears reluctant, but eventually gives in by permitting all his sons to attend the feast, which in some ancient MSS is described in an additional clause: 'and Absalom made a banquet like the banquet of a king'.[1] The remark is important for its possible innuendo that Absalom was angling for recognition as next in line after Amnon for the throne (*cf.* 1 Sa. 25:36, where the same expression is used of Nabal). The death of Amnon would thus fulfil a dual purpose for Absalom, who ordered his servants on his authority to murder Amnon, though Amnon was crown prince representing the king, half-brother of Absalom, and an invited guest. Such treachery as this merited the most extreme penalty. It is understandable, therefore, that the assassins

---

[1] LXX and 4QSam[a]. The translators of the JB, NEB and GNB have incorporated the addition into the text. *Cf.* Gordon, 'David's Rise and Saul's Demise', p. 46 n. 32.

needed extra reassurance, *Fear not . . .*, and the remaining princes fled on their royal mules for their lives, fugitives from Absalom.

30–31. In the sudden panic and terror a messenger took a garbled account of events to the palace, *Absalom has slain all the king's sons*, and even more emphatically, *not one of them is left*, as if to compensate for a degree of uncertainty. The king, however, takes the *communiqué* at its face value and is overwhelmed with grief. Had he not contributed to this terrible event by permitting all his sons to leave the capital, and by releasing Amnon in particular? The king's courtiers mourned with their prostrate king.

32–33. But one of their number claimed to have insight into the event. Jonadab, who had given Amnon the benefit of his advice two years previously, could confidently assert that Amnon alone had been killed. He was convinced that this was Absalom's vengeance for the rape of Tamar, an act from which he distances himself.[1] On this ground he endeavoured to stand aside from the mourners, and, somewhat vainly, reassure the king. Amnon's death alone was sufficient cause for his father's grief.

34. *But Absalom fled*: While messengers were reaching Jerusalem, he was making his escape in the opposite direction. Meanwhile, the watchman reports the approach of a large crowd *from the Horonaim road*. The name is based on the LXX and refers to Upper and Lower Beth-horon, to the north-west of Jerusalem. The LXX adds, 'The watchman went and told the king, "I see men in the direction of Horonaim, on the side of the hill" ' (NIV, which incorporates this addition into the text). The details enable the reader to enter into the suspense caused by the lack of hard information.

35–36. Jonadab recognized the princes and pointed out that he had been right. Everyone else at court mourned for the dead prince.

37. *But Absalom fled, and went to Talmai*, his grand-father on his mother's side, who was *king of Geshur*, a buffer-state

---

[1] Fokkelman 1981, p. 109, points out that Jonadab could not have predicted how Tamar would react, nor how Amnon would choose the most severe option: 'I consider it improbable that the Jonadab of 13:4–6 had already cynically premeditated rape.' His proposed deception, 'admittedly not very morally elevated', was meant to secure a private meeting between Amnon and Tamar.

between Israel and Syria, to the north of Gilead (2 Sa. 3:3). There he escaped being brought to justice, but at the same time he forfeited any likelihood of inheriting the throne of Israel. His father, meanwhile, continued in mourning *for his son*: for Amnon, presumably, though there is ambiguity here.

38. *So Absalom fled*: the repetition, which often strikes the Western mind as redundant, should be interpreted as a device which provides a window into the mind of the narrator: the situation has reached deadlock. King David is powerless to punish the offender; Absalom is unable to return. The reader is curious to know how the problem is resolved *after three years*, for mention of the duration of Absalom's stay in exile implies his return.

39. This verse forms a transition between the events just related and new developments in the next chapter. The Hebrew has been described as 'untranslatable',[1] and some emendation is inevitable, but the sense is that the passing of time took the edge off bitter feelings. David had to come to terms with the loss of Amnon because he was dead. Absalom, however, might as well have been dead so far as his father was concerned; David longed to see him but did not recall him. His love and his sense of justice found no place of reconciliation, so, torn between the two, he did nothing. It is significant perhaps that David, who rightly refrained from taking action against Saul in his younger days, became blameworthy as king for failing to execute justice within his own family. One reason had to do with his own failings, which he could see being reproduced in his sons; another arose out of his love for his sons, who nevertheless had no scruples over deceiving him into doing what they wanted, and involving him in their evil plans. Already the prophecy of Nathan that the sword would never depart from his house was working out in David's experience.[2]

---

[1] Driver 1913, p. 235. The verb is in the feminine form, which implies a feminine noun as subject, hence the emendation of 'David' to the word *rûaḥ*, 'spirit', which is not very different in the consonantal text.

[2] 2 Sa. 13:39 permits another translation, which reverses the meaning: 'David longed intensely to march out against Absalom, for he was grieved about Amnon, that he was dead' (K. Jongeling, quoted in Fokkelman 1981, p. 126). While this is a possible way of taking the Hebrew, it is hard to see why, if David was going to march against Absalom, he should not have done so without waiting two full years. The passing of time made action more rather than less difficult. Moreover, Joab's stratagem would make no sense if Jongeling's interpretation were correct.

iii. Joab's daring initiative (14:1–33). The impasse which left Absalom, now the heir presumptive, in exile could not be permitted to continue indefinitely, and yet the king did nothing; among the king's advisers none was better placed than Joab to influence the king, but even he hesitated to appeal directly to David, preferring the employment of a judicial parable, like the one Nathan had used (2 Sa. 12:1–6), put into the mouth of a woman seeking special protection from the king. In this way he could catch the king unawares, and be more likely to attain his end.

1. The ambiguity noted in 2 Samuel 13:39 arises again in this verse because *the king's heart went out to* (Heb. *'al*) is more naturally translated 'against' Absalom (*cf.* Dn. 11:28, 'against [*'al*] the holy covenant'). The supreme judge felt obliged to punish the murderer. The obligation weighed the more heavily in view of the fact that Absalom was heir to the throne. In his case above all, justice needed to be seen to be done. Yet for all that, David was reluctant to take up arms and capture his son. Ironically the time was coming when that son would take up arms against his father.

2–3. Joab's device enabled the king to see the situation objectively, and thus, with a new slant on the matter, come to a decision. *Tekoa* was only five miles from Bethlehem, and was the home of one of David's heroes (2 Sa. 23:26). Joab evidently knew both the place and this *wise woman*, who had the skill to act a part and persist even with the king himself until he had taken her point. Though Joab prescribed her dress and her words, she needed all her wit and tact to parry the response of the king, which could not be foreseen. In that she is to pretend to have been *mourning many days for the dead* she can count on the sympathy of the king who has not forgotten the death of Amnon.

4–5. The woman comes to present her case directly to the king, who is accessible to citizens whose complaint has not been settled to their satisfaction by the local judges. *Help, O king* (Heb. *Hôšiʿā*, 'save') is the cry of the widow who, having no defender, finds herself powerless, and cries out for protection.

6–7. *Two sons . . . one struck the other and killed him*: the parallel case in his own family cannot have failed to remind David of his own sorrows. *The whole family has risen against your handmaid*, requiring justice according to the law by which the victim of a murder was to be avenged: 'he who struck the blow shall be put to death' (Nu. 35:21). Those who called for the death penalty had justice on their side, but the mother loved her son, in whom all her future, and that of her dead husband, was bound up. He was her one remaining *coal* in a dying fire. Joab had skilfully portrayed the conflict that had immobilized the king. How would the king react?

8–11. The royal judge wishes to dismiss the case as promptly as possible, with the assurance, *I will give orders concerning you*, but the woman is not to be so easily shrugged off. *On me be the guilt . . .* : by taking the guilt upon herself, the woman implies that she remains vulnerable in the face of the family's demands, which the king has not yet taken sufficiently seriously. Though the king undertakes to deal with anyone who becomes aggressive towards her, she requests this on oath, *that the avenger of blood slay no more*. The avenger (Heb. *gō'ēl*) will be intimidated by the mention of *the Lord your God*, and will take seriously the word of the king, who pronounces *As the Lord lives . . .* , and so protects the life of the son. From this point on, though he does not realize it, David is committed to protecting the life of Absalom, against the death penalty for fratricide.

12. Even now, the woman still has ahead of her the most delicate part of her commission, to make the application to the king and his son, and for this she requests further permission to speak.

13. The blunt attack on the king, *Why then have you planned such a thing . . .* , gives the reader a shock, as it must have given David a shock. What is he supposed to have done against *the people of God*, his subjects? The woman accuses him concerning the exile of *his banished one*, the son who had caused him agonies, and so probes the wound of the king.

14. *We must all die*, and yet the woman in her story had been unwilling that her one remaining son should die. The king had decreed mercy; just so *God will not take away the life of him* [*David*] *who devises means not to keep his banished one an outcast*. This courageous woman dares to speak of the mercy of God and contrast that with the king's want of mercy towards his son, which is tantamount to 'quenching his coal' (v. 7) and spilling *water . . . on the ground*, in other words, causing his premature death. She claims to speak on behalf of all the people who are looking for the king to devise some means of bringing the exile home.

15–17. At this point the woman changes her tack, returns to her own story, and becomes deferential in her address to the king, whom she depicts as a deliverer, a man of insight *like the angel of God*. Her prayer for God's presence with the king makes it unlikely that David will take exception to the hard things she has said, yet it points to hard decisions in which the king will need the help of the Lord his God. Cleverly, she has moved again from her own concerns to those of the king, but in a context of reassurance.

18–20. By this time the king had begun to wonder what lay behind this long interview. Intuitively, he sensed that he had not yet got to the bottom of the affair, and suspected the interference of his uncle, Joab. It is a tense moment as the king puts his question, and the woman acknowledges the king's astuteness before admitting that Joab had indeed been the author of her role play. But his motive had been *to change the course of affairs* by delivering the king from an impasse; thus he was acting as *your servant*, and the woman is *your handmaid*. With a flattering reference to the wisdom of the king, the woman brings her audience to an end. Her fictional story has done its work and she has achieved her purpose.

21–24. Joab, who had evidently been following the whole episode closely, took her place, and heard the royal pronouncement, *Behold now, I grant this*. The king knows he has been tricked into a course of action he cannot now avoid, because it is backed by his oath, but he makes no protest at Joab's audacity; instead he gives Joab the responsibility of bringing back to Jerusalem *the young man Absalom*. David persists in thinking of his son as a youth (Heb. *naʿar; cf.* 2 Sa. 18:5, 12), and so failing to give him the status to which his manhood entitled him, while at the same time being too lenient in his attitude towards the crime committed by Amnon. For this reason, he cannot bring himself to accept Absalom back into his presence, but continues to show his disfavour by banishing him to *his own house*. Though in reacting to the widow's story David has allowed compassion to triumph over strict justice, in applying the principle to his own circumstances he cannot quite bring himself to go so far. As it turned out, this worked against David's best interests, because his son resented his father's limited and reserved acceptance of him, and reacted with hostility.

25–27. The situation was not helped by the physical

attractiveness of Absalom, which set him in a class apart. He was so handsome that he put everyone else in the shade. The extravagant description conveys the impression that this man was totally taken up with his appearance, especially with his hair, which he cut annually and carefully weighed, recording the statistics by the royal weights (about 5½ lb., or 2.5 kg.). Ironically, it was his hair that would on a future occasion cause his death. Mention of his sons and lovely daughter suggests the popularity of this proud and good-looking family, but the name *Tamar* acts as a warning reminder of Absalom's raped sister, after whom his daughter has been named.

28–31. The insight into Absalom's personality increases our sense of unease that for two whole years David, by having no dealings with Absalom, gave him ample opportunity to undermine the authority of the king, and encourage support for himself. His self-seeking would be fuelled by his sense of outrage that he had been brought back to the capital only to be snubbed by his father, while the public thought highly of him. Joab's double refusal to respond to his summons was the last straw, and the blazing field of barley both symbolized Absalom's rage and brought Joab hurrying to his home, demanding an explanation.

32–33. Absalom knows how to force his way through opposition. Joab, who had only half succeeded in his first attempt to reconcile Absalom with his father, had been reluctant to be further involved, but Absalom sees in Joab his only hope. He had, after all, been the one who brought him back from Geshur, but in the event his return had achieved nothing. Now, after five years, he wants Joab to take a message to ask for an audience with the king, *and if there is guilt in me, let him kill me*. Absalom appears to be arguing that he is free from guilt (*cf.* 1 Sa. 20:8); he may have persuaded himself that he was avenging a wrong through killing Amnon, and that he would not have had to punish his brother if his father had done his duty, and had passed sentence on Amnon. The fact that David had not done so was ground for thinking that he would not have Absalom put to death either.

The king granted Absalom an audience; the brief and formal description is in itself significant. Though it ends *the king kissed Absalom*, there is no attempt to bridge the gulf between father and son. Each sees the guilt of the other, and is cold and unforgiving, but at least a small step has been taken towards

256

reconciliation: Absalom has come into the king's presence and has prostrated himself before him. The question is, will he in future remain loyal to the king? The king has kissed his long-lost son, but, in the absence of conversation between the two, how much does that indicate? When Joseph revealed himself to his brothers there was much weeping and exchange of news; Joseph had prepared himself for the meeting by facing up to his own experience of God's goodness, which enabled him genuinely to offer his brothers his forgiveness (Gn. 45:1–15). In the case of Absalom and the king, the relationship remained virtually deadlocked, neither side having the spiritual incentive to break it.

iv. Absalom's rebellion (15:1–37). 1. *After this Absalom got himself a chariot . . .* : though he had manipulated his way into the king's presence, Absalom was far from satisfied, and deliberately set out to undermine the authority of his father by building up his own prestige. In this his sense of theatre and his flair for publicity, together with his already impressive public image, ensured a high degree of success. Jerusalem's terrain was highly unsuitable for chariots and horses. Absalom's decision to use them distinguished him as an innovator, but the fifty runners ahead of his chariot prevented any great speed, and achieved instead unprecedented grandeur for an ambitious prince.

2–5. Absalom the politician had a predetermined policy which he ruthlessly pursued. He would *rise early*, a sign of keenness and diligence. (Was late opening a characteristic of David's court of justice?) Positioning himself at a strategic point close to a city gate, Absalom attracted attention by taking a close interest in strangers entering the city. The conversation sums up his customary approach, guaranteed to impress the Israelite who has come to the capital with a grievance. Here is someone ready to listen, and eager to right the country's wrongs. In this way he captures the popular vote.

But Absalom goes much further. His information, *there is no man deputed by the king to hear you*, is misleading, even deceitful, in its intention, because these people have come to put their case before the king, and it is clear from the way the woman of Tekoa was received (2 Sa. 14:4–7) that the king dealt personally with those who asked for his ruling. There may, for all we know, have been delay, but a deputy for the king had not been in question. Absalom's audacity in saying to these strangers, *Oh that I were judge in the land!*, indicates what an inflated idea he had of his own abilities. Uppermost in his mind, of course, was his own importance rather than the responsibility of making just judgments in hard cases. It suited his purpose to make out that everyone was in the right. Finally Absalom is depicted receiving homage as though he were king, but what a king! He receives his subjects with a handshake and favours each suppliant with a kiss. 'But this conjures up the situation in which his father became reconciled to him! . . . Now he is enjoying the reverse situation hundreds of times over and in so doing he is already secretly experiencing his own kingship.'[1] In his own mind he is already king.

On the surface, it seems strange that David should have permitted all this subversion to take place. Given the unmistakable pageantry, it is inconceivable that David did not know what Absalom was doing, but did he feel secure in his hold on the hearts of his people, and judge that he could safely tolerate the play-acting of his upstart of a son?

6. Absalom's 'play-acting' was an expression of his deep resentment against his father, and should have been taken by David with all seriousness, for *he stole the hearts of the men of Israel*, who did not see through the pretentious self-advertisement of Absalom. For the masses self-interest outweighed any lurking suspicion as to his motives. Did he not favour 'the poor in the land' and intend to work out justice for all?

7–8. *At the end of four years*[2] all Absalom's well-laid plans to rebel came to fruition. He had plenty of perseverance, and could bide his time. His last words with his father made a show of piety, but they had a hollow ring. Why had Absalom waited four years before giving thanks for his return? *Hebron* could have been explained as important to him because he was born there (2 Sa. 3:2–3). It was also the place where David had begun his reign, but that point does not surface as David listens to his son's carefully planned speech, in which *the Lord* features three times. Absalom had requested leave once before to take away most of the court to a feast (2

[1] Fokkelman 1981, pp. 166–167.
[2] Translators and commentators are virtually unanimous in preferring the evidence of some LXX MSS, the Syriac and Josephus for 'four', in preference to the Hebrew, which reads 'forty'.

Sa. 13:23–27); this time he does not even invite the king, but intends to deprive him of most of his supporters, as before. Even so, David appears to suspect nothing.

9. *Go in peace* is David's very last word to his son, who ironically goes away to prepare for war against his father.[1] Since he went with royal approval, suspicions as to his activities would be allayed, and he would gain time for a nation-wide muster of supporters.

10–11. From this point on, Absalom takes control, his *secret messengers* posted in such a way that *the trumpet* (Heb. *šōpār*, 'ram's horn') will resound throughout the land as each takes up the call with the words, *Absalom is king at Hebron!* The *coup d'état*, announced almost simultaneously in this way to all the tribes, makes any opposition appear useless. Meanwhile, the *two hundred men from Jerusalem who were invited guests* suspected nothing, and therefore gave the proceedings a genuine air of normality. By the time they realized what was happening, they were swept up in the confusion of events, powerless to intervene.

12. *Ahithophel the Gilonite, David's counsellor*, was grandfather of Bathsheba (*cf.* 2 Sa. 11:3 with 23:34). He was not in Jerusalem but in *Giloh*, which was a village close by, in the hills to the north of Hebron, having turned traitor to the king. All his skill and experience were at the disposal of Absalom, to the dismay of the king (v. 31). Meanwhile, Absalom was *offering the sacrifices*, and ostensibly worshipping the Lord his God, but his mind was on his own immediate future, and the steadily increasing numbers of his supporters. While the guests were enjoying their feast, they were being gradually hemmed in on all sides by new arrivals. Absalom's strategy had been impeccable, ensuring the success of his conspiracy against his father, many of whose best men were in Hebron, involved (whether they liked it or not) with Absalom.

13. The king learnt about his son's revolt not from the ram's horn signal but from some loyal messenger, who had observed the extent of Absalom's following.

14–16. David ordered immediate evacuation of the city, because he was in no position to defend it. Reassured of the

---

[1] Wiseman, 'Is it peace?', p. 323, points out that ' "Go in peace" may have had, at least originally, a range of meaning within the covenant making procedures . . . the predominant use appears to be as the *conclusio* of successful negotiations'.

loyalty of his servants, the king and all his household, apart from ten concubines, who were to look after everything, fled from the royal palace of cedar which David had built. In these verses and those that follow, David is repeatedly and deliberately referred to as *the king*.

17–18. Once out of the city, the king halts to take stock, and to make sure who is accompanying him. It is a true march-past, a review of long-valued servants and troops, whose years of allegiance made them doubly precious in such an emergency. It is instructive that the foreign troops (*cf.* the commentary on 2 Sa. 8:16–18) are singled out for special mention. They are loyal when even David's own son deserts.

19–23. David refuses to take for granted the willingness of a newcomer to endure the rough living and the dangers which lie ahead for the fugitive king. *Ittai the Gittite*, from Gath, and therefore a Philistine, is an exile who has chosen to come with a group to throw in their lot with David, who realizes that they would not have bargained for the turn of events. He therefore offers Ittai the chance to return and serve in a more normal way in the city. Such thoughtfulness in a time of stress shows David at his best. The words *steadfast love* (Heb. *ḥesed*) and *faithfulness* (Heb. *'emet*), so reminiscent of the divine covenant and so contrary to David's current experience, are nevertheless what he wishes for this Philistine soldier. From his response, Ittai reveals himself to be a believer, for whom love and faithfulness were paramount. His moving oath of loyalty *for death or for life* does much to make up for the treachery of the conspirators, and to encourage David at the nadir of his fortunes.

Mention of *all the little ones* serves as a reminder that whole families were fleeing the city. Already the procession had reached an obvious landmark, 'the last house' (v. 17) before *the brook Kidron* to the east of the city.[1] David was making for the east side of the Jordan, a journey which took the refugees over the Mount of Olives into *the wilderness*, the inhospitable region made famous by Jesus in the parable of the Good Samaritan.

24. Last of all, David makes a decision as to the part to be

---

[1] In v. 17 the NIV (*cf.* AV), instead of 'the last house', has 'a place some distance away', based on the Targum, the Aramaic version of the Old Testament. The Hebrew expression is unusual, hence the uncertainty. *Cf.* BDB, p. 112.

played by the ark of God and by those who serve the ark, the priests *Abiathar* and *Zadok*, and *the Levites* who accompany them. Abiathar had proved trustworthy over many years (1 Sa. 22:20–23); Zadok is first named in 2 Samuel 8:17, where he and Abiathar's son are recorded as priests. The Hebrew text begins the verse with Zadok, as though he were in charge of the ark; Abiathar's name is mentioned later (*cf.* AV, RV, NEB, GNB), almost as an afterthought: 'The priest Abiathar was there too' (GNB). 'Abiathar offered sacrifices' (NIV) makes good sense.[1] A makeshift altar, a small fire, and grain offerings would be possible in the emergency, as an accompaniment to prayer for the king's protection and victory.

25–26. *Carry the ark of God back into the city* indicates that David has no superstitious feelings about the need to have the presence of the ark with him. In the moment of crisis, David firmly believes that his future is in the hands of God, who will bring about his return to Jerusalem or his downfall, according to his good pleasure. Similarly, Absalom will not be helped by the presence of the ark in Jerusalem; 'deliverance belongs to the Lord' (Ps. 3:8, which, according to the heading, is a psalm relating to this incident), not to the presence of a sanctuary in or of itself. All the same, the ark of God was a most precious symbol which was irreplaceable; enshrined in its holy place, it represented the presence of Israel's God in the midst of his people. David's hope was to *see both it and his habitation*, for then he would know he had found *favour in the eyes of the Lord*. For David, it was an act of faith to send the ark back, and it was at the same time an act of surrender to whatever the Lord saw fit to do.

27–29. David sends Zadok with the commission, 'Look', which may be more than an interjection (*cf.* mg.); the NIV has 'Aren't you a seer?', while the NEB says 'Can you make good use of your eyes?' The latter makes best sense, but there may have been deliberate ambiguity, for this was no private conversation. David needed informers, and he sent the priestly group to act as his spies in the city, *in peace* (*cf.* v. 9). They would assess the situation and send word to David *at the fords of the wilderness*, one of the usual crossing points of the Jordan.

30–31. There was no time to lose, yet the steep ascent of

[1] *Cf.* Fokkelman 1981, p. 455, for a justification of his translation 'Abiathar made a fire offering'.

the Mount of Olives, still within sight of Jerusalem, could not be hurried. Indeed it became the occasion for an outpouring of emotion, first on the part of the king, and then taken up by the people with him, in solidarity with his humiliation. A further blow was the news of Ahithophel's defection, evidently regarded as a triumph for Absalom, to judge by David's heart-felt prayer, which he went on to supplement with such action as he was in a position to take.

32. The brow of the Mount of Olives afforded a panoramic view of Jerusalem. Understandably, it was a place *where God was worshipped* (indicating perhaps that there was a 'high place' on the summit), and there God's answer to prayer appeared in the person of *Hushai the Archite* (*cf.* Jos. 16:2) who turned out to be a loyal friend and servant, dismayed and mourning over the fate of the king.

33–37. His appearance at that very moment prompts David to send him on a special errand. Among the refugees he would be *a burden*, perhaps on account of his age or infirmity, but at the court of Absalom he would be an invaluable ambassador to counter the suggestions of Ahithophel. In collusion with the chief priests and their sons, he could keep the king informed of all that was planned at the highest level. His arrival in Jerusalem *just as Absalom was entering* from the south seemed providential: David's friend and confidant would soon be in action.

v. David's encounters and Absalom's plots (16:1 – 17:29). Evacuation of the city had been so urgent that there had been no time to plan provisions for the long journey ahead. The welcome sight of food could scarcely fail to cheer the king, and predispose him to be generous in return.

1. *Ziba, the servant of Mephibosheth*, represented the family of Saul, which might have been expected to attempt to seize the throne after David's departure. Instead, here was a most acceptable gift, designed to meet a pressing need, and sufficiently ample for the large number of people involved. Since Ziba was appointed to farm Mephibosheth's land, the produce was probably part of the owner's harvest, and hardly Ziba's to give (2 Sa. 9:10).

2–4. In the heat of the moment, David takes Ziba's answers to his questions at their face value, and deeply resents the apparent treachery of Jonathan's son, to whom he had shown special kindness (2 Sa. 9:1–13). If Ziba was trying to curry favour with the king he succeeded. The land which had belonged to Mephibosheth became his own, but the allocation came under review when David returned (2 Sa. 19:24–30).

5–8. A little further on, at the village of *Bahurim* in Benjamite territory (*cf.* 2 Sa. 3:16), David came under verbal abuse from another of Saul's relatives. *Shimei* was on a path parallel to the one being taken by David, on the opposite side of a ravine (v. 13), so that he could hurl both insults and stones at David across the divide. He wishes David out of the land, calling him *you man of blood*, that is, a murderer, and *you worthless fellow*, or good-for-nothing (*cf.* 1 Sa. 1:16), who deserved all he was getting because he had taken Saul's place as king. Now David's son will take his place as king: *the Lord has given the kingdom* to *Absalom*. This angry opponent of the king, who took on single-handed all the royal retinue, was wise to keep his distance; his claim to know the Lord's mind was negated by his abusive language. Only time and events could prove the validity of such a claim, which meanwhile should have rendered him inviolable, but as he could not be sure of this he kept his distance!

9. Nevertheless, it was to be expected that one of David's soldiers would want to defend the king, and nip in the bud such subversion. Joab's brother *Abishai*, noted earlier for his impetuous reactions (1 Sa. 26:8), was all for decapitating the assailant without delay.

10–12. The king's quiet authority and control denotes true greatness. He will not retaliate, but will instead take constructively the possibility that the Lord is speaking through Shimei, and accept the abuse in that light. The reasoning of verse 11, which all his men are to note, takes the heat out of an ugly incident. For once the sons of Zeruiah did not get the better of the king (*cf.* 2 Sa. 3:39), who saved the life of the one who was cursing him, and put his own case into the hands of Lord for his judgment.

13–14. Not that the abuse stopped. The pelting with stones and clods of earth continued, inflicting wounds, not least to the heads of those hit by them, but there could be no stop for rest until the end of the day's journey. *At the Jordan* is not in the Hebrew text (*cf.* AV, RV, NIV), but is taken from the LXX. The Jordan was David's safety barrier (2 Sa. 17:22), the only question being whether he travelled so far before nightfall.

15. The scene now changes to Jerusalem, where Absalom is in the process of installing himself, with the help of Ahithophel, who had already joined him (*cf.* 2 Sa. 15:12). *And Ahithophel with him* was tantamount to saying that Absalom was sure to succeed because this adviser never put a foot wrong (v. 23).

16–19. The intervention of *Hushai the Archite, David's friend*, took Absalom by surprise, for he had not gone so far as to invite his father's personal adviser to defect. Hushai's double *Long live the king!*, music in the ears of ambitious Absalom, raised no question in his mind, despite their ambiguity as to who was king (*cf.* 1 Ki. 1:25, 31, 34, 39). Absalom's double question reveals his misgivings, but he does not notice that there are two ways of taking the answer of Hushai, who again avoids mentioning names. Hushai is indeed remaining loyal to his master, David, chosen by the Lord and the people, but Absalom in his vanity fails to see that inference; does he really think he is the one whom the Lord has chosen, or does he take the Lord's name as merely pious talk? By asserting that he will serve his master's son, Hushai lays stress on the very relationship which Absalom has severed.

Should it not be his son?: indeed it should, if he were loyal to his father. As it is, Hushai will serve Absalom while at the same time being loyal to Absalom's father. Hushai has kept his integrity, Absalom has been blinded by his own egoism, and the reader is permitted to see one example of the outworking of God's providence.

20–22. For the moment, Absalom asks advice only of Ahithophel, who is forthright, decisive and ruthless: *Go in to your father's concubines* . . . Whereas Hushai had spoken positively of the father-son relationship, Ahithophel advises action which will demonstrate beyond doubt the gulf between Absalom and David. While it may have been customary in the ancient Near East for the king of a new dynasty to take the harem of the previous monarch, it was certainly not acceptable that a son should break the taboo against intercourse with his father's wives and concubines (Lv. 18:7–8). Ahithophel may have been shrewd, attractive and influential, but he revealed his true colours in the advice he gave on this occasion. True, the prophet Nathan had said, 'I [the Lord] will take your wives . . . and give them to your neighbour' (2 Sa. 12:11), and Ahithophel may have known of the prophecy, but it took some nerve to implement those words. The link with David's adultery is clearly made; David was reaping what he had sown. He had failed to punish the sin of Amnon, and now Absalom was taking his enmity against his father to its furthest extreme. By invading his father's most intimate and private world, and doing so blatantly and publicly, he would indeed make himself odious to his father, and to all right-minded people in Israel.

23. There is irony in this comment on Ahithophel's standing with David and Absalom. His advice was accepted with all the authority normally reserved for the word of God himself! Since both David and Absalom acted on his advice, he was virtually running the country. How was Hushai going to compete successfully with him?

The outcome of Absalom's rebellion depended on the strategy adopted at the planning stage, and now that he had two counsellors, Absalom had to choose between two different ways of achieving the desired victory.

17:1–4. Ahithophel volunteered his second piece of advice. He was not going to be outnumbered with his twelve chosen battalions, representing perhaps the twelve tribes united against their king. He would set out immediately in order to capture David while he was weak and disorganized, and likely to be deserted by his men. *I will strike down the king only*, is a slip of the tongue, surely, in referring to David as 'the king', yet Ahithophel sees clearly his objective. Once David is dead, those who were with him can safely be allowed to return, and Israel *will be at peace*. The simile *as a bride comes home to her husband* is not in the Hebrew, but has been introduced from the LXX; probably it should be omitted, because it is inconsistent with Ahithophel's matter-of-fact style (so AV, RV, NIV). Ahithophel's plan convinced the council of war, and it was accepted.

5–6. Absalom, however, had second thoughts, and was curious to know what his other, unbidden, adviser would say, though he had not been included in the inner cabinet. There is delay while Hushai is fetched and as Absalom brings him up to date with the discussion thus far, so that he can give his considered opinion.

7–10. Hushai, who has to think on his feet, makes the general judgment that Ahithophel's advice *is not good*, and then proceeds to give his reasons, based on David's track record.

265

By starting *You know . . . your father and his men*, Hushai trades on the fact that, as a son of the royal house, Absalom could not deny the prowess of his father, which had become proverbial. Hushai proceeds to weave a web of conjectures, throws in some emotive comparisons with a raging she-bear, before which even the lion-heart quails, and suggests the deadly part which rumour can play in exaggerating a small setback till it becomes defeat: *a slaughter among the people who follow Absalom*. In this way, Absalom's confidence in Ahithophel's scheme is undermined, and fear of his father's might and courage inculcated.

11–14. Hushai now proceeds to construct his proposal, which depends on total mobilization from *Dan to Beersheba*, and involves the presence of Absalom in person. Moreover, the aim is total destruction of David's company, made possible, if Hushai has his way, by the huge numbers of men at his command. They will saturate the area *as the dew falls on the ground*, permitting none to escape. Given the support of *all Israel*, even a city where David was hiding could be demolished and its stones dragged away. Hushai's speech is a master stroke, winning over Absalom and his supporters by subtle play on his fears, and also by giving importance to the inspiration of his presence with his army. Ahithophel would see immediately the weakness of all that Hushai had propounded, but everyone else was convinced by his arguments, which won the day.

At this point the narrator permits himself a comment in which he reveals his judgment that from Absalom's standpoint Ahithophel had given *good counsel*. The fact that Absalom disregarded it for the advice of Hushai, which was designed to protect David, he saw as an example of the Lord's intervention in order to overthrow Absalom, for by following Hushai's advice Absalom went to battle and lost his life. He had been persuaded by a speech that pulled the wool over his eyes, one full of vague references: 'some other place' (v. 9), *some place where he is to be found* (v. 12), *a city* unnamed (v. 13), at least one ambiguity (whose people fall in v. 9?), and an obvious contradiction between the picture of David as a mighty man at the beginning (v. 8) and his overthrow at the end, trapped by superior numbers. When had David ever been worried by the sheer size of the forces against him? Nevertheless, Hushai's rhetoric won over the war cabinet; Absalom saw himself at the head of a huge, victorious army, and the delay necessitated by further recruitment of reinforcements gave David the opportunity to shape his troops, recover strength, and decide on the terrain advantageous to him in the coming battle. But first he needed news of Absalom's intentions.

15–16. The spy network came into operation. Hushai wisely conveyed the advice given by both Ahithophel and himself, and advised David to prepare for the worst and cross the Jordan before nightfall. Absalom might change his mind!

17–20. The priests were under suspicion of supporting David, hence the ploy of stationing the two runners, *Jonathan and Ahimaaz*, at *En-rogel*, 'the spring of the fullers' or 'wanderers' or 'spies', outside the city, and possibly frequented daily by the maid as she fetched water[1] (thus her journey would not arouse suspicion). But the men were spotted and reported to Absalom. The *man at Bahurim*, the place through which David had passed (2 Sa. 16:5), must have been a known sympathizer, loyal to the king in Benjamite territory; his well, covered and camouflaged, provided safety for the spies (*cf.* the similar, equally successful, ruse in Jos. 2:6).

Nothing was known of it: a point worth making; a village community normally knew everything that happened, if only through the children playing in the streets. By directing Absalom's envoys to search beyond the village, the man's wife sent them on a wild goose chase. *Over the brook* (Heb. *mîkāl*) is an uncertain translation, because the word occurs only here in the Hebrew Bible, hence the possibility, 'They passed by the sheep pen towards the water' (NIV mg.).

21–22. Though delayed, the spies safely reached David, who immediately took the advice to cross the Jordan, despite the darkness of the night. With that barrier between himself and Absalom, the king had room for manoeuvre.

23. The fact that David got across the Jordan put paid to Ahithophel's plan of campaign to capture the king before he could reach Transjordan. By his delay, Absalom had forfeited the advantage, and the seasoned strategist Ahithophel knew that, since David would now regain control, there was no longer any future for him. Ahithophel would face death for

---

[1] The common factor between all these possible meanings is the Heb. verb *rāgal*, 'to foot it', 'go about as a slanderer or spy'. The fuller trampled the cloth in water to clean it. The appropriateness of the name of the spring would not escape the Heb. reader.

treason against the king. Calmly he accepted the situation, and resolved what he would do. The steps he took all contribute to the picture of a very calculating statesman, totally aware of all that is at stake, who follows to its bitter conclusion the path of logic and reason. This man of iron coolly took the time to return to Giloh, make sure all his affairs were in order, and only after that committed suicide by hanging himself. It was a tragic end for an undoubtedly able man, who at one time had been an invaluable counsellor to David (2 Sa. 16:23) but who had turned traitor.

24–26. *David came to Mahanaim,* a place of some importance on the east of the Jordan, where Ishbosheth had been crowned king (2 Sa. 2:8–9). Here, while Absalom was going through a coronation ceremony (2 Sa. 19:10), and mustering support from *all the men of Israel,* David had the opportunity to become organized for battle. The commander of Absalom's army was *Amasa,* Joab's cousin (*cf.* 1 Ch. 2:16–17), son of *Ithra* or Jether (NIV), a variant of the same name, an *Ishmaelite.* The RSV prefers this reading, found in some LXX manuscripts and in 1 Chronicles 2:17, to the Hebrew's 'Israelite', which adds nothing to the sense. *Abigal* and *Zeruiah* appear to have been half-sisters to David, since their father was *Nahash* and not Jesse. The reason for the family history is to enable the reader to appreciate the animosity between Amasa and Joab as they commanded the opposing forces. Mention of *Gilead,* where Absalom and his army encamped, raises the question of the sympathies of the inhabitants.

27–29. In one long sentence, these verses reveal the practical concern of three leaders in the region for David and his company. *Shobi the son of Nahash from Rabbah of the Ammonites* must have been more like his loyal father than the ruthless Hanun, who succeeded to the Ammonite throne (2 Sa. 10:1–4); *Machir* has been mentioned as host to Mephibosheth before David invited him to Jerusalem (2 Sa. 9:4); and *Barzillai* was an old man, the head of an important family in Gilead, who was loyal to David (*cf.* 2 Sa. 19:31–40). These three men of substance brought produce from their land, together with *beds, basins, and earthen vessels,* saying, *The people are hungry and weary and thirsty in the wilderness.* Such generous and thoughtful gifts represented a concern for the king which was so deep that it had to express itself in tangible, practical help.

vi. The defeat and death of Absalom (18:1–33). 1–4.
Battle is now imminent, and David inspects his troops, who
are split up into three divisions, each under a general: Joab
has to share the command with his brother Abishai and Ittai
the Gittite (*cf.* 2 Sa. 15:19–21), but as it turned out Joab
proved to be as independent and impetuous as ever (vv. 9–16).
David's intention to lead the army into battle does not meet
with the consent of the troops. Their argument agrees with
that of Ahithophel (2 Sa. 17:2–3); David is the target at which
the enemy army is going to aim, and therefore he should
remain behind the lines, and provide support from the city.
The king proceeded to review his troops from the city gate as
they marched to battle in companies and battalions.

5. Great stress is laid on the king's final command; it was
heard not only by the three commanders but also by *all the
people*: *Deal gently for my sake with the young man Absalom*, or as we
might say, 'Go easy with my boy Absalom, to please me.' The
king expected his army to be victorious, but he could not bear
the thought of the possible death of his son. In view of all that
David had gone through, it is easy for the onlooker to blame
him for being too soft with the rebel son, but the father still
longs for reconciliation with a repentant Absalom (Ps. 103:13).

6–8. This succinct description of the ensuing battle divides
into two parts: verses 6–7a depict the advance of David's men
towards the army of Absalom and the defeat of the latter by
David's troops, but in the middle comes the telling detail, *and
the battle was fought in the forest of Ephraim*. From this verse
comes the information that much of Gilead was covered in
forest at that time. David had arranged that the battle should
take place in this terrain, where the experience and courage
of each individual soldier counted more than sheer numbers.
Verses 7b–8 lay stress on the great loss of life, with the middle
clause, *the battle spread over the face of all the country*, explaining
the effect that the wooded landscape had on the battle,
removing all sense of direction so that soldiers wandered
aimlessly and got lost. 'The Transjordan landscape gives
everything it has to offer to the hungry David and his people
in the form of food (17:28sq) through the agency of the inhabitants, the three friends of the king, but it consumes Absalom's
supporters, outdoing the sword in hunger.'[1] Indeed, all nature

[1] Fokkelman 1981, p. 240.

conspires to prosper the cause of the king and defeat the rebel, even though the latter has the support of 'all Israel'.

9. The part played by nature has not yet been fully told. In the hide-and-seek battle, Absalom comes face to face with danger from some of David's men, who watch the royal mule walk away from under his rider, leaving Absalom with *his head caught fast* in an oak (*cf.* Is. 2:13; Zc. 11:2). The traitor hangs there helplessly, so the soldiers have no need to fight the king's son, but neither do they rescue him. The great tree, inanimate though it is, has proved more than a match for the pride of Absalom.

10–11. Someone who caught sight of the situation ran to report his news to Joab, *Behold, I saw . . .* , to which Joab sarcastically replied using the same words, 'Behold you saw . . .', but why had he not killed their enemy? Joab's intended reward of money and *a girdle* implied promotion (*cf.* 1 Sa. 18:4).

12–15. This man from the ranks is admirable in his resistance to bribery. Even *a thousand pieces of silver* would not have induced him to kill the king's son after the king had given his explicit orders within the hearing of Joab and everyone else. This ordinary soldier is admirable also in that he respects and obeys the king's command; his general, by contrast, takes the law into his own hands, shoots and pierces Absalom's heart. This, according to the standards of the soldier, was treachery (v. 13a). Joab's ten armour-bearers *surrounded*, *struck* and *killed* Absalom, so completing the treacherous deed, but the soldier points out that, had he done the same thing, he would have been found guilty of treason, and Joab would not have defended him. This man did not fear to speak his mind.

The part played by Joab here demands an explanation in view of the lead he took in Absalom's favour a few years earlier (2 Sa. 14:1–3, 21–22). At that time it seemed that Joab considered the return of Absalom to be a political necessity: his exile was a cause of unrest, and Joab had wanted to 'change the course of affairs' (2 Sa. 14:20). In the event, the outcome was disappointing, for little was changed. Absalom and his father were never truly reconciled, hence the plotting which ended in the rebellion. What could be gained now by sparing Absalom's life? Would the king react any differently to him after such an insurrection? It seems likely that Joab, impatient with David's indulgence towards his son, thought it wisest to terminate the life of the insolent young prince while he had the chance. Ultimately this was also in the best interests of the country, so far as Joab could judge. Providence certainly played into his hands, and the death of Absalom brought the battle to an end, so preventing further bloodshed.

16–17. Joab is now firmly in control of David's men, whom he recalls and restrains from pursuing their brothers who had supported Absalom. All that remains is to bury there and then in the forest the body of the rebel, his grave marked only by a huge cairn of field stones, which would in a relatively short time cease to be identifiable. It was an ignominious end.

18. Absalom had shown during his relatively short lifetime a characteristic interest in his continuing fame after his death by building a *monument* to himself. His choice of *the King's Valley* is in keeping with his aspirations to rule, but by setting up his own monument Absalom declared that he feared he would not otherwise have a memorial. *I have no son* contradicts 2 Samuel 14:27; presumably he lost his three sons while they were still of tender years. The verse testifies to sadness that a man of such early promise should have failed to achieve what even the commoner takes for granted: continuing significance through his posterity. All that bears Absalom's name is a stone.[1]

Four paragraphs full of suspense span the distance between the battle lines and the king, waiting anxiously for news in the gate of the city of Mahanaim.

19–20. *Ahimaaz the son of Zadok*, one of the two runners from Jerusalem to the Jordan (2 Sa. 17:17), was impatient to continue his messenger role, and carry to the king what he considered to be good news. Joab, who knew David better, was fully aware that the king would be interested only in what had happened to Absalom, and that for him the news would be anything but good.

21–23. For this reason Joab chose a foreigner to take the message. For him it would be merely a duty, and his words would not be emotionally charged. But Ahimaaz was not to be so easily deterred. In his enthusiasm for the king's interests, and believing that David would see the Lord's hand in the outcome of the battle, he insisted on going to the king, and

[1] The landmark pointed out to tourists as Absalom's tomb in the Kidron Valley goes back only to the first century AD. It is not to be confused with Absalom's monument.

271

in his eagerness proved to be the faster runner.

24–27. The scene switches to the king, anxiously waiting for news. He sits *between the two gates*, the inner and outer city gates, between which there were seats for gatherings of the elders in the shadow of the high walls. The watchman in the turret above reported to the king everything he could discern: one runner on his own will bring news (good news is implied), but why another? The tense and worried king draws reassurance from recognition that Ahimaaz *is a good man, and comes with good tidings* (Heb. *ṭôḇ*; the 'good' is emphasized). Joab had wanted to spare the king just such a disillusionment.

28–30. *All is well* (Heb. *šālôm*) sums up the message of Ahimaaz as he prostrates himself before the king and blesses God for the defeat of the king's enemies. To the king's enquiry about Absalom, he pretends not to know the answer; his vague reply only intensifies David's anxiety.

31–33. The Cushite has the official news for the king, and he expresses it objectively and yet kindly. He refers to Absalom along with all the enemies of the king, omitting his name and avoiding the word 'dead'. Yet his meaning is clear, and David, overcome with grief, goes up to one of the guardrooms in order to give himself to weeping for his son. If David had led the fighting men, as he had intended (v. 2), instead of being shut up to his own thoughts, he might have avoided the emotional impasse which prevented him from appreciating all that his army had endured in order to achieve victory. David was one degree removed from reality if he imagined that he could have saved both the throne and the life of his son. Maybe he had no such illusion, but was torn by the love which continued to well up within him at the thought of his son's great potential. Hence his passionate outburst. *Would I had died instead of you, O Absalom, my son, my son!* There was another consideration, and that was David's own contribution through his adultery to the problems of the family. He was not without guilt himself, and consciousness of the fact will have added to his torment.

Fokkelman draws attention to a deep change that has taken place in David by contrasting him at the time when he withdrew from Jerusalem with the David who hears news of the battle that saved him the throne. On the Mount of Olives (2 Sa. 15:30–37), though he is under attack, 'Politically and emotionally, he is realistic and adequate. He is himself, he is whole.' But the father who had never taken steps to correct this ambitious and spoiled son is indulging in self-torment when, in 2 Samuel 18:33, he expresses the wish that he had died in Absalom's place. 'It reveals a huge and terrible hole in that part of David's soul where there should be self-confidence and where a sound feeling of self-esteem belongs.'[1] In other words, when allowance has been made for all that a loving father goes through on the death of his son, there remains an aspect of David's behaviour which is unsound. He can no longer bear to face reality, and takes refuge in a wish that he could not fulfil, and that leaves him with negative feelings that block any way forward. It is this barrier that Joab has to help the king to surmount.

vii. Breaking the deadlock (19:1–40). While the king was still far from the capital, submerged in his grief, the army was unrewarded and the country was leaderless. It was a dangerous situation in which some upstart could attempt to seize power; and in the absence of any prophetic word, Joab played the key role in the difficult task of bringing the king to a better mind.

1–4. Joab cannot altogether have been surprised by the news that the king was grieving for his son (2 Sa. 18:20), but for the victorious army it was hard to accept that the king had no word of appreciation for their valour in battle. In the circumstances, there had been no tangible reward either, in the form of spoils. The king could not have ignored the army more completely if it had returned defeated, such was his isolation. Having *covered his face*, he could not see other people; and while *he cried with a loud voice*, he could not hear what anyone wanted to say to him. He wished to be quite alone.

5–6. *Then Joab came into the house to the king*: he knew he had to break into David's misery and isolation if David were to have any credibility as king. He was testing to the limits the loyalty of his followers. Joab is suitably brutal in order to shake David into acknowledging the situation: he finds four ways of pointing out that the king's behaviour is abnormal, overturning all accepted standards. i. People who have saved his life and the lives of his wives and children David has rewarded with dishonour. ii. The reason is that David has

---

[1] Fokkelman 1981, pp. 262–263.

turned the commandment to love his neighbour into hating him (*cf.* Lv. 19:18). iii. *Commanders and servants are nothing to you*: Joab himself is included among those who have been ignored for their pains in achieving victory. iv. Taking David's attitude to its logical conclusion, David would sacrifice all his followers if Absalom could only live. The hard-hitting sequence is calculated to bring the king face to face with the reality that he cannot bring Absalom back (*cf.* David's own realism when Bathsheba's baby died, 2 Sa. 12:22–23).

7. Having uncovered the outrage, Joab proceeds to point the way forward: *Arise, go out and speak kindly to your servants*. Immediate action is called for, both to shake the king out of his lethargy, and also, even more importantly, to retain the allegiance of the army. Joab has repeatedly drawn attention to 'this day', 'today' (five times); the crisis is such that the king must act straight away, or lose all his supporters *this night*. Joab's oath *by the Lord* adds solemnity to the fact Joab is urging upon the king.

8a–c. *Then the king arose, and took his seat in the gate*, but by this time there were no onlookers to greet him. The passive verb, *the people were all told* (*cf.* v. 1, 'It was told Joab . . .'), continues the sense of anticlimax, and though the king took his seat in the gate, ready to receive the homage of his people, the impression is strong that he had achieved this only with difficulty. No mention is made of his speaking kindly, nor indeed of his speaking at all. But *all the people came before the king* and saw his face (contrast v. 4), with its evidence of suffering and grief, and we sense that the crisis has been averted. His supporters will remain loyal.

The king has complied with Joab's direction, but what is going on deep down? How is he taking the high-handed attack of his general who, though he had undoubtedly saved the day, had presumed to direct the king, not with kindly understanding, but with harsh words that were guaranteed to wound? This long-standing comrade-in-arms, who had played his key role in many a battle, and had obeyed the king's order to set Uriah the Hittite in the hottest area of battle (2 Sa. 11:14–15), had now disobeyed orders and killed the king's son. How much further would he go in defying the king? How much further should he be permitted to go?

8d–10. Meanwhile, the situation in the country at large is confused. People are divided as to their leader; there is a general consensus that they want the king to return, but no-one takes the initiative to recall him. There appears to be political naïvety in the inference that a new king can be anointed and followed as an experiment; if it fails the status quo can be restored! *The king* now refers to David. There is no other, and the people who have been duped by the usurper know they cannot do without him. Within a week or two, untold harm has been done, and there will be need for great skill in rebuilding confidence between the king and his subjects.

11–15. *The word of all Israel*, that they were asking for his return, reached the ears of the king, who, instead of accepting gratefully the change of allegiance by grasping the outstretched hands, looked to his priestly allies in the capital to rally the support of his own tribe. By taunting Judah with the readiness of the other eleven tribes to receive him, David is driving a wedge between Judah and the rest, whereas he would have been wise to unify the kingdom by rising above tribal factions and loyalties. David the king has suffered such a series of blows to his confidence that he feels in desperate need of those he knows and loves to restore his equilibrium. Joab has failed him at this level, and on his own David cannot rise above the state of shock in which he finds himself. Nevertheless, he can still take the initiative of demoting Joab, and replacing him by another of his family, his cousin Amasa (see 2 Sa. 17:25), who had commanded the army of Absalom. Thus David upheld Absalom's appointee at the expense of Joab, and at the same time offered an olive branch to those who had recently supported Absalom.

The appeal of David to the tribe of Judah resulted in his unanimous recall to the throne, and a formal ceremony at the Jordan. *Judah came to Gilgal*, between Jericho and the Jordan, where Joshua made his first camp in Canaan (Jos. 4:19–24), where Samuel regularly ministered (1 Sa. 7:16) and Saul had his kingship confirmed (1 Sa. 11:15). Gilgal had had connections with all the tribes, but on this occasion only Judah was officially invited *to meet the king and to bring the king over the Jordan*. The effect of such partiality could only be divisive. Certain individuals, however, who had good reasons of their own for contacting the king, made certain of an audience at the first opportunity.

16–17. Political changes made all the difference to the

allegiances of *Shimei*, who had insulted David only a short time before on his outward journey (2 Sa. 16:5–8). This time the description makes no mention of Shimei's relationship to King Saul; instead the emphasis is on his haste and on the company with which he surrounds himself. Not only is he accompanied by a thousand people of the tribe of Benjamin, through whose territory the king will be travelling, but he also contrives to time his arrival with that of the Judahites, and of *Ziba* and his men, who had succeeded in convincing the king of his loyalty by the presents he produced in the king's time of need (2 Sa. 16:1–4). The intense competition between all these groups to prove their loyalty calls in question their sincerity. Why does each one find it necessary to rush down in order to be first to arrive?

18–20. In the case of Shimei, the answer is obvious: he feared for his life, and hoped he would find safety in numbers, so he rushed across the water at the fords to offer his services to the king, who will be carried, together with his household, across the river. But first he presents his petition, *Let not my lord hold me guilty*, though Shimei admits he *did wrong*. The ground of his petition is his confession, *I have sinned*, and his appeal is to the change that has brought him, *the first of all the house of Joseph*, to David. By this he refers to the tribes other than Judah, which he implies will follow his lead, and *come down*, literally but also figuratively, by changing their allegiance and returning to their rightful king.

21–23. Abishai, certain that his first instinct had been right (2 Sa. 16:9), wants Shimei executed forthwith, for having *cursed the Lord's anointed* (Heb. *mᵉšîaḥ*). Suddenly David comes to himself. He identifies Abishai as *an adversary*; he distances himself from *the sons of Zeruiah*, and asserts his authority: *I am this day king over Israel*. David takes the risk of granting Shimei on oath a free pardon, though he had behaved in a thoroughly despicable way, and David never trusted him (1 Ki. 2:8). Solomon was saddled with removing him from all possibility of seditious plotting against the throne (1 Ki. 2:36–46).

24–25. Another person who was anxious to put his record straight was *Mephibosheth*, Jonathan's son, whom David had made a permanent member of his household (2 Sa. 9:13). As such, he should have accompanied the king in his exodus from Jerusalem, but Ziba his steward had turned traitor and had maligned him (2 Sa. 16:1–4). David, however, was at a loss, not knowing what to believe. The appearance of the man, especially his untrimmed beard, gave unambiguous evidence of the genuineness of his claim to have been grieving for the king's return.

26–28. Mephibosheth, who had been seriously disadvantaged by his lameness, genuinely pays homage to the one he calls *my lord the king* (five times, vv. 26–30). He acknowledges his utter dependence on the king, asks for nothing except what the king sees fit to do, and puts himself in the king's hands.

29–30. David finds himself in an embarrassing situation. He had been so grateful for Ziba's gift of provisions on the outward journey that he had believed the story about Mephibosheth's aspirations after the throne and had given all Saul's lands to Ziba, in a sudden fit of gratitude (2 Sa. 16:4). Ziba had already arrived to declare his allegiance (v. 17), but now David, confronted with Jonathan's son, whom he has wrongly suspected of subversion and deprived of his rightful lands, is torn as to what he should do. Impatiently, he decrees, *you and Ziba shall divide the land*. The decision sounds just, but in fact it unjustly favours Ziba, who has obtained the property by deception, and it deprives Mephibosheth, who because of his disability deserved to be defended against those who would take advantage of him, of half his estate. The one who comes out of the incident unscathed is the crippled Mephibosheth, who rises above financial considerations and takes genuine pleasure in the return of his lord the king in safety (Heb. *bešālôm*, *i.e.* with peace and security fully restored). It is sad to see David's grudging response to the genuine warmth of Jonathan's son, who has himself suffered, and who understands what the king has had to endure.

31–33. The third individual singled out for special mention, *Barzillai the Gileadite*, is altogether devoted to the king, having used his riches to meet the material needs of all David's household and army during their stay in Mahanaim (*cf.* 2 Sa. 17:27–29). Despite his age, he takes the journey to the Jordan in order to escort the king on his way, and the king, desiring to return his hospitality, invites him to a place with the king at court in Jerusalem. The site of *Rogelim* is unidentified.

34–37. This loyal but independent farmer wants to end his days in his own home, and he pleads that his increasing infirmities will burden the king unduly. Moreover, he has

277

done nothing to deserve such a reward. On these grounds, he politely refuses the king's intended honour, and requests that he may return to his city and remain close to the family grave. But he takes the opportunity to introduce to the king *Chimham*, who according to some LXX manuscripts is his son (*cf.* NEB, JB mg., GNB). This is in keeping with 1 Kings 2:7; there was also a place called Geruth Chimham, near Bethlehem, meaning 'the lodging-place of Chimham' (Je. 41:17). Barzillai asks the king to do for Chimham *whatever seems good to you*.

38. The king gladly accepts Chimham, but invites Barzillai to propose *whatever seems good to you*; David offers him 'an open cheque'.

39–40. The parting took place on this friendly note, and Barzillai returned home with the king's blessing, while the king had the reassurance of a staunch ally in Gilead, and found his own well-being restored in the generous gesture he had been able to make to Chimham. But the tribal support was divided.

e. Discontent in Israel (19:41 – 20:26)

41–43. The northern tribes felt keenly their exclusion from the ceremony in which the king was escorted over the Jordan on his way to Jerusalem. Though they *came to the king*, the dialogue takes place between the two main tribal groups, the king, whose responsibility it had been to notify everyone, opting out.

Those accused, the Judahites, defended their action, thereby admitting they had 'stolen the king away'. As tempers rose, they repudiated the idea that there had been any favouritism or material inducement involved. Israel's counter-argument was their greater numerical strength, and the fact that the first suggestion to bring back the king had come from Israel (2 Sa. 19:10). David's discrimination in favour of his own tribe had driven a wedge between Judah and the rest, which once again brought war to the land.

20:1–2. The self-appointed leader of the disaffected tribes, *Sheba, the son of Bichri*, took advantage of the discontent, and declared independence for Israel, under his own leadership. *All the men of Israel withdrew from David*, but only temporarily, as it was to prove on this occasion (*cf.* 1 Ki. 12:16, when the fragile union broke down once and for all).

278

3. The return of David to the capital is described only in terms of the unfortunate concubines, who remained in virtual widowhood, a reminder to the end of David's life of the horror perpetrated by Absalom (2 Sa. 16:20–23).

4–6. Amasa's first assignment as commander of the army (2 Sa. 19:13) revealed his shortcomings. His failure to appear within *the set time* with the army ready for operations filled David with alarm, lest he also had turned traitor, and Sheba was given time to make headway in the north by capturing *fortified cities*.

7–10. Abishai, commanding the standing army, and Joab were sent into the field to pursue Sheba, and at Gibeon's *great stone* it is Joab who comes to the fore. Indeed the Hebrew in verse 7 reads 'Joab's men' (*cf.* RSV mg.). Though he had been dismissed, he was not so easily excluded from the action, and he had his own reason for wanting to eliminate Amasa, the cousin who had been promoted in his place. Posing as a friend, he treacherously killed his rival (*cf.* 2 Sa. 3:27). At such close range it is not surprising that he achieved his purpose *without striking a second blow*; this experienced soldier was skilful with his weapons, and ruthless in his self-interest. He could brook no rival.

11–13. The pursuing army was aghast at the sight of general Amasa's gruesome body; everyone halted in order to weigh up what had happened and how to proceed, but Joab's man on duty made sure that all the people got the message: Joab was in control of the king's army, though all unbeknown to the king! Once the corpse was removed, there was no obstacle to prevent the total army's pursuit of Sheba under Joab's leadership. Abishai disappears from the record, unable to hold his own once Joab had asserted his authority.

14. The trek was a long one to the very north of Israel's territory, where Sheba was finally run to ground in *Abel of Beth-maacah*, modern Tell Abil on one of the headwaters of the Jordan, and thirteen miles (20 km.) north of Lake Huleh. The use of the name Abel in verse 18 and in the Egyptian Execration Texts implies that Beth-maacah is an alternative, possibly Syrian, name for the place.[1] Another suggestion is that they may have been twin towns on either side of the

---

[1] *Cf. IBD* 1, p. 2 map; p. 3 under 'Abel of Beth-maachah'. *NBA*, pp. 43, 45.

stream.[1] In that case, only one would have been fortified. In the walled city the fugitive took refuge, supported only by *the Bichrites*, Sheba's own tribe. The RSV has adopted an emendation here (*cf.* the RSV mg., 'Heb. *Berites*', and AV, RV, NIV), because the name 'Berites' is not otherwise known.

15. The siege tactics described here are typical. The *mound against the city* wall enabled the attackers to approach by a gentle gradient and to pound the vulnerable upper part of the wall with improvised battering rams, in an effort to breach them.[2]

16–17. In the middle of the attack, terrifying to those within the city, an unexpected intervention occurred. *A wise woman* called for Joab. To judge by Joab's immediate response, which would entail a lull in the attack, it must have been possible to identify her in some way as a representative of the city, the leader of its council. Having identified Joab, she ascertained that he was prepared to put his mind to what she was about to say. The long introduction indicates the importance of her words.

18–22. Her city, Abel, had an honourable reputation in Israel as a centre for wise advice, and she quotes the proverb, *Let them but ask counsel at Abel*. The woman identifies herself as typical of the best traditions in Israel: she is *peaceable and faithful*. Joab, by contrast, she accuses of two crimes: *You seek to destroy a city which is a mother in Israel*, of which she is the mother-figure, and of which the villages around are the 'children' (*cf.* Zc. 9:9). If he succeeds, Joab, whose name means 'Yahweh is father', will commit the second crime of depleting the Lord's inheritance. Joab is piqued, and denies that he has any such intention. He seeks only the one man who has risen up against the king. The woman has the power to speak for the whole community when she states that Sheba will be beheaded, and his head *thrown . . . over the wall* as proof positive that the execution has been carried out. Thus the war comes to a satisfactory end with a minimum of casualties, thanks to the intervention of a 'wise woman', who drew out of the military leader the answer she wanted, and saved her city. In

[1] E. C. B. MacLaurin, 'Qrt-'ablm', *PEQ* 110 (1978), pp. 113–114.

[2] Excavations at Lachish have revealed just such a siege ramp at the southwest corner of the city; *cf.* D. Ussishkin, *Excavations at Tel Lachish 1973–1977, Preliminary Report* (Tel Aviv: University Institute of Archaeology, 1978), plates 1 and 21).

an earlier incident, another 'wise woman' had co-operated with Joab and had undertaken the delicate task of bringing the king to a new viewpoint (2 Sa. 14:1–20). Both these episodes shed light on the diplomatic role played by women at the period of the early monarchy.

And Joab returned to Jerusalem to the king, brazening out the murder of Amasa, and his self-appointment to command the army in the place of Abishai, whom the king had appointed. All this he expected to get away with in the light of his success in ending the insurrection against King David. At this point, the reactions of David are omitted, but on his death-bed they were made clear to Solomon, who was warned, 'do not let his grey head go down to Sheol in peace' (1 Ki. 2:6). Though Sheba's rebellion had been quelled, and David could only be thankful that this second attempt to strike at his throne had been overcome, he was saddled with a general who persisted in killing men whom the king had put in authority, and taking over the command of the army. The problem was that Joab was capable and confident, and came home victorious, but from the point of view of the king, he was a murderer whom he could not bring to justice. Joab had killed Abner (2 Sa. 3:27), Absalom (2 Sa. 18:14) and now Amasa (2 Sa. 20:10). David can hardly have welcomed him with open arms, and yet he had saved the kingdom.

23–26. A list of the officers of the crown, similar to that in 2 Samuel 8:15–18, but relevant to the later period, brings the section to an end. The differences between the two lists are worth noting: i. the omission of David's name in connection with administration of the law may be significant (*cf.* 2 Sa. 15:3–4); ii. a new development is a department of *forced labour*, ominous in view of the trouble to which it was to lead (1 Ki. 11:28; 12:12–16); iii. David's sons are no longer said to be priests, understandably so, in view of their activities, as recorded in the intervening narratives; *Abiathar* would appear to be the son of Ahimelech, named after his grand-father. But first in the list was Joab, *in command of all the army of Israel*, a towering figure, whose ability and strength seemed not to diminish with the passing of the years.

2 Samuel 11 – 20 has covered a period of David's reign which he might well have wished to omit from the records. Why did it have to be included?

From the historian's point of view, 2 Samuel 1 – 10 contains material more relevant to his purpose.[1] Yet 2 Samuel 11 – 20 proceeds with slow and deliberate pace, punctuated with direct speech; the carefully constructed narrative gives prominence to David's grave offence and all that followed from it. Affairs of state are shown to be closely bound up with personal relationships; sinful liaisons have repercussions that rebound far beyond the private lives of the individuals concerned. At the same time David, though forgiven by God, found himself handicapped by his own past and unable to discipline others; moreover, his own children never came to terms with what their father had done.

In other words, the narrator has invited the reader to pay particular attention to the social and psychological aftermath of adultery, as well as to the obvious fulfilment of God's judgment as pronounced by the prophet Nathan (2 Sa. 12:10–12). Though David's kingdom was retained intact, David lost the control he had earlier had over men and affairs. The implications for people in positions of leadership are likely to be especially significant, and yet they are important for all, for 'as an artistic masterpiece of universal and transtemporal value', the figure of David makes contact still with the reader. The highest qualities of David '(as shown or as violated by him) . . . are the same as those of our own human existence. This narrative art has a didactic quality about it . . . It transmits profound wisdom . . .'[2] To concentrate on the historical aspect of David's reign, therefore, and to stop there, is to miss the point of the book. What we are meant to find is guidance to live by, a clue to the deceptions that distort our understanding of what is beneficial and what ought to be done. In other words, these chapters, like many more, are meant to be 'a lamp to my feet and a light to my path' (Ps. 119:105).

IV. EPILOGUE (2 Samuel 21:1 – 24:25)

A further selection of literature representing different periods of David's life brings our book to a conclusion. The six episodes here form a concentric pattern (A, B, C, C[1], B[1], A[1]) with poems written by the king at the centre, on either side

---

[1] Bright devotes thirteen pages to 2 Sa. 1 – 10, and only four to 2 Sa. 11 – 20; see Bright, pp. 190–202 and 203–206 respectively.
[2] Fokkelman 1981, p. 424.

an account of great warriors who served the king, and at the beginning and end natural disasters which struck during David's reign. In a skilful way, these chapters summarize what has gone before, yet without mere repetition. At a deeper level, they present Israel's greatest king as a man who both inherited problems from his predecessor and created them himself (A, A¹); who fought and achieved his victories with the help of many others who are celebrated here (B, B¹), and whose joy and strength was his God, whom he praised with total abandon because everything he was and everything he had achieved was to be attributed to the faithful Lord God of Israel (C, C¹).

A. A legacy from the past (21:1–14). When Israel suffered famine for three years in succession, David presumed that the Lord was saying something to his people through the disaster. He was not mistaken.

1. The underlying cause of the failure of the rains was a broken covenant. When Joshua was invading Canaan and destroying its inhabitants, he was taken in by *the Gibeonites*, who pretended to have come from a distant place beyond the area claimed by Israel, whereas their city was only a few miles north of Jerusalem. The peace treaty he made with them was binding for all time, despite their trickery: the Gibeonites were to be allowed to live (Jos. 9:15). In an incident unrecorded in the narrative about Saul, he had evidently been so rash as to break the covenant by putting Gibeonites to death, and had gone unpunished. *Bloodguilt* therefore remained on Saul and his family.

2. Gibeon was close to Gibeah, Saul's city, and had a famous shrine at which Solomon offered inaugural sacrifices when he became king (1 Ki. 3:4). Saul *in his zeal* resented the permission given to foreigners, Amorites, to serve even in a menial way at the shrine of the Lord (Jos. 9:27), and therefore put some Gibeonites to death. The name *Amorites* is used as a general term for the inhabitants of Canaan.

3–6. The king is eager to take action in order to relieve the country of the famine, and asks the Gibeonites, *how shall I make expiation . . . ?* The seriousness with which the Gibeonites regarded the breaking of an oath is indicated by their reply. Money would not provide compensation, but only the giving of life for life. The answer of the Gibeonites illustrates the meaning of the Hebrew *kipper*, 'make expiation', in a secular context as opposed to its use in sacrificial ritual. Saul had committed the wrong, and, since Saul was dead, seven of Saul's family should be handed over *so that we may hang them up before the Lord*. Justice was seen, not in any abstract way, but as the requirement of the Lord, whose land they inhabited, 'and no expiation can be made for the land . . . except by the blood of him who shed it' (Nu. 35:33). The shedding of blood will bring about reconciliation between the Gibeonites and Israel, *that you may bless the heritage of the Lord*.

Gibeon on the mountain of the Lord (v. 6) is a correction of the Hebrew, which reads, 'Gibeah of Saul, whom the Lord did choose' (AV, *cf*. RV, NIV). The LXX, on which the emendation is based, may have 'corrected' an unlikely but original meaning, on the grounds that Gibeon and Gibeah are easily confused.

7–9. David did not shirk the heart-rending task of selecting seven grandsons of Saul; *Rizpah* was a concubine (2 Sa. 3:7) who had two sons; *Merab* was Saul's daughter. The RSV has preferred the alternative name to the Hebrew Michal, who was said not to have had any children (2 Sa. 6:23); it was Merab who married Adriel (1 Sa. 18:19). The death of these seven men *in the first days . . . of barley harvest* (a reference to the time of year rather than suggesting that there was any harvest to reap) was evidently long remembered.[1]

10–14. The hope that rain would fall and break the long drought, as a result of her sacrifice, prompted Rizpah to mourn beside the bodies of her dead sons until rain came. David, moved by her example, decided to make amends for the suffering caused; he arranged for the honouring of the bodies of Saul and Jonathan, which had been buried after the battle of Gilboa in Jabesh-gilead (1 Sa. 31:8–13). The transfer of their bones, together with those of the men who had been hanged, to the tomb of Saul's father *Kish*, provided public testimony to the respect in which the king held the family of his royal predecessor. *Zela* is one of the places listed among the fourteen in the hill country to the north-west of Jerusalem (Jos. 18:28); it is likely to have been the birthplace of Saul.

---

[1] The so-called Gezer Calendar, a roughly inscribed stone from the tenth century BC, divides the year according to the farmer's main tasks, and mentions 'barley harvest', which takes place in our March/April. *Cf. DOTT*, pp. 201–203; *IBD* 1, art. 'Calendar', pp. 222–224.

After that God heeded, because justice had been done and honour had been satisfied, a note which recurs in 2 Samuel 24:25.

B. David's giant-killers (21:15–22). This section puts a little more detail into the account of David's wars against the Philistines, described in the important summaries of 2 Samuel 5:17–25 and 8:1. Four incidents are recorded here, of which all except the first appear again, with differences of detail, in 1 Chronicles 20:4–8. It seems likely that a roll of honour was kept, in which outstanding acts of bravery, some of which are quoted here, were written and handed down to posterity. The concise style of writing is appropriate for an official honours list.

15–17. *The Philistines had war again* reads like an extract from such a chronicle of exploits. King David, worn out by the battle, was in danger of death. His opponent, *one of the descendants of the giants* (Heb. *rāpā*, singular, *cf.* NIV's 'Rapha', so treating the word as a family name; the RSV assumes a connection with *rᵉpā'îm*, plural, *cf.* Dt. 2:11; Jos. 17:15), expected to kill David.[1] His spear, though heavy (7½ lb. or *c.* 3.5 kg.), was only half the weight of that belonging to Goliath (1 Sa. 17:7). Nevertheless, Abishai attacked the formidable soldier and killed him, so saving the king's life. David had a narrow escape, hence the ruling made by popular consent, that this was to be his last appearance as leader of the troops in battle, *lest you quench the lamp of Israel*. The king was the focus of the nation, the source of its policies, the one responsible for keeping the covenant of the Lord (*cf.* 1 Ki. 11:36; 15:4). The metaphor is suggested by the ever-burning lamp in the sanctuary, which is itself a symbol of Israel's dependence on the favour of the Lord, but also of the light revealed by the Lord for the blessing of the people of Israel and of the nations (*cf.* 2 Sa. 22:29, but see also the lampstand in Zechariah's vision and its meaning, Zc. 4, esp. vv. 6, 14). *Abishai*, Joab's brother, had had his moment of glory, despite his eclipse by the headstrong Joab.

18. *Gob* is unknown outside this passage; the LXX and Syriac have 'Gath', while 1 Chronicles 20:4 has 'Gezer'. Another

---

[1] Considerable differences exist between some translations (*e.g.* JB, NEB) and the RSV in vv. 15–16. The changes adopted by some modern translators go back to J. Wellhausen, *The Text of the Books of Samuel* (1871), quoted in Driver 1913, pp. 270–271.

Hushathite, or inhabitant of Hushah, a place near Bethlehem, identified with the modern Husan, is named in 2 Samuel 23:27.

19. This verse is a difficult one because, on the face of it, David is denied the honour of killing Goliath. 1 Chronicles 20:5 reads 'Elhanan the son of Jair slew Lahmi the brother of Goliath the Gittite'; but since 'Lahmi' is part of the Hebrew word 'Bethlehemite', this is likely to be a very early attempt to deal with the problem. The Chronicles verse does, however, suggest that *Jaareoregim* should be translated 'Jair the weaver' (*cf.* NIV mg.). The same word occurs at the end of the verse, translated *weaver's beam*. Who then is this *Elhanan*? The most likely suggestion is that it is David under another name, his family's name for him as opposed to his throne name; in that case Jair must be the equivalent of Jesse.[1]

20–22. The fourth of the huge Philistine champions *taunted Israel*, as Goliath of Gath had done (1 Sa. 17 uses the same verb in vv. 10, 25–26, 36, 45, where it is translated 'defy'). David's nephew, the son of his brother *Shimei*, or Shammah (1 Sa. 16:9), or Shimeah (2 Sa. 13:3), emulated his uncle's prowess by killing the giant. *They fell by the hand of David* makes best sense if at least one of the four was killed by David, though some of his picked troops were responsible for the other triumphs.

C. One of David's great psalms (22:1–51).

This song of thanksgiving occurs as Psalm 18 in a slightly variant form. The two Hebrew versions enable scholars to make a comparative study of the two texts, which provide evidence of early spelling and grammatical constructions.[2] By 'early' is meant pre-exilic, probably not later than the ninth to eighth centuries BC, and possibly even Davidic:

> The literary associations . . . point to a relatively early date for the composition of the psalm. Finally, the inclusion of the poem in II Sam, along with the 'Last Words of David'

---

[1] For a very clear statement of the problems and their possible solution, see D. F. Payne, 'The Elhanan Problem', *NBC*, pp. 318–319. He points out that, in view of the textual problems, it is a precarious argument to insist that 2 Sa. 21:19 contradicts 1 Sa. 17.

[2] A detailed comparison is made by F. M. Cross, Jr., and D. N. Freedman, 'A Royal Song of Thanksgiving: II Samuel 22 = Psalm 18', *JBL* 72 (1953), pp. 15–34.

(itself a very archaic poem) shows that an old tradition associated the psalm with the early monarchy. A tenth century date for the poem is not at all improbable.[1]

No other king of Israel or Judah is more likely to have been the author.

This vivid, spontaneous poem sustains to the very end its feeling of exultation at all that the Lord has done. Here is David at his best, before his lapse into adultery numbed his spiritual awareness (vv. 18–25). The psalm may be divided to show the following structure: proclamation (vv. 2–4); summary (vv. 5–7); flashback (vv. 8–31); report (vv. 32–46); vow (vv. 47–50); praise (v. 51).[2]

1. This verse corresponds to the heading of Psalm 18. Mention of deliverance *from the hand of Saul* suggests that the psalm would have been composed soon after the battle of Gilboa, while the realization was still fresh that the Lord had wonderfully fulfilled the promise implied at David's anointing (1 Sa. 16:1–13).

2–4. A torrent of metaphors proclaims to the world that David has found his God to be a rock of ages, utterly dependable in all kinds of dangerous situations, infinitely resourceful in delivering his servant from death. A number of the metaphors recall particular incidents by the word chosen: *my rock* (v. 2, Heb. *sela'*) is the word used in 1 Samuel 23:25–28; *my fortress* (Heb. *mᵉṣûdâ, cf.* Masada, the name of Herod's well-known fortress by the Dead Sea) recalls 1 Samuel 22:4; 24:22 and Jerusalem itself (2 Sa. 5:7); *God, my rock* (v. 3, Heb. *ṣûr*), is the word used in 1 Samuel 24:2. David's praises celebrate actual deliverances which he and the men with him could authenticate. That he has lived to become king is proof of the power of the Lord to save the one who takes refuge in him.

5–7. In brief, David's testimony is to the efficacy of prayer in times of *distress* (Heb. *ṣar*, 'straits'), when he was being assailed by all the combined forces of death's dark powers, personified in his human enemies. Wonderfully, God *heard my voice . . . my cry*, distinguishing the individual's need amid all the cries that reach his ears.

---

[1] *Ibid.*, p. 20. *Cf.* D. Kidner, *Psalms 1 – 72*, TOTC (Leicester: Inter-Varsity Press, 1973), p. 90; Gordon 1986, p. 304; Watson, p. 40.

[2] Watson, p. 167, suggests that this is the structure common to individual psalms of praise, of which other examples are Pss. 30; 40; 66:13–20.

8–16. In answer to the cry of one person, he, the Lord, Israel's covenant God, Yahweh, harnessed all nature to make way for his triumphal entry to the scene of his servant's plight. The vivid imagery, reminiscent of that of Moses' song after the Exodus (Ex. 15:1–18), and of the manifestations at Sinai of the Lord's awesome presence (Ex. 19:9, 16–20), no doubt owes something to the poetry current in Canaan, especially in poetic technique.[1] But the concept of God and nature moving in concert to answer prayer for one man is bold almost beyond belief, if it were not affirmed in Scripture. The Lord *is* in control of the world of nature, and causes it to do his bidding.

17–20. David, at the receiving end of this divine intervention, found that a strong hand *from on high* rescued him from those who were too mighty for him. *The Lord was my stay*, or 'support', the one on whom he could safely lean. The *broad place* (v. 20) contrasts with the 'straits', 'tight corners', of verse 7; the pressure has been lifted and David is free to live a more normal life.

21–25. Since the Lord has marvellously rescued him over and over again, David concludes that his behaviour in relation to Saul must have been pleasing to the Lord, as David had intended it should be. He had *kept the ways of the Lord*, refusing to kill his pursuer, and waiting for the Lord to vindicate him. Now that vindication had come, and therefore he could safely conclude that he was right with God (*cf.* Ps. 66:18–19). There is a righteousness according to the law, which does not fall into pride or hypocrisy (*e.g.* Lk. 1:6; Phil. 3:6), and the Lord honours it.

26–31. This is the theme of verses 26–28, as David has observed the outworking of God's providence, not only in the affairs of the nation, but also in his dealings with individuals. *With the crooked thou dost show thyself perverse*, or 'shrewd' (NIV), is well illustrated by the Lord's dealings with Jacob (Gn. 29:23; 30:35–36; 31:7), but all with the purpose of making him a changed man (Gn. 32:28).

---

[1] Watson, p. 6. The Ugaritic tablets, whose language is closely related to Hebrew, were written down 'in approximately 1400–1350 BC', though the compositions 'are very probably much earlier'. 'As Ugaritic poetry is chiefly narrative in character it cannot be directly compared with Hebrew poetic texts. Even so . . . they share a common poetic technique and in many respects would appear to belong to the same tradition of versification.'

A humble people: the adjective (Heb. *'ānî*) implies 'unjustly afflicted', 'needy', as opposed to the *haughty*, who are self-sufficient and their own final authority. David delights in the light he receives from the Lord, and acknowledges his need of it (*cf.* 2 Sa. 21:17). With his God, he can go on the attack against *a troop* or 'run through a barricade' (NIV mg.), the Hebrew word has both meanings.

I can leap over a wall (Heb. *šûr*): this unusual word for 'wall' (*cf.* Gn. 49:22; Jb. 24:11, both poetry) may suggest a metaphorical rather than a literal wall, though David certainly scaled both. Verse 31 looks back to the opening words of the psalm. Having reviewed how fully every prayer had been answered, David asserts even more emphatically the perfection of the Lord's way and promise and safe-cover; *the promise of the Lord proves true*, the verb means 'stands the test of fire', like precious metal. What is more, it is available to *all those who take refuge in him*. There is no élitism here.

32–36. The 'report' section opens with a question which is virtually a profession of faith. Though others may claim to worship the only God under another name, the test lies in the character of the God revealed to his servants. David is convinced that there is none like *the Lord*, Yahweh, who had proved to be *a rock* (Heb. *ṣûr*) in the long and eventful life of Moses (Dt. 32:4, 31), and has proved to be equally dependable to David, as he has scaled the heights of Judah on foot, as sure and fleet of foot as a hind. This prowess, together with strength and skill with the bow, resulted from much practice, but David was aware how much he owed to the Lord, who is the subject of all the verbs here. *Thy help made me great* is the reading confirmed by 4QSam[a].[1] The familiar 'thy gentleness' (AV, RV, RSV mg.) would have been 'thy humility' in any human context, and has been a little suspect. Nevertheless, there is an element of condescension on God's part in answering our prayer, and 'you stoop down to make me great' (NIV), which fits in with the thought expressed in verses 7–20, is part of the truth David is expressing.

37–43. The part played by the Lord alternates with the part David himself played in defeating his enemies. They had trusted other gods and were not in line with the plan of the

---

[1] Ulrich, *The Qumran Text of Samuel and Josephus* (Missoula: Scholars Press, 1978), p. 140.

Lord to deliver David; it is for that reason that *he did not answer them*.

44–46. The establishment of David as king is part of the background. This too is the Lord's doing: *Thou didst deliver me from strife with the peoples* or 'with my people' (Heb. *cf.* RSV mg.). There was plenty of occasion for strife, as developments during the later part of David's reign were to show, but early on external enemies had to be dealt with, and this preoccupation kept Israel from internal dissension (2 Sa. 8:1–14).

Foreigners came cringing to me: the verb is that of Deuteronomy 33:29, 'Your enemies shall come fawning to you'; having seen the God of Israel at work, they know they have to capitulate.

47–50. *The Lord lives* throbs with conviction based on all that David has been relating in his poem. One specific answer to prayer can bring home the fact that the Lord lives (*cf.* Hannah's song, 1 Sa. 2:1–10); David had countless occasions to which he could point, and which he summarizes now. David therefore vows to do all in his power to extol the Lord *among the nations*. Little did he know that the time would come when the nations would translate his words into every language of the world, and use his poems to worship the same living Lord (*cf.* Paul's use of David's vow in Rom. 15:8–9).

51. The climax of the poem celebrates the link between the living Lord God, in whose hand is all authority and power, and *his king* (*cf.* 2 Sa. 7:16). David had received the promise of an ongoing dynasty through Nathan, but, since David would not live for ever, it would pass to *his descendants* – better 'offspring', which is a singular collective noun like the Hebrew (*cf.* Gal. 3:16) – and points ahead to the coming Christ. The blessings of which David had been aware in his experience were to become even more specific and unmistakable in Christ (*cf.* v. 29 with Jn. 8:12; v. 30 with Phil. 4:13; v. 31 with Jn. 16:23–24).

C¹. The last words of David (23:1–7). *Oracle of David* (Heb. *nᵉ'um Dāwid*) indicates that David is speaking as a prophet, and uttering a divine word. This is expressly stated in verses 2–3. The poem has been studied in some detail by H. Neil Richardson, who draws attention to its structure and imagery, its place 'within the framework of the Davidic covenant theology, as we know it from its earliest expressions', and 'a limited number of forms . . . consistent with what we know of the earliest poetry of Israel'.[1] Its theme is the rule of the righteous king, and the Lord's covenant with David (2 Sa. 7:4–16).

1. The introduction to the poem is a fourfold portrait of the writer. He describes himself not in terms of human achievements but in relation to his God, who caused him to become king. *The anointed of the God of Jacob* says much in few words: the 'God of Jacob' is the one who transforms twisted human material, so David thinks of himself as in need of transformation (not like the kings of Egypt, for example, who considered themselves divine), yet he is 'anointed' (Heb. *mešîaḥ*) as the Lord's designated ruler, whose attributes should match those of his God. *The sweet psalmist of Israel* or, better, 'Israel's beloved singer' (NIV mg.).[2]

2–3b. Before the divine word is cited, a fourfold ascription makes certain that the Lord is known to be its source. In the LXX the third line reads 'God of Jacob' with 'Rock of Israel' in the fourth, an attractive possible parallel with the end of verse 1 (*cf.* JB).

3c–4. The Lord commends one who *rules justly over men*, who is 'just' (Heb. *ṣaddîq*) like God himself (Ps. 11:7), who rules *in the fear of God*, upholding with all his might everything that God upholds. Such a ruler, says the Lord, is to be compared with three lovely experiences common to mankind everywhere: the early morning, when light dawns, the warmth of the sun on a cloudless morning, and rain that enables grass to sprout even after long drought (*cf.* Ps. 72:6). All three elements are necessary for healthy growth of plants, without which all life would cease; and for society the righteous ruler has an equally vital part to play: 'May he have dominion from sea to sea', says the psalmist, and 'may he live for ever' (Ps. 72:8, 15). Lasting peace and security, as well as conservation of natural resources, depend on long-term justice and mercy exercised by godly leaders. They find their resources in God and in his Christ, who will indeed 'reign for ever' (Rev. 11:15).

5–7. David, meditating on the divine word, sees it in the

---

[1] H. N. Richardson, 'The Last Words of David: Some Notes on II Samuel 23:1–7', *JBL* 40 (1971), pp. 257–266. Quotations from pp. 265–266.

[2] Richardson, 'Last Words of David', p. 261, refers to studies on parallel terms in Ugaritic and suggests the translation 'the beloved of the Guardian of Israel', which continues to point to his God, and avoids any hint of self-praise.

light of Nathan's prophecy (2 Sa. 7:12–16). David's house, kingdom and throne had been declared sure for ever in *an everlasting covenant, as ordered and secure* as a legal document, because it depends on the word of the Lord, which cannot prove false. It follows that, since David seeks to rule justly, all his *help* (Heb. *yiš'î* from *yeša'*, 'welfare', 'salvation') and *desire* (Heb. *ḥēpeṣ*, 'deepest longings') will be brought to fruition according to the Lord's promise. When Jesus went about proclaiming 'the kingdom of God is at hand' (Mk. 1:15), David's aspirations were at last to be realized; the very name 'Jesus' spoke of salvation (Mt. 1:21).

But godless men are all like thorns: just as the farmer had to clear his land of thorn bushes, and contrive, without injuring himself, to make a fire of them, so David saw the implications of judgment for those who opposed God's cause. Like thorns, they were not only useless but dangerous, choking the growth of all that was good (Mt. 13:7, 22; *cf.* Is. 33:12; Heb. 6:8). In the light of God's word to him, David saw clearly in his old age how people's destiny becomes polarized either for or against God. This poem is David's 'last word', his final legacy.

B¹. More citations for bravery (23:8–39). It was fitting that the names of those who distinguished themselves in defence of Israel and of King David should be recorded in the account of his reign. The king would never have achieved so much without his loyal and valiant heroes. The corresponding passage in Chronicles (1 Ch. 11:10–47) sometimes elucidates the Samuel text.[1]

8–12. The *three* were honoured above the rest, and named in order of precedence. The name of the first is given in a variant form in 1 Chronicles 11:11, and is different again in the LXX; the remainder of verse 8 is also problematic (*cf.* RSV mg., NIV mg.). *Josheb, Eleazar* and *Shammah* had all stood their ground in single combat when the remainder of the army had fled. Their valiant stand had proved the turning-point from defeat to victory, but their survival alone against enemy onslaught could have but one explanation: *the Lord wrought a great victory*. In the case of Shammah, food supplies were being threatened; *Lehi*, one of the places on Israel's border with the

---

[1] For more detail, see B. Mazar, 'The Military Elite of King David', *VT* 13 (1963), pp. 310–320.

Philistines, had been the scene of one of Samson's exploits against them, and the place where the Lord delivered him from dying of thirst (Jdg. 15:14–20). The exploits celebrated here sound very like the border raids of the time of the judges.

13–17. This incident refers to the wilderness period of David's life, when his headquarters were at *the cave of Adullam*, the *stronghold* in the hills to the west of Bethlehem, his home. Some Philistines had *encamped in the valley of Rephaim* southwest of Jerusalem (2 Sa. 5:17–25), and since it was *about harvest time* their intention was probably to steal food from the fields. That the Philistines could penetrate so far east as to set up their garrison at Bethlehem indicates the weakness of Israel, and explains David's discouragement. In expressing a wish for a drink from the well at Bethlehem, David was longing for normality, peace and home, but three of his thirty officers took him literally and risked their lives to bring him water from Bethlehem's well. The story of such devotion to a leader became part of Israel's literary heritage, especially as the leader was humble enough to admit that only the Lord was worthy of such sacrifice. That is why *he poured it out to the Lord* as a libation: it represented the life-blood of three brave men.

18–19. No mention is made of Joab except as brother of *Abishai*, probably because, as army commander (2 Sa. 8:16; 20:23), he was in a class apart. Though Abishai commanded the army for a short time, he was no match for Joab (2 Sa. 20:6, 10b–22). Even so, he had his own claim to renown as *chief of the thirty* or 'three' (Heb.). If 'three' should be read here, we have to surmise that there was a second group in addition to those of verses 8–12.

20–23. *Benaiah* had distinguished himself in three great deeds. The word *ariels* is a transliteration of the Hebrew word, the meaning of which is not known (*cf.* Is. 29:1–3). 'He struck down two of Moab's best men' (NIV, *cf.* NEB) is based on an alleged parallel use of the word 'ariel' in an Egyptian papyrus, where it appears to mean 'armed leader'.[1] The *lion* trapped in a pit amid snow would have been particularly dangerous because of hunger. The *Egyptian*, *a handsome man*, is described in 1 Chronicles 11:23 as particularly tall, and the man's stature is to the point here, hence 'a huge Egyptian' (NIV). Having

[1] A. Zeron, 'Der Platz Benajahus in der Heldenliste Davids (II Sam 23:20–23)', *ZAW* 90 (1978), pp. 20–27.

disarmed the Egyptian, Benaiah killed him with his own spear. This prowess won him oversight of the king's bodyguard (2 Sa. 8:18; 20:23).

24–39. This list of the 'thirty' illustrates the ability of David to hold the allegiance of men from very different backgrounds. As might be expected, a number of his closest supporters came from the hill country of Judah, where David fought many of his early battles. Places such as *Bethlehem*, *Tekoa* (2 Sa. 14:2) and the *Carmel* south of Hebron (1 Sa. 25) are familiar enough, but *Paltite* (v. 26) indicates Beth-pelet, near Beersheba (Jos. 15:27), *Hushathite* (v. 27) Hushah, south-west of Bethlehem, while *Netophah* (v. 28) and *Gilo* (v. 34) were also in Judah. *Anathoth* (v. 27), however, was in Benjamin's territory, and *Gibeah* (v. 29), was Saul's own city, while *Pirathon* and *the brooks of Gaash* (v. 30) were probably in Ephraimite country (Jos. 24:30), and the *Ithrites* (v. 38) were connected with Kiriath-jearim, west of Jerusalem (1 Ch. 2:53). In addition, several of the 'thirty' were foreigners: *Maacah* (v. 34) and Ammon (v. 37) were allied as enemies of David (2 Sa. 10:6), and *Uriah* was a *Hittite* (v. 39), though his name meant 'Jahweh is my light'.

Thirty-seven in all: thirty-six names are mentioned in verses 8–39, so maybe Joab was the thirty-seventh. The *thirty* was a title rather than an exact figure, though it is likely that people who fell in battle were replaced, and we know that Asahel and Uriah died untimely deaths (2 Sa. 2:23; 11:17). All these men were renowned in their lifetimes and honoured by the king they served.

A¹. Divine judgment again falls on Israel (24:1–25).

This last episode in 2 Samuel shows David in a moment of weakness and Israel in need of correction. More important matters are at stake than David's reputation, though his repentance and concern for the good of his people result in a positive gain for both David and Israel.

1. *Again* refers back to 2 Samuel 21:1–14, with which it has similarities (*cf.* 2 Sa. 21:14 with 2 Sa. 24:25). The parallel account in 1 Chronicles 21 shows how theological thought had developed over the years, and attributed to 'Satan' or 'an adversary' what was earlier attributed to *the Lord*. Perhaps Paul had these two accounts in mind in 2 Corinthians 12:7; the 'messenger of Satan' works by divine permission. David accepted responsibility for his action (v. 10), acknowledging it to have been sinful, but if the thought of numbering Israel had been put there by the Lord, the Lord would seem to be working against himself. It would be possible to translate 'one incited David . . .', but the standard translations reject this way out of the difficulty. It is not immediately obvious to the modern reader what was wrong in numbering the people. A census from time to time is accepted as necessary for many purposes; in David's case, the intention was probably to raise a standing army, contrary to the traditions of the period of the amphictyony. He therefore needed to know the potential strength of the fighting forces available (v. 9), as in Numbers 1:2–3, where a census is actually commanded. There may have been superstitious fears attached to counting heads, as if inviting a disaster to reduce the number;[1] but in the case of David, the sin appears to lie in self-sufficient pride, the very opposite of the attitude that typified him in the psalm of 2 Samuel 22 and in his 'last words' of 2 Samuel 23. Accepting that David lapsed here and acknowledged his fault, we return to verse 1 and ask what the narrator was wanting his readers to grasp from his thought-provoking way of introducing the incident. Was he not drawing attention to the mysterious way in which God's plan for human history takes in even the lapses of God's servants?

2–3. The reaction of Joab to David's orders implies a reluctance to take a census, because the strength of the nation's population was a kind of barometer of the Lord's favour (Gn. 12:2; 2 Sa. 7:9–11). As such, it was not to be 'read' so as to justify human pride in human achievements, or to boost royal ambitions.

4–9. The army commanders went *to number the people of Israel*, implying 'to enrol the fighting men of Israel' (NIV). The route they took started east of Jordan, where the river Arnon formed the southern border with Moab. *Aroer* was 'on the edge of the valley of the Arnon' (Dt. 2:36, where another town in the gorge is also mentioned). Reuben was the first tribe to be enrolled, therefore, followed by *Gad*, whose territory included the city of *Jazer* (Jos. 13:25) and the district of *Gilead*. Working their way northwards the officers made *Dan* a turning-point

---

[1] *Cf.* Ex. 30: 11–16. Gordon 1986, p. 317, refers to possible inferences from Mari, where the word for 'census' meant literally 'purification'.

(*cf.* v. 2), but mention of *Kadesh in the land of the Hittites* would have doubled their journey northwards and is therefore an unlikely emendation of the unknown Hebrew name *Tahtim Hodshi* (NIV). Kadesh Naphtali is more likely, but the place in question should be to the east rather than the west of Dan. Though *Sidon, Tyre and the cities of the Hivites and Canaanites* were not reckoned part of Israel, David counted these cities as part of his empire (*cf.* 2 Sa. 5:11–12; 1 Ki. 5:1,6), and therefore expected them to provide soldiers for his army. The process of enrolment, which ended at *Beersheba*, was timed precisely, and the number of troops was registered separately for Israel and Judah, so indicating an administrative division which was to become significant (1 Ki. 12:19–20). The word *thousand* is likely to be used here in its military sense, 'contingent' (*cf.* the commentary on 1 Sa. 4:2). If this is so, the figures cannot be used with any accuracy as a basis for estimating Israel's population at the time of David.

10. After the event, *David's heart smote him* (*cf.* 1 Sa. 24:5); he had a tender conscience, and prayed immediately for removal of the *iniquity* (Heb. *'āwon*) or guilt and its consequences, having first confessed his sin.

11–14. *The prophet Gad*, who had given David sound advice during his outlaw period (1 Sa. 22:5), was officially recognized at court as *David's seer*, as the prophet was called at that period (1 Sa. 9:9). He acted as a kind of chaplain to the king, communicating to him the message of the Lord, and in this case putting to him three possible disasters, of which he was to choose one.[1] The choice is *three years* (though the Hebrew has 'seven', the 'three' of 1 Ch. 21:12 and the LXX seems likely to be original), *three months* or *three days* – the shorter the period, the more intense the suffering. David, in his dilemma, decided according to a principle: his dependence on the Lord's mercy, which he had learnt to trust (*e.g.* Ps. 40:11), as opposed to man's inhumanity, which he had reason to distrust.

15–16. The spread of an inexplicable, incurable and fatal disease is dreaded still, and the imagery of the destroying

[1] Parallels have been drawn between the prophetic utterances at David's court and prophetic sayings at Mari, a city on the Euphrates, in the time of King Zimrilim, a contemporary of Hammurabi. If the examples quoted by W. Beyerlin, *Near Eastern Religious Texts relating to the Old Testament* (London: SCM, 1978), pp. 122–128, are typical, the resemblances are minimal, though the importance attached by Zimrilim to prophets is instructive.

angel bringing death but halting at Jerusalem provides a vivid picture of intense fear suddenly relieved. David's city was to be spared, as happened again in the time of Hezekiah (2 Ki. 19:34–35), so giving rise to the popular belief that the Temple and city were inviolable (Je. 7:4–15).

The Lord repented of the evil: the verb (Heb. *yinnaḥem*) means 'to suffer grief over', 'the Lord was grieved because of the calamity' (NIV). David's trust had not been misplaced, because in judgment the Lord had remembered mercy. In the Chronicles account, David is specifically said to see the angel of the Lord, sword in hand, threatening Jerusalem (1 Ch. 21:16a); our account implies as much. From his vantage-point in the city, David could see that the divine visitation had reached *the threshing floor of Araunah the Jebusite*, evidently one of the well-known landowners remaining in the vicinity of Jerusalem after David's capture of the city.[1] The word of the Lord to the angel he presumably did not hear.

17. This prayer of David is remarkable in that he not only admits for the second time that he has been at fault (v. 10), but goes so far as to invite the judgment of the Lord on himself and his family (the personal pronouns are emphatic) in order that *these sheep* may be spared. The imagery of the king as shepherd of his people alerts David to responsibility rather than privilege, and to self-sacrifice for the sake of others.

18–19. The divine response came through the prophet Gad, not directly to David. Araunah's threshing floor was to be the site of sacrificial offerings on an altar which David was to erect. The first the owner knew of it was the arrival of the royal procession in obedience to the Lord's command.

20–21. *When Araunah looked down*: threshing floors were usually on a height, in order to catch every breeze; some area to the north of David's city is indicated, and the site of the Temple, overlooking the Kidron valley, would certainly make good sense, though in this account no mention is made of the Temple (contrast 1 Ch. 22:1). The threat of death from plague made the bargaining over the price of the threshing floor unusually urgent, so that the sacrifices could be offered.

22–23. The pressure of circumstances, and the fact that he

---

[1] The name Araunah is preceded here by the definite article in Hebrew, as though it were a title. G. W. Ahlström, 'Der Prophet Nathan und der Tempelbau' *VT* 11 (1961), pp. 113–127, has argued that Araunah was the last Jebusite king of Jerusalem.

was negotiating with the king, put Araunah in a difficult bargaining position; though he offered for nothing all that David requested and more, he would not have been expecting to be taken at his word (*cf.* Gn. 23:11–16), where Ephron casually lets drop the sum he expects in payment, despite v. 11). *The Lord your God accept you* is more than a pious wish; it is a matter of life and death.

24. For this reason, David is anxious to fulfil his obligations both to Araunah and to his God, and the principle he enunciates, *I will not offer burnt offerings to the Lord my God which cost me nothing*, is valid for all time.

Fifty shekels of silver: though Abraham paid four hundred shekels of silver for the field of Ephron, there is no suggestion that David underestimated the value of the threshing floor, which was to become the site of the Temple.

25. Having purchased the threshing floor, David was able to build his altar and sacrifice his burnt offerings and peace offerings. As in 2 Samuel 21:1–14, obedience resulted in removal of the threat to Israel, and prayer was answered. The population had been depleted by seventy thousand, but the whole country had been given a salutary reminder of spiritual realities: true prosperity was to be found in dependence upon their faithful covenant Lord, and on him alone.

David's story is not quite finished. The events of his last days are related in connection with Solomon's succession, and are therefore included in 1 Kings, but even so, the narrative of David's life has been a long one, covering a total of about forty chapters of 1 and 2 Samuel. Even during Saul's lifetime, it is David who holds the reader's interest, so that the space allotted to Saul in 1 Samuel 16 – 31 is largely dominated by David. Right at the beginning of this book, we commented about the amount of space given to Saul and David in the Old Testament. In view of the fact that only three chapters (2 Sa. 13 – 16) relate exclusively to the reign of Saul, the question becomes confined to the person of David: Why should forty chapters be devoted to him?

In the first place, people must have had a desire to write about David. The early tenth century BC has been reckoned a period of remarkable literary activity: indeed Leonhard Rost calls the Succession Narrative 'the finest work of Hebrew narrative art',[1] a judgment with which it is not difficult to concur. Strictly, however, we have no means of knowing whether other works of similar quality were produced at that time, or in succeeding centuries. Only the biblical narratives survive, and they paint a picture of an outstanding person, courageous, generous, warm-hearted, outgoing and appreciative of others. He was, moreover, a man who inspired loyalty, and with the help of his supporters accomplished much: the establishment of Jerusalem as Israel's capital, and the uniting of the twelve tribes into a state which could hold its own in the international scene. Israel's cities had their defences strengthened, and by the end of David's reign preparations were in hand for the building of the Temple in Jerusalem. All this accounts in part for David's greatness.

In what sense, however, was he 'a man after [the Lord's] own heart' (1 Sa. 13:14)? He is depicted in Scripture as entirely human, hampered by weaknesses that were the counterpart of his strengths: in particular he was indulgent towards his sons and, on occasion, towards himself. Unlike Saul, David received rebuke by humbly admitting his faults; when Nathan or Gad delivered a message of judgment, the prophet's condemnation was accepted as the word of God. In other words, the Lord was king; David was merely the Lord's vicegerent, exercising delegated power. His successors, who for the most part failed to conform to this role, were pointed back to David, for whose sake the dynasty was permitted to continue until the kingdom was swept away by the Babylonians. Even then, hopes were kept alive by the promise of Nathan to David, 'Your house and your kingdom shall be made sure for ever before me; your throne shall be established for ever' (2 Sa. 7:16). The New Testament takes up the theme when Jesus is introduced as a descendant of David; indeed the very first verse of Matthew's Gospel makes the point, 'The book of the genealogy of Jesus Christ, the son of David . . .'

[1] L. Rost, *The Succession to the Throne of David* (Sheffield: JSOT Press, 1982), p. 115.